A
TRAVELLER'S
WINE GUIDE
TO

*Italy*

To Jane,
whom I met in Italy over a
glass of Barolo

# A TRAVELLER'S WINE GUIDE TO

# Italy

## Stephen Hobley

Foreword by Donatella Cinelli Colombini

Photographs by Francesco Venturi

INTERLINK BOOKS
An imprint of Interlink Publishing Group, Inc.
New York

This revised and updated edition first published 2004 by **Interlink Books**, an imprint of Interlink Publishing Group, Inc., 46 Crosby Street, Northampton, Massachusetts 01060.

Edited by Keith Bambury, Laura Brown, Philip Clark and Tony Raven

Photographs by Francesco Venturi (except where otherwise credited)

Maps by AND Map Graphics Ltd., Carte Blanche, Andrew Green and Simon Green

**Library of Congress Cataloging-in-Publication Data**
Hobley, Stephen.
  A traveller's wine guide to Italy/ Stephen Hobley: photographs by Francesco Venturi.
    p. cm. – (Traveller's wine guides)
  Includes bibliographical references and index.
  ISBN 1-56656-409-3 (pbk.)
  1. Wine and wine making – Italy – Guidebooks. 2. Italy – Guidebooks.
  I. Title. II. Series.
  TP559. I8H58 1997
  641.2'2'0945 – dc20              96-45975
                                        CIP

The *Traveller's Wine Guides* were conceived and produced by Philip Clark Ltd., 53 Calton Avenue, London SE21 7DF, U.K.

Printed in Singapore for Imago

**ACKNOWLEDGEMENTS**
Philip Clark Ltd. would particularly like to thank Joanne De Luca, Tony Raven and Kerry Brady Stewart for checking the proofs, and Keith Bambury for his editorial help and invaluable technical assistance.

The author would like to thank: Roberto Bava for help in contacting his fellow wine producers; Paolo Valdastri for enlightening comments on the Livorno and Pisa section; Giampaolo Pacini for introducing some hidden parts of Tuscany; Ursula Thurner and Donatella Cinelli Colombini for their support and enthusiasm. The wine producers who helped by suggesting sights to visit as well as providing information about their own visiting hours and conditions are too numerous to mention individually, but without them, this book would have been impossible to put together.

**COVER**
Designed by Janet James and Chris Legee

Main illustration: Vines and citrus groves on the cliffs near Amalfi, Campania. (Photograph: Mick Rock/Cephas Picture Library)

Foreground photography by Darius

Road map of Italy: 1:200,000 edited by Touring Club Italiano. Reproduction authorized 23.5.96.

**TITLE ILLUSTRATION**
The city of Orvieto in Umbria looms through the early morning mist over cypresses and olive trees. Orvieto is sited on a natural fortress of volcanic rock. (Photograph: Alan Williams)

**PHOTO CREDITS**
**Maureen Ashley MW** 131
**Azienda Agricola Contucci** 99
**Azienda Agricola San Felice** 92
**Casa Vinicola Collavini** 64
**Casa Vinicola Umberto Fiore** 30
**Casa Vinicola Roberto Kechler von Schwandorf** 71
**Co-operativa Locorotondo** 117
**Co-operativa Monte Schiavo** 110
**Italian Trade Centre, London** 78
**C. Penna (Bava Collection)** 14, 25
**Mick Rock/Cephas Picture Library** 124-5
**Alan Williams** 22, 33, 35, 41, 56, 57, 84/85, 76, 77, 79, 89, 101, 126, 130, 132
**Zefa Picture Library** 38/39, 44

# Contents

# How to Use this Book

The greatest change since the last edition of this book is the growth of the Internet. Now so much information is available to help the wine traveller plan his trip that it would be foolish not to start by consulting the websites of the wineries in the area to be visited. Some areas, Tuscany and Sicily in particular, have excellent regional websites. Nevertheless this book is only a starting point.

To get the best use out of this book, you need:
a) a good set of maps. The most useful are the 1:200,000 series produced by the Touring Club of Italy, the TCI.
b) to plan ahead. Wine tourism in Italy is still a relatively new concept and most producers prefer to be contacted before a visit by telephone, fax or e-mail.

Remember, however, that these are guidelines rather than rules. This is Italy. It may not be necessary to book every visit. Enthusiasm and a smile on the part of the visitor wins round all but the most hardened or hard-pressed Italian. There is always an element of serendipity in any unplanned meeting for winemaker and visitor alike.

Equally, many producers have stated that there is a charge for tasting. This is not a rigid law either. It makes sense to charge organized groups for a tasting. In that way, everyone knows where they stand, and local cheeses and salami are often part of the package too. But individual wine enthusiasts can build a rapport with the winemaker that goes beyond the strictly commercial.

## Booking ahead

Advance booking by fax or e-mail is easier (see page 141 for suggested wording). Areas used to general tourism, such as Tuscany and the Veneto, have a long tradition of sales at the winery to the general public anyway.

However, it is undoubtedly true that you will receive a better tour of the winery if you contact them in advance, especially if your visit is to involve more than just purchasing wine.

The itineraries in this book are, of course, in no way obligatory, and deviation from the sequence of visits suggested does not matter at all.

The main text describes areas to go to – for example the Langhe in Piedmont, the Franciacorta in Lombardy, and Chianti Classico in Tuscany – rather than individual wine producers to visit (except where the producer is exceptionally important or where space has permitted).

## The blue information panels

More often, the information about individual wine producers, wine shops and wine exhibitions is to be found in the blue information panels by the side of the main text. All the producers – and shops – detailed in these panels are recommended for the quality of their wines, but the list is, of course, by no means fully comprehensive.

The panels will provide you with information which should be helpful when visiting a winery. The symbols used (see the explanatory panel, right) let you know what to expect.

Most wine companies offer tours on the tacit assumption that a small purchase at least will be made. Visits to a winery (see pages 12-13) can be an education and a great pleasure; a real interest is always rewarded.

Wine to be tasted will vary from the honestly cheap and cheerful to the expensive and carefully crafted.

Just like any other businesses, wineries are usually open during office hours only. Most of them are closed on Sundays, in the month of August, and between Christmas and the New Year.

## INFORMATION PANEL SYMBOLS

**D** Dutch spoken
**E** English spoken
**F** French spoken
**Fi** Finnish spoken
**G** German spoken
**J** Japanese spoken
**S** Swedish spoken
**Sp** Spanish spoken
**TF** free wine-tasting offered
**TP** paid-for wine-tasting
**WS** wine for sale
**B** booking required
**b** booking advisable

**EP** *Enoteca pubblica* local government-sponsored wine exhibition center, sometimes including museum and restaurant
**ER** *Enoteca regionale* regional wine exhibition center, the most important type of *Enoteca pubblica*
**\*** Member of *Movimento del Turismo del Vino* (see below)

## MOVIMENTO DEL TURISMO DEL VINO

The national Movement for Wine Tourism in Italy is run by wine producers and has as its aim the development of wine tourism for the benefit of visitors and tourists alike. Two Open Days every year see hundreds of wineries make a special effort to attract visitors:
Cantine Aperte –
(last Sunday in May)
Calici di Stelle –
(August 10)
Fax: 0577 849356
www.wine.it/mtv/

# Foreword

by Donatella Cinelli Colombini, President of the *Movimento del Turismo del Vino*

This book takes you to vineyards that look like gardens, with roses planted at the end of each row of vines; to wineries with their own museums attached; to cellars beneath Renaissance villas; to castles and to entire medieval hamlets with wine barrels in place of inhabitants. So many wonderful wines, all with their own story to tell.

Stephen Hobley shares with you his experience of the places where great Italian wines are made; very few people can help the traveller to understand these areas as he can. Learning about them is a rewarding task: just look carefully at the gently rolling hills where the vines grow, at the cellars with their wine casks, and listen to the producers and the cellarmasters who welcome you. Many of the smaller producers will press you to taste their wines in their own homes. In Italy, whoever goes into a cellar as a potential customer leaves it as a friend.

The wine traveller does not have to be an expert. It is enough to have some enthusiasm for the subject, to love being in the country, and to have just a little spirit of adventure. Some of the places recommended in this book are as yet unused to wine tourism and to some extent you will be a pioneer.

This book takes you to places where the scenery seems to come straight out of a Renaissance painting, where you eat and drink well, often at a very reasonable cost. Wine tourism can be integrated into a traditional holiday in Italy, and combined with a visit to Florence, Venice, Rome or the Mediterranean resorts. It is enough to remember that in the Uffizi Gallery you are less than an hour away by car from a producer in the courtyard of whose castle you will be able to taste wine while admiring the bas-relief by Donatello.

After the crush of the alleys and piazzas of Venice, it is a relief to visit a villa designed by the great architect Sanmicheli and surrounded by vineyards that produce an excellent white wine. Those who like archaeology can admire the Forum or the Colosseum, but there are also wine cellars built out of old Roman cisterns and at least one vinification tank carved out of stone over two thousand years ago. Wine tourism gives you the opportunity to enhance your holiday in Italy with something new, something a bit different and a pleasure at the same time.

When you return home and invite your friends to dinner, you will be able to serve wine bought in Italy and tell your guests: "This is one of my discoveries; it comes from a Tuscan villa that has a collection of rare farm animals that the owner is trying to save from extinction." What you need not explain is that the wine cost you less than a bottle of table wine from your local shop. This must be one of the secrets closely guarded between you, a pioneer of wine tourism, and the wine producers of Italy.

*Donatella Cinelli Colombini*

# Introduction _____

Italy has never lacked style. Lamborghini and Ferrari, Gucci and Armani – these are all internationally revered names. The Italian sense of style and the Italian way of living are generally much admired. And Italian food and the Mediterranean diet have made an impact worldwide. To many foreigners, however, Italian wine is just something to drink with spaghetti or pizza at home. It is difficult to understand in a world enamored of the simple tastes of Chardonnay, Cabernet and oak.

But, as the Californians say, "ABC – Anything But Chardonnay", meaning "I shall die of boredom if I have to drink another full oak Chardonnay." Anyone who holds any prejudices about Italian wines is in danger of missing out on a whole glorious new world of tastes, from superb native Italian grapes, such as Sangiovese (in Chianti, Vino Nobile di Montepulciano, and Brunello di Montalcino) and Nebbiolo (in Barolo), to new interpretations of the classic international grapes (Chardonnay, Cabernet, Pinot Noir and Sauvignon).

As exports grow and domestic consumption declines, a combined total of 860,000 hectares (2.1 million acres) of vineyards produce about 60 million hectoliters of wine every year. (That is over 1.5 billion gallons.) Italy and France vie to be the biggest producers every year.

In Italy, wine is more than a drink. It is also part of the geography, history and general culture of the country. Perhaps there is no other country in the world where wine tourism and gastronomic tourism are so varied.

Each region, every town even, has its own wines and foods, a variety of preparations that have been handed down from generation to generation, so that, just as there is no such thing as Italian Food, there is no such thing as Italian Wine. It is all regional.

Regional does not, however, mean provincial. Just like every other country in the Old Wine World, Italy is busy re-examining its local heritage at the same moment as it is assessing the new possibilities brought by internationally

successful grapes as well as production methods – principally, maturation in the small French new oak *barrique* (cask) rather than the traditional large old Slavonian oak barrel. Wine producers realize that both export and education are vitally important.

This is where the wine tourist comes in – you. Be assured of your welcome in Italy. The Italians are naturally hospitable, but they are also well aware that the long-term future of Italian wine is bound up in the communication of the pleasures of the Italian table, food and wine, to an audience.

Look out for the current band-wagons: aging in *barriques* – this lends a vanilla taste to the wine and makes it more "international"; the rediscovery of local grape varieties; the introduction of international grape varieties – Cabernet Sauvignon and Chardonnay, for example; and the increase in sales of sparkling wine.

There has never been a more exciting time to discover Italian wine.

Bolzano

NORTH
CENTRAL
ITALY
Trento

FRIULI-
VENEZIA
GIULIA

Aosta

VENETO
Venice

NORTH-
WEST
ITALY
Milan

Verona

Trieste

Turin

**ADRIATIC
SEA**

Genoa

VIA EMILIA

Bologna

Florence
Pisa

Ancona

TUSCANY

Perugia

Siena

CENTRAL
ITALY

Pescara

l'Aquila

Rome

Campobasso

**ADRIATIC
COAST**

Naples
Bari

SARDINIA

Potenza

Taranto

**MEDITERRANEAN
COAST**

Lecce

*TYRRHENIAN
SEA*

Cagliari

Catanzaro

Palermo
Messina

**SICILY**

*Pantelleria*

# The Classification of Wines

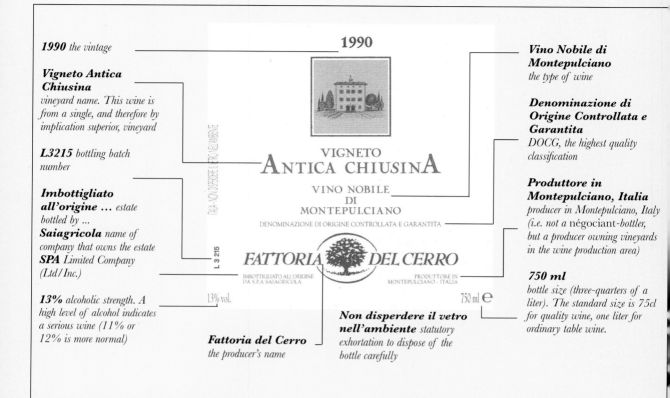

**1990** *the vintage*

**Vigneto Antica Chiusina**
*vineyard name. This wine is from a single, and therefore by implication superior, vineyard*

**L3215** *bottling batch number*

**Imbottigliato all'origine** ... *estate bottled by ...*
**Saiagricola** *name of company that owns the estate*
**SPA** *Limited Company (Ltd/Inc.)*

**13%** *alcoholic strength. A high level of alcohol indicates a serious wine (11% or 12% is more normal)*

**Fattoria del Cerro**
*the producer's name*

**Non disperdere il vetro nell'ambiente** *statutory exhortation to dispose of the bottle carefully*

**Vino Nobile di Montepulciano**
*the type of wine*

**Denominazione di Origine Controllata e Garantita**
*DOCG, the highest quality classification*

**Produttore in Montepulciano, Italia**
*producer in Montepulciano, Italy (i.e. not a négociant-bottler, but a producer owning vineyards in the wine production area)*

**750 ml**
*bottle size (three-quarters of a liter). The standard size is 75cl for quality wine, one liter for ordinary table wine.*

*(On label:)*
1990
VIGNETO ANTICA CHIUSINA
VINO NOBILE DI MONTEPULCIANO
DENOMINAZIONE DI ORIGINE CONTROLLATA E GARANTITA
FATTORIA DEL CERRO
IMBOTTIGLIATO ALL'ORIGINE DA S.P.A SAIAGRICOLA
PRODUTTORE IN MONTEPULCIANO - ITALIA
ITALIA - NON DISPERDERE IL VETRO NELL'AMBIENTE
L 3 215
13% vol.
750 ml ℮

## Reading the label

Ultimately, the producer's name is always a more reliable guarantee of quality than any official qualification on the label, but knowledge of a few basic terms helps in predicting what a wine should be like.

As more and more wines are brought into the official DOC system, the days when it seemed that Italy's best and worst wines were labelled *vino da tavola* are now at an end, and labels are beginning to mean more.

## (DOCG) Denominazione di Origine Controllata e Garantita

The top classification and the one with most significance for quality as well as for tipicality. Independent tasting commissions verify the quality of wine at this level and relatively few wines are included.

The reds are Barbaresco, Barolo, Brachetto d'Acqui, Gattinara and Ghemme from Piedmont; Brunello di Montalcino, Carmignano, Chianti, Chianti Classico and Vino Nobile di Montepulciano from Tuscany; Sagrantino di Montefalco and Torgiano Riserva from Umbria; Taurasi from Campania; and Valtellina Superiore from Lombardy.

The whites are Albana di Romagna from Emilia-Romagna; Asti, Moscato d'Asti and Cortese di Gavi from Piedmont; Franciacorta from Lombardy; Recioto di Soave from the Veneto; Vermentino di Gallura from Sardinia; and Vernaccia di San Gimignano from Tuscany.

*(Seal:)*
COLLIO
C 017051 1
CONTROLLO DELLA QUALITÀ
INCARICO VIGILANZA DM 26.11.1975
CONSORZIO TUTELA VINI
COLLIO D.O.C. VQPRD

### DOC (Denominazione di Origine Controllata)

The cornerstone of the Italian system, DOC regulations set maximum yields from the vineyards, maximum yields in terms of must from the grapes, minimum alcohol levels, and precise geographic origins. Entire regions can have umbrella DOC's (Piedmont is the most important) and tiny areas can have their own denomination (Loazzolo in Piedmont is Italy's smallest DOC, with only five producers).

### IGT (Indicazione Geografica Tipica)

Similar to French *vin de pays*. The first wines in this category appeared only in 1996. This is the base of the Italian wine quality pyramid, whose apex is DOCG and whose middle is DOC.

IGT can be granted to specific geographic areas and producers can declare varieties on the label if they are typical of the region. Most of the old super *vino da tavola* wines (wines in the super premium category that obeyed no rules at all – such as Italy's famous first international Cabernet-based blockbuster, Sassicaia) are now classified as IGT. Sassicaia, confusingly enough, is now plain DOC.

### Vino da Tavola

A *vino da tavola* is now only a true "table wine" with no vintage and firmly relegated to the bottom of the quality pyramid.

## Types of producers

**Tenuta, Castello, Podere, Fattoria:** traditional agricultural estates more or less devoted to wine production.

**Azienda Agricola:** a wine estate producing its own grapes. It will

*Labels strive for elegance at the same time as following strict formulas about relative sizes and importance of script. The Mithas Valpolicella Superiore label (above) combines image and message on one label. By contrast, the Countacc! label (right) ignores regulations – this is the front label of the bottle, but all the regulatory information is on a hidden back label.*

generally consider itself superior to the following:

**Casa Vinicola:** winemakers using bought-in grapes. They will argue that by buying in grapes they control what they get with greater accuracy.

**Co-operativa:** a co-operative.

## Basic wine terms

**Bianco, Rosso, Rosato** red, white, rosé.

**Classico** from the heartland of the traditional production area. By implication (and usually in fact) better than others in the region.

**Superiore** with slightly higher alcohol and, for reds, aged longer.

**Riserva** aged longer and therefore necessarily of higher quality.

**Spumante** sparkling wine, usually made in the cheaper tank method rather than bottle-fermented.

**Talento** generic term for all bottle-fermented sparkling wines (except Franciacorta).

**Vigna** single vineyard.

**Vino biologico** organic wine.

**Vino novello** new wine, to be drunk as young as possible, as with French Beaujolais Nouveau.

# Visiting a Winery

**HINTS FOR MOTORISTS**
This book is not intended to encourage drinking and driving in any way. Italian law is rightly strict in its sanctions against motorists who offend in this respect. To help your motoring to be worry-free, here are a few useful points to bear in mind:

**Speed limits**
**In town:** 50km/h (31mph)
**Out of town:** 90km/h (55mph)
**Main roads:** 110km/h (68mph)
**Motorways:** 130km/h (81mph)

**Alcohol limit:** 80mg per 100ml of blood

**Motoring tips**
• Service stations are usually closed during the lunch hour (longer in summer) and all day on Sunday. Exceptions are the 24hr motorway services and the automatic cash machine pumps on some forecourts.
• Always pay cash for fuel.
• Illegal parking in Rome can carry a prison sentence.
• Stick to motorways for longer distances; local roads are invariably congested except in deep country.
• Traffic police can demand heavy on-the-spot fines for speeding or for not wearing a seat belt.
• Carry your driver's license and passport with you at all times.

*The vineleaf insignia of the Associazione Enotecnici Italiani (Italian Association of Wine Technicians). The AEI are experts on the technical analysis of wine.*

## Booking a visit

Most wineries require some notice of an impending visit, for practical reasons. *In extremis*, however, if you arrive without warning and express interest, you will find Italians never less than courteous and always willing to help you if possible.

Booking can be made by fax, e-mail, telephone or letter (see page 141 for a sample letter/fax/e-mail in Italian). It is sometimes sufficient to express interest, but most wineries accept visitors on the understanding that some purchase will be made, however small.

## Types of visit

*Co-operatives* These vary considerably in size and outlook. In general, it is those that are proud of their wines, and keen to show that being a co-operative is no handicap to making good wines, that are most ready to welcome foreign visitors.

Some co-operatives, however, concentrate solely on bulk wine for local consumption and are less interested in visitors.

*Private companies* The grandest companies, the Antinoris and Ruffinos of the Italian wine world, are not generally orientated towards the public.

It is the medium-sized and especially the smaller Italian producers who are often the most rewarding to visit. The wine producer is often also the owner of the company, although he will probably have a consultant wine expert (an enologist) for the technical aspects of winemaking. Many producers are total enthusiasts who are dedicated to promoting their wines. Like most enthusiasts, they are fascinating to talk to on their subject.

*Enoteche* Enoteche means "places of wine." Two types are mentioned in this book (see page 6).
**1.** "Public Exhibition and/or Tasting Center" – usually run by local government. The general purpose is educational. Booking may be necessary for a guided tour.
**2.** The equivalent of a "Specialist Wine Shop" – a commercial enterprise. Like any shop, booking is not necessary and tasting is not usually offered, although if the shop doubles as a wine bar it will, of course, provide wine by the glass and at least a range of snack food.

## Tasting wine

It is very helpful to take notes when you taste wine, so that you can build up a sort of reference system, and thus more easily compare one wine with another tasted some time before. It is useful to examine at least three aspects of the wine:

**Color** A light white is lighter in color than a heavier white. A young red is brighter than an older red.

**Nose** Much of the taste of a wine can be predicted from its smell. The perfume of the wine itself is part of the sensory pleasure of drinking. Tasters differentiate between the primary aromas of fruit from the grapes or wood from the barrel and the secondary aromas of the mature, fully integrated, wine.

**Taste** Does the wine balance the taste of the grape with the tannin (in red wines) or with the alcohol and the acidity? Is there a particular aftertaste to the wine?

Don't forget though that wine is to be enjoyed. If you like it, say so, and try to find a reason why.

If not, the reason why you didn't like it is equally important.

**Spitting** Don't feel embarrassed to ask for a spittoon, *sputacchiera* – all professional tasters spit tasting samples out – but don't feel obliged to do so either. Enjoy tasting.

## The process of winemaking
### White wines

1. White (or red) grapes are broken away from their stems by machine.
2. A press crushes the grapes to extract the juice. This is separated from the skins and pumped into a fermentation vat (usually of stainless steel, and equipped for temperature control).
3. Fermentation ends. Sweet wine results when it is stopped before all the sugar in the grapes turns into alcohol. Vice-versa for dry wine.
4. When fermentation is complete and the wine has been drained (racked) off the sediment (lees) and clarified (fined), it is stored in large vats (often made of glass-lined concrete) until bottling.

### Red wines

1. After crushing and de-stemming, the grapes are put into a vat to ferment.
2. Fermentation lasts until the sugar is used up, about a fortnight.
3. Racking and fining, as for white wines, above.
4. The wine is aged: in stainless steel for light wine, large barrels for a heavier wine, small barrels (*barriques*) for special wines that require the vanilla flavors of wood.

### Sparkling wines

The process of fermentation usually provides the bubbles. The most expensive and prestigious way of doing this is to give the wine a natural second fermentation in the bottle itself in what used to be described as the "Champagne method," but now has to be called simply "bottle-fermentation." Italians sometimes call this the *metodo classico*, or *metodo tradizionale*. Talento is the generic name for sparkling wine made by this method.

Less expensive is the "Charmat" or tank method, which uses a single stainless steel fermentation vat to induce bubbles in the wine, a whole tankful at a time.

Really cheap sparkling wine is produced by adding carbon dioxide to an ordinary wine, just like the bubbles in most mineral water.

Price is a good rule of thumb with sparkling wine, but such is the confusion in the Italian sparkling wine industry that the generic word *spumante*, sparkling wine, has acquired negative connotations.

The extent of this trend is indicated by the fact that Asti Spumante – now DOCG (see page 10) has dropped the "Spumante" from its name.

**TASTING WINE – THE BASICS**

*1. Hold the glass to the light to assess the wine's color.*

*2. Smell the wine.*

*3. Swirl the wine in the glass to liberate the flavor.*

*4. Sip the wine and move it around inside your mouth.*

*5. Spitting accurately is not easy. (Practise beforehand with a glass of water!)*

# North-West Italy

North-west Italy comprises two areas of lesser importance in wine terms, Valle d'Aosta and Liguria, and one area which produces some of the finest wines in the world – Piedmont. Valle d'Aosta and Liguria are both mountainous areas, and they present extreme difficulties for the cultivation of vineyards. Wine in the Valle d'Aosta is produced with enormous effort from steeply sloping terraces which are clearly visible on both sides of the narrow Dora Baltea valley.

Similarly, in Liguria, a boat trip around the headlands of the Cinque Terre or east of Savona towards the French border will reveal yet more precipitous vineyards in more hand-cultivated terraces. Unfortunately, the wines of both areas tend to be relatively expensive, precisely because of these difficulties of production. But wine quality continues to rise in both regions despite a dramatic decline in viticulture in the last few years.

Each of the three regions has a distinct character. The Aostans have always regarded themselves as an independent mountain people, while the Ligurians have a proud seafaring heritage that goes back to the Genoese trade empire in the Middle Ages. But it was the Piedmontese who unified Italy, under King Victor Emmanuel (from 1861), and who still view the results with a somewhat amused detachment.

Piedmont is the Burgundy of Italy. It has a proud ducal past, its wines are produced on innumerable small holdings according to ancient traditions, and few people claim to understand the *cru* (single vineyard) nature of its most famous wines, Barolo and Barbaresco. But even a lowly trattoria will produce a very drinkable opaque wine, normally one of the house reds: Dolcetto and Barbera. Their characteristic slight *pétillance* is not a sign of bad winemaking, but rather of how Italians like their young red wines.

The major change in recent years is the rise to importance of white wines, Chardonnay particularly, as well as the more local Gavi, Erbaluce, Favorita and Arneis.

Also included in this section is a part of Lombardy, the sparkling wine-producing area of Oltrepò Pavese.

*Fields and vineyards near the wine town of Asti create geometric patterns in shades of green.*

Other DOC/G vineyard areas

Domodossola
*L. Maggiore*

Mont Blanc
Tunnel

*AOSTA*

Morgex

Aosta

AOSTA

*Gran Paradiso*
*National Park*

*L. Orta*

GATTINARA

Biella

Varese

A8

Ticino

A4

Milan

*L. Viverone*

ERBALUCE
DI CALUSO

A5

A4

Vercelli

Novara

*LOMBARDY*

Susa

A32

Pavia

A7

Po

A21

Turin

Cocconato

Po

Casale
Monferrato

Moncalvo

A26

Stradella

OLTREPÒ
PAVESE

Castelnuovo
Don Bosco

Vignale
Monferrato

M
O
N
F
E
R
R
A
T
O

A21

Pinerolo

Po

Rocchetta
Tanaro

Asti

Alessandria

Tortona

Costigliole d'Asti

Nizza Monferrato

BARBARESCO

Santa Vittoria d'Alba

Canelli

Acqui
Terme

A26

Gavi

A7

Bra

Alba

Santo
Stefano
Belbo

ASTI/
MOSCATO
D'ASTI

GAVI

*PIEDMONT*

BAROLO

Ovada

L
A
N
G
H
E

Dogliani

Cuneo

Genoa

A6

*LIGURIA*

A12

*Stura di Demonte*

*Tanaro*

Savona

CINQUE
TERRE

A10

Levanto

Monterosso al Mare

Riomaggiore

La Spezia

*LIGURIAN SEA*

DOLCEACQUA

Dolceacqua

Imperia

Ventimiglia

# Valle d'Aosta

**AYMAVILLES**
**Az Agr Les Crêtes*** Loc Villetos 50. Tel: 0165 902274. Fax: 0165 902758. (Costantino Charrere). 0830-1200, 1430-1900. Property includes 18th-century mill and olive mill. E.F.TP.WS.B.
**Cave des Onze Communes*** Fraz Urbains 14. Tel/Fax: 0165 902912. (Dino Darensod). F.TP.WS.B.

**CHAMBAVE**
**Co-op La Crotta di Vegneron*** Piazza Roncas 7 (near Fenis). Tel/Fax: 0166 46670. (Andrea Costa, Rino Lillaz). Sat 0800-1200. F.TP.WS.B.
E-mail: lacrotta@libero.it

**DONNAS**
**Co-op Caves de Donnas*** Via Roma 97. Tel: 0125 807096. Fax: 0125 804481. (Giulio Follioley). F.TP.WS.B.
E-mail: donnasvini@tin.it
www.donnasvini.com

**MORGEX**
**Co-op Cave du Vin Blanc de Morgex et La Salle*** Loc Les Iles. Tel: 0165 800331. Fax: 0165 800401. (Raffaella Scaldaferro, Gianluca Telloli). Mon, Tue, Thu, Fri 1000-1200, 1600-1830. E.F.TF.WS.B.
E-mail: caveduvinblanc@hotmail.com

**QUART**
**Maison Vigneronne Frères Grosjean*** Fraz Ollignan 1. Tel: 0165 765283. (Vincenzo Grosjean). F.TP.WS.B.

**VILLENEUVE**
**Az Vit Renato Anselmet & Figli*** Fraz La Crête. Tel: 0165 95217. (Renato Anselmet). F.TF.WS.B.
E-mail: renato.anselmet@tiscalinet.it

Since 1947 Valle d'Aosta has been an autonomous region within Italy with the same local government freedoms as the similarly mountainous border regions of Trentino and Alto Adige. Signs in Aosta are usually bilingual and the dialect of the local people is an almost impenetrable mixture of Italian and French that is more readily understood by the mountain dwellers on the French side of the border than by other Italians.

Valle d'Aosta is well known to skiers for its resorts at Courmayeur and Cervinia and to naturalists for the Gran Paradiso National Park. It is not well known for its wine even in Italy, but the whole area is now classified as a single DOC (see page 10).

Considering the fact that Valle d'Aosta is by far the smallest producer of wines in Italy with just over 650 hectares of vineyards in all, and that those wines that have survived the pressures of modern economics count among some of Italy's most interesting rarities, the dedication of the whole area exclusively to quality production is justified in both wine and socio-economic terms.

After all, if the surviving vineyards fell into disuse, the physical appearance of the whole valley would change as the laboriously-maintained mountain terraces crumbled away.

## The Aosta Valley

The Aosta Valley is famous for its chain of castles leading down to the Piedmontese border. There are 130 in all; some are now no more than ruined watchtowers, others were splendidly restored in the last century. The castles of Issogne and Fenis, both restored by the architect of Turin's incredible Borgo Medioevale, Alfredo d'Andrade, are most attractive; the fortress of Bard is forbidding. Fenis also has a museum of local history, the *Museo dell' Arredamento Valdostano*.

Some wines are made throughout the valley. Gamay is a light quaffable red made from the same grape as Beaujolais. Müller-Thurgau is made from the international grape of the same name. The same applies to Pinot Nero, but, unusually, it is also possible to find this as a white wine.

### La Valdigne

The narrow valley of the Valdigne extends some 27km (17 miles) from Mont Blanc until just before Avise. The only vine that grows in this area, an indigenous one called Blanc de Morgex or Blanc di Valdigne, has the useful qualities of being able to survive at higher altitudes than other vines and of being resistant to the deadly disease phylloxera. The area produces a good white aperitif wine called Blanc de Morgex et de la Salle. The town of Morgex is the commercial center, and La Salle has a notable castle.

### La Valle Centrale

This area extends from Avise to St Vincent, where the road and the Dora Baltea river suddenly plunge southwards towards Piedmont. About 16km (10 miles) further on is the village of Arvier, with its intriguingly named Enfer d'Arvier, a light red wine with a pleasingly bitter aftertaste.

Still on the SS26 and a few miles after Aosta are the villages of Nus and Chambave, which give their names to two wines, which can be either red or white. Chambave in its white version is made from the Moscato grape. In its most prized form it can be made from partly dried grapes and have a formidable alcoholic content.

Torrette, the other particular DOC wine of the Valle Centrale, is a dry, slightly bitter red wine made principally from the Petit Rouge, another of the grapes indigenous to the Valle d'Aosta.

## La Bassa Valle

The 25km (15 miles) of the Bassa Valle extend from St Vincent to the border with Piedmont. The vineyard terraces cloak the valley slopes.

It is when one nears the border with Piedmont that the land of classic Nebbiolo-based wines begins with the red wines called Arnad-Montjovet and Donnas.

These are made from the same grape as their heavier cousins Barolo and Barbaresco, but they are not aged for so long and can be much subtler wines. They are also very difficult to find outside their own areas of production.

*The steeply-terraced vineyards of the Valle d'Aosta are clearly visible both from the fast* autostrada *and the winding* superstrada. *Viticulture here is laborious and expensive.*

17

# The Enoteche of Piedmont

The wine traveller in Piedmont is exceptionally fortunate; the system of public and private *enoteche* and *botteghe del vino* provides extensive opportunities for tasting and learning about wine.

The difference between the two types of wine showplace is one of size and scope. An *enoteca* will certainly display the wines of its area, but it will also often have a restaurant designed to serve complementary local foods and a museum of winemaking implements.

The *bottega* tends to be more modest, more specialized, often staffed by the growers themselves, and perhaps only open at the weekends.

There is a double pleasure in visiting the *enoteche* of Piedmont: they are all sited in monuments of historic interest that have been restored to serve as showcases for the local vinous heritage. Four of them are in castles, one is in a deconsecrated church, and two are in historic *palazzi*.

### The castle of Barolo

It was, in fact, the annual Barolo tasting at the castle of Barolo that introduced me to the delights of Italian wine. My casual visit to a small village in the Langhe, whose wine I had certainly heard of but which I had never really explored, led me to the annual tasting of all 70 or so Barolos on display in the Enoteca for the sum of 5000 lire. The combination was enchanting – the highest quality Italian wine presented in a historic castle in one of the prettiest parts of Piedmont. I have been addicted ever since and still regard Barolo as the finest wine in the world.

### Grinzane Cavour

If there is time to visit only one of these *enoteche* or *botteghe*, then that should be the Enoteca Regionale at Grinzane Cavour, near Alba. This is an imposing castle dating from the mid-13th century, which, as the name recalls, was once the property of the great statesman of the *Risorgimento*, Camillo Benso di Cavour. The prototype of the *enoteche* system, it was opened in 1971 as the showplace for the best wines and grappas of Piedmont.

A restaurant within the castle serves Piedmontese specialties, and its museum has interesting historical displays on coopering, distilling, and truffle hunting.

### Botteghe

There are many *botteghe del vino* in Piedmont, although most are only open weekends. More are being established as

*The castle of Barolo is one of the nine Piedmontese* enoteche. *On display are over 100 different varieties of Barolo, Italy's "King of Wines and Wine of Kings." The castle also contains a hotel, school and museum.*

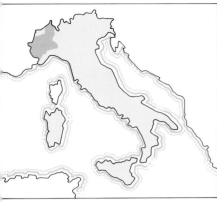

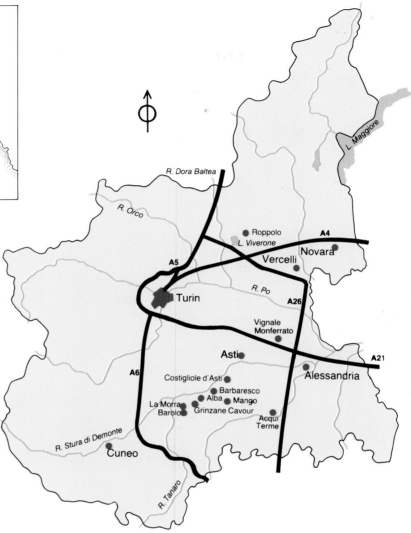

**GRINZANE CAVOUR**
**ER Piemontese**
**"Cavour"** Via Castello 5.
Tel/Fax: 0173 262159.
Closed Tue, Jan. Guided
tours. Museum. Restaurant.
Tel: 0173 262172.
E.F.G.TP.WS.b. E-mail:
enotecavour@libero.it

**MANGO**
**ER Colline del Moscato**
Piazza XX Settembre, 19.
Tel: 0141 89291. Fax: 0141
839914. 1030-1300, 1500-
1800. Closed Tue.
Restaurant. Hotel.
E.F.G.TP.WS. E-mail:
enotecamango@infinito.it

**ROPPOLO**
**ER della Serra Castello
di Roppolo** Tel: 0161
98501. Fax: 0161 987510.
Thu 1600-1830; Fri-Sun
0930-1200, 1500-1900.
Hotel in castle. E.F.TP.WS.
E-mail: enotecadellaserra@
interbusiness.it

**VIGNALE
MONFERRATO**
**ER Palazzo Callori**
Piazza del Popolo. Tel/Fax:
0142 933243. Mon, Wed-Fri
0900-1300, 1330-1630; Sat,
Sun 1000-1200, 1500-1830.
Historic 15th-century
*palazzo, infernotto* cellars.
Restaurant. E.TP.WS.
E-mail: palazzocallori@
libero.it

small groups of wine-growers band together to take advantage of the growing public interest in genuine handmade products of the countryside, of which wine is only one. Many of the *botteghe* also act as wine bars, the one at Nizza Monferrato is a good example, and serve *spuntini* (snacks) and local food specialties to go with the wines.

An increasing nostalgia for the countryside, combined with interest in *agriturismo* – vacationing in the country rather than in the traditional skiing or beach resorts – has created greater willingness on the part of the winemakers to exhibit their wines.

Perhaps the most interesting of the *botteghe* is the Cantina Comunale of La Morra (see page 29). This is in the heartland of Barolo production, where every south-facing hill has its carefully-manicured Nebbiolo vineyard. You can find details of local vineyard walks here. La Morra itself is unique in having a statue not to a winemaker but to *Il Vignaiolo*, the vine-grower.

# Turin and its Vicinity

*The Royal Hunting Lodge at Stupinigi on the outskirts of Turin. Those who think of the city as mainly industrial are amazed by the range of its architectural masterpieces.*

### COCCONATO D'ASTI
**Bava\*** Strada Monferrato 4. Tel: 0141 907083. Fax: 0141 907085. (Paolo Bava). 0830-1230, 1400-1900. E.F.Fi.G.TE./TP.WS.b. E-mail: bava@bava.com www.bava.com

Piedmont may be more famous for its successful industries, FIAT and Olivetti; but for the wine lover it signifies the great Italian wines of Barolo and Barbaresco and exciting new styles of Barbera and Dolcetto. In fact Piedmont is particularly rich in wine; it boasts more than 40 DOC and DOCGs and the whole area is the first major wine-producing zone in Italy to create its own umbrella DOC appellation system.

## Turin and its vicinity
The city of FIAT, Juventus and La Stampa is often disparaged by Italians from outside Piedmont, and its bypass system is successful enough for it to be missed as a matter of course by the motorized traveller. But it has many attractions. This is the lovely arcaded city where Michael Caine was filmed in *The Italian Job*. It should be visited for its museums, palaces and churches, often built in a wonderfully extravagant

Torinese Baroque style. It also has some of the finest Liberty-style buildings in Europe, dating from around the turn of the century, and an Egyptology Museum second only to Cairo's.

### Terra dei Santi

Leaving Turin to the south-east by the SS10 to Chieri, you can make a brief stop at Superga, an extraordinary 18th-century basilica that looks out over the city and houses the Savoia Mausoleum.

Chieri is rich in 15th-century churches (S. Domenico, S. Giorgio, the Duomo), and is a center for the production of a traditional Piedmontese wine that is rarely seen abroad, Freisa. The name comes from its strawberry-like bouquet and in both its sweet and dry versions it can be a sparkling red wine, not unlike a good Lambrusco: equally it can be made as a still wine with moderate aging power, like Dolcetto.

After Chieri, a detour to Pessione leads to the fascinating Martini & Rossi winery and museum. The most impressive exhibits are the carts used to transport barrels for the new vintage's wine, all marvelously carved with appropriate scenes of Bacchic revelry.

The whole area is sometimes called the *Terra dei Santi* because of its associations with Turin's famous philanthropic priest Don Bosco, and the missionary S. Giuseppe Cafasso.

### Fruit, wine and music

Malvasia di Castelnuovo Don Bosco is a sweet sparkling red that makes an excellent summer aperitif or, even better, livens up a fruit salad with a festive splash of aromatic wine.

I have to thank Roberto Bava, wine producer at Cocconato d'Asti, for introducing me to this combination of fruit and wine with his own Malvasia. Roberto's favorite theory is that the tastes of different wines can be matched with the sounds of different musical instruments; Malvasia is light, festive and summery – a piccolo, maybe? Cocconato is well worth a visit anyway for its fine hilltop views, its two good restaurants, and the rest of the Bava symphony orchestra of wines.

### Chocolate and *I bicerin d'Turin*

Turin is also one of the world capitals of chocolate. Dynastic links between the royal families in Turin and in Vienna, together with a common cultural flowering in the early 19th century, meant that Vienna developed its coffee houses and chocolate cake at the same time as Turin developed the *bicerin* (pronounced "bik-yer-i," and meaning "little cup" in Torinese dialect).

The *bicerin* consists of hot chocolate, a small jug of hot coffee (both originally very expensive), and a small jug of hot milk. All three elements are left in their jugs so that the customer can mix them to taste in a large cup. Anyone ordering the *bicerin* in a café had the right to share a table with anyone else taking part in the same ritual. A whole ceremony developed around the *bicerin* in the coffee houses of Turin, and a special selection of 14 sweet biscuits evolved (called *I Bagnati*, literally "the bathed ones"), each with its own name, to accompany the substantial drink.

Discover the typical handmade Torinese chocolates, *gianduiotti*, in one of the marvelous mahogany, mirrors and gilt chocolate shops of Turin: the *bicerin* can be experienced, with all its ceremony, in several coffee houses.

## MONCUCCO

**Bottega del Vino and Trattoria del Freisa** Via Mosso 6. Tel: 011 9874765. Fax: 011 9927144. Mon, Thu, Fri 1500-2400; Sat, Sun 0900-2400. Closed Tue, Wed. Restaurant and wine shop. E.F.TP.WS.b.

## PESSIONE DI CHIERI

**Museo Martini di Storia dell'Enologia** (Martini Museum of the History of Enology). Tel: 011 94191. Fax: 011 9419324. Book one week ahead for free guided tour and tasting. E.F.G.TF.WS.B.

## TURIN

### CHOCOLATE: SHOPS AND CAFÉS

**Al Vej Bicerin** Via Carlo Alberto 27. The complete *bicerin* experience.
**Baratti & Milano** Piazza Castello 29. Torinese gilt, mirrors and mahogany.
**Pfatisch** Via Sacchi 42. Turn-of-the-century time capsule with own chocolate workshop below the bar/ *pasticceria*.
**Stratta** Piazza San Carlo 191. Exquisitely packaged *gianduiotti* chocolates. E-mail: strata@tiscalinet.it

# Asti

*Moscato vines in the Asti heartland of the Belbo valley.*

## Asti wines

Asti's great rival is Alba. While Asti has its historic Palio celebrations involving horse-racing every year, Alba has an almost parodic *Palio degli Asini* – donkey-racing. But in wine terms, the advantage seems to belong to Alba; how could Asti Spumante (now called simply Asti) match the splendors of Barolo?

The answer is, it can't; but if the occasion is right, it is actually much more appropriate. Asti is fun, Barolo is serious; Asti is light and low in alcohol. Asti is the drink Italians celebrate with – together with a good *panettone* cake – chilled, of course, and served in a flute glass to preserve the bubbles and concentrate the enormous floral bouquet.

Asti is not the only wine of the region, either. The two other principal wines are Dolcetto d'Asti and Barbera d'Asti. Here again, there is the comparison with Alba. True to type, Dolcetto d'Alba and Barbera d'Alba are more serious than their Asti counterparts; the Alba producers are probably making Barolo too, and there is often something of the "junior Barolo" feel about them. The Asti versions are more nervy, brighter, sharper, more fun even.

It is Barbera d'Asti that is creating the news at the moment in the region. Producers have discovered its affinity with new oak. In fact, the naturally high acidity of the grape marries well with the vanilla cloak conferred by aging in new oak *barriques* and the consequence is that Barbera has been transformed in the space of a decade from a wine that was unwanted to the smartest bottle in the restaurant.

## South of Asti

The town of Asti itself is bigger and more commercial than Alba, as befits its status. It has a cathedral that is the supreme example of Piedmontese Gothic architecture, an impressive art gallery and a museum of the *Risorgimento*.

From Asti go south-west to Costigliole d'Asti, with its wonderful castle. It used to belong to the Contessa di Castiglione, who became mistress to Napoleon III of France, and is visitable by arrangement with the Cantina dei Vini di Costigliole d'Asti, the Enoteca belonging to the local producers' association (see page 18 for details).

From Costigliole go to Castagnole Lanze to browse in the Bottega del Vino shop, and then to Mango, to see the splendid castle and Enoteca Regionale (see page 19 for details). In medieval times it was the vital center of the area strategically commanding the ancient Roman *Magistra Langarum* road linking Piedmont with Liguria. It now contains a restaurant and an Enoteca dedicated to Moscato wines and Piedmontese sparkling wines in general.

Follow the Belbo valley north-east to Santo Stefano and visit the birthplace of Cesare Pavese (1908-1950), the author who made the valley famous.

The next stop is Canelli, the commercial center for Asti and a pretty hillside town, very conscious of its place in wine history. Further up the valley, Nizza Monferrato has an active Bottega del Vino (open Fri-Sun) and the Bersano winery and museum with its collection of prints and wine artifacts dating from the 17th century.

Return to Asti, maybe via Rocchetta Tanaro (see page 35), where the Bologna family make a range of pioneering Barbera wines, including the famous *barrique*-aged Bricco dell'Uccellone. The local foods to discover here include *Lingue di Suocera* (mother-in-law's tongues) bread (thin, crisp and flavorsome!), and the *Tirà*, a ring-shaped cake.

### Loazzolo

Loazzolo, in the hills above the Belbo valley, is one of Italy's newest, smallest and most fashionable DOC areas. Inspired by the enologist Giancarlo Scaglione, a small band of producers have revived a long-abandoned wine type. This is Moscato Passito, a rich dessert wine made from partially dried grapes picked from sparsely-planted vineyards and small outcrops of vines dangling over steep drops, which are very picturesque, and very difficult to cultivate. As interesting as the wines in this mountainous area are the traditional cheeses of Loazzolo and nearby Roccaverano.

The village of San Giorgio Scarampi has a Bottega del Vino (open every day except Monday).

*Castello Gancia in Canelli. Gancia were the pioneers of sparkling Asti in the last century.*

**LOAZZOLO**
**Az Agr Forteto della Luja\*** Reg Bricco Rosso 4. Tel/Fax: 0141 831596. (Silvia Scaglione). 0800-1900. E.F.TP.B. E-mail: fortetodellaluja@imarinol.it

**NIZZA MONFERRATO**
**Bersano\*** Piazza Dante 21. Tel: 0141 720277. Fax: 0141 701706. (Carla Cavallo). 0900-1200, 1400-1600. Museum. E.TF.WS.B. E-mail: wine@bersano.it www.bersano.it
**Bottega del Vino Vineria "La Signora in Rosso"** Palazzo Crova, Via Crova 2. Tel: 0141 793350. Fri-Sun 1100-1300, 1700-0100. Wine bar. TP.WS.

***For further addresses, see page 35.***

# Monferrato

## The Basso Monferrato

From Asti go north to the Basso Monferrato. This area, between the Tanaro valley in the south and the Po valley in the north, is largely undiscovered and contains sleepy towns on the top of gentle hills covered with vineyards and woods. It cannot fail to charm.

Sometimes, indeed, it may even be a little kitsch. At the village of Callianetto, near Castell'Alfero, the villagers celebrate a character from the popular 18th-century *commedia dell' arte* theatre. This is Gianduja, a canny peasant who delights in poking fun at the pomposities of local worthies. The figure of Gianduja leads the local

*Moscato grapes at harvest time in vineyards near Alba. Not all of them will go towards the making of sparkling Asti – the still Moscato d'Asti is increasingly popular as a dessert wine.*

carnival procession of costumed girls from his native *ciabot* (cottage). Gianduja is now, of course, famous the world over because of the *gianduiotti* chocolates of Turin (see page 21).

## Grignolino

The first wine town is Portacomaro, which has its own Bottega del Vino sited in the solitary tower that remains of the town's castle. It specializes in Grignolino and, a rarity indeed, Grappa di Grignolino.

Grignolino is a classic Piedmontese wine that is much undervalued – partly by the producers themselves, because of the difficult nature of the grape. It is almost a rosé wine in color, but it has the structure of a full-bodied white wine. Needless to say, it is an excellent accompaniment to the rich local foods, especially the cheeses. But it is difficult

to manage enologically, and poor versions of this wine are too common. As usual, the producer is the guarantee of quality, not the regulations that make this a DOC wine.

Nearby Castagnole is the home of a unique and rare red wine called Ruchè di Castagnole Monferrato, a dry aromatic red that is light in color with a distinct hyacinth-like bouquet. Piedmont is full of such local curiosities that need a leading wine producer to take under their wing and promote as a re-discovery of an ancient heritage, which indeed they are.

Vignale Monferrato is only about 10 kilometers (6 miles) away and has the Enoteca Regionale (see page 19) in Palazzo Callori specializing in Barbera and Grignolino.

### Frassinello

Frassinello, towards Casale, has two castles. The Castello di Lignano, a winery as well, is particularly striking with its round medieval tower faced with alternate bands of tufa rock and brick. Casorzo is another one of those Piedmontese localities with its own specialty wines; in this case Malvasia di Casorzo d'Asti, a pale pink wine that is usually sweet and either fully sparkling or lightly *frizzante*.

### The Fair of the Fattened Ox

Moncalvo is the local market town and is famous for its food; *bollito*, delicious boiled meats, is a specialty. In fact, this is one of the few towns in Piedmont to retain its *Fiera del Bue Grasso* (Fair of the Fattened Ox), a festival day when a garlanded ox is the center of a procession. Moncalvo was important enough in medieval times to have the right to mint its own coins. The remains of the old castle form two sides of Piazza Carlo Alberto. The

*Most of the men and women who actually do the work of vine-tending throughout Italy belong to the older generation; what will happen when they have gone? Their children work in the towns. Their work is essential, and the question is increasingly pressing.*

church of San Francesco, built in the Lombard Gothic style, contains notable paintings by Guglielmo Caccia.

North of Moncalvo there are wine producers to visit at the castle of Salabue and at Crea, the site of a remarkable Santuario, consisting of terracotta figures in a series of shrines, a sort of religious theme park from centuries past.

### The infernal regions

Towards Casale, the commonest building stone is tufa. Blocks of this soft material form the walls of farm buildings, and conversely wine cellars are excavated from it, the famous *infernotti*. These secret wine cellars, also called *crutin* in local dialect, are difficult to visit because of continuous use, but the Enoteca at Vignale has its own *infernotti*, which can be visited to get an idea of these sanctuaries of wine.

**TREVILLE**
**Pavese Livio*** Regione Bettola. Tel: 0142 487215. Fax: 0142 487045. 0800-1200, 1400-1800. E.F.TF.WS.B. E-mail: liviopav@tin.it www.liviopavese.com

**QUARANTI**
**Bottega del Vino "Brachetteria"** Via al Castello 2. Tel/Fax: 0141 793939. 0900-2400. TP.WS.

**PORTACOMARO D'ASTI**
**Bottega del Grignolino** Piazza Marconi 18. Tel: 0141 202666. Restaurant closed Mon. Bottega/wine bar Sat, Sun and public holidays 1000-1230, 1500-1930. TP.WS. (B for restaurant.)

**SERRALUNGA D'ALBA**
**Bottega del Vino** Tel: 0173 613604. Fax: 0173 613101 E.F.TP.WS.b.ER. E-mail: bdv.serralunga@ areacom.it www.bdv-serralunga.com

# Alba

**BRA**
**Cantina Ascheri Giacomo*** Via G Piumati 23. Tel: 0172 412394. Fax: 0172 432021. (Maria Cristina Ascheri). 0900-1200, 1500-1700. *Osteria.* E.F.Sp.TE.WS.b. E-mail: ascherivini@tin.it

**ALBA**
**Az Vit Ceretto** Loc San Cassiano 34. Tel: 0173 282582. Fax: 0173 282383. (Roberta Ceretto). Mon-Fri 0800-1100, 1400-1700. E.F.G.TE.B. E-mail: ceretto@ceretto.com www.ceretto.com
**Pio Cesare** Via Cesare Balbo 6. Tel: 0173 440386. Fax: 0173 363680. (Augusto Boffa). 0900-1200,1500-1800. Closed weekends. E.F.TP.B. E-mail: piocesare@piocesare.it
**Prunotto** Reg San Cassiano 4/G. Tel: 0173 280017. Fax: 0173 281167. (Gianluca Torrengo). 0800-1230, 1330-1700. E.F.Sp.TE.B. E-mail: prunotto@prunotto.it www.prunotto.it

## Towards Alba

Alba is the capital of the Langhe, a wonderful area full of gently rolling hills with medieval castles and villages perched upon them. It is best visited in the autumn when truffles perfume the streets, the vines have turned russet color and the new vintage froths in the vats.

In many ways Alba is the epitome of the Italian Experience. Churches built in warm red medieval brick, arcades, bars with gilt and glass, shops full of homemade cakes and biscuits, the aromas of mushrooms and truffles, and trattorias with ample menus. It is a marvelous center for excursions into the winelands that surround it – the Roero and the Langhe.

## Roero

North of the Tanaro river from Alba lies a hidden area of soft hills with soft and subtle wines. This is the land of two unique white wines: Arneis, fashionable with a distinctive almondy aftertaste; and Favorita, just

becoming known outside the area. The local red wine is made from Nebbiolo, the same grape that is used for Barolo, but here it makes a lighter style Roero DOC or Nebbiolo d'Alba with moderate aging capability.

Visit the town of Bra for the finest Baroque churches in Piedmont and the unexpected delight of the Osteria Murivecchi, a wine bar/trattoria in the courtyard of the Ascheri winery serving local foods with the Ascheri wines. Canale d'Alba in the north of the Roero region has the Enoteca Regionale for Roero wines (see page 18). It is also well known for its nougat.

Santa Vittoria d'Alba is the site of the enormous Cinzano factory and a town with a "secret," according to the movie that tells the true story of how the inhabitants walled up the town's hillside cellars to hide their wine from the occupying Germans.

## Barolo

From Alba turn south to the land of Barolo, a triangular area with its points at Alba, Cherasco and Dogliani. Just outside Alba, on the way to La Morra, is Roddi with its fine 15th-century castle and unique truffle-hound school. (Training is based on the eagerness of a hungry dog to find food – in this case bread rubbed with truffles. Lucky dog!) The nearby castle of Verduno was once King Carlo Alberto's private Barolo-producing estate and is now a winery and hotel (see page 29).

## Barolo styles

Barolo, the wine, has a reputation for being something of a tannic monster, needing years to soften out. This reflects the inexpert application of old-fashioned vinification techniques

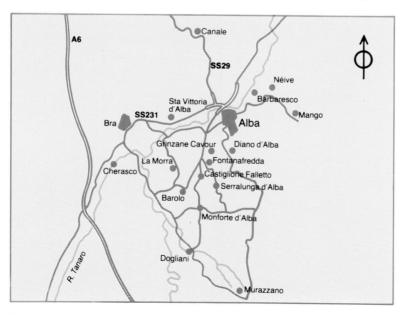

when the wine would be fermented for as long as a month with the mass of grape skins continually submerged under the must, increasing the tannin levels all the time. The resulting wine needed at least five years in large Slavonian oak barrels to shed its mouth-puckering tannicity, even before bottling, and even then it rarely recovers.

Modern practice favors a much shorter fermentation with the necessary color from the grape skins maximized by a process called *rimontaggio* (pumping the must back over the skins) while minimizing the harsh tannins that come from a more lengthy process. The wine is then put in barrel for the minimum two years, often with a short time spent in new oak *barriques* that give a characteristic vanilla-oak flavor, masking the tannins and adding a velvety touch to the wine.

Which style of wine is better? If handled expertly by a master winemaker like Aldo Conterno, the old style is incomparable, full of many layers of flavor and lasting for ever. Equally, a modern master, such as Bruno Ceretto, will produce wines that are a pleasure to drink from their very first year and gain in complexity as they age. Personally, I prefer my Barolo without new oak vanilla, but the style is very popular and very international.

Try Barolo for yourself at the Enoteca Regionale at Grinzane Cavour (see pages 18-19). This is an excellent place to learn about Piedmontese wines and truffles and, preferably, to consume both.

## La Morra

Like Burgundy, the Barolo-producing area is divided into sites that have long been recognized as producing

*Vineyards encircle the wine town of Barbaresco, which lies north-east of Alba.*

### BAROLO
**Marchesi di Barolo*** Via Roma 1. Tel: 0173 564400. Fax: 0173 564444. (Donata Patrito). Mon-Fri 0900-1700; Sat, Sun 0900-1200. Old bottles of Barolo from 1938. Guided tour. E.F.G.Russian. TF.WS. (B for weekends). E-mail: marchesi.barolo@ marchesibarolo.com www.marchesibarolo.com
**Cantina Bartolo Mascarello** Via Roma 15. Tel: 0173 56125. (Bartolo Mascarello). 0900-1200, 1430-1830. F.G.TF.WS.b.
**Az Agr Luciano Sandrone** Via Pugnane N4. Tel/Fax: 0173 56239. E.F.TP.WS.B. E-mail: info@ sandroneluciano.com www.sandroneluciano.com

**CASTIGLIONE
FALLETTO**
**Az Agr Vietti** Piazza
Vittorio Veneto 5, 12060
Castiglione Falletto (CN).
Tel: 0173 62825. Fax: 0173
62941. 0830-1200, 1400-
1800. E.TF.WS.B.
E-mail: vietti@il-vino.com
www.vietti.com

**DOGLIANI**
**Az Agr Abbona
Annamaria\*** Fraz
Moncucco 21, 12060
Farigliano (CN). Tel/Fax:
0173 797228. 0900-1200,
1400-1800. Wonderful views.
F.G.TF.WS.b. E-mail:
annamaria.abbona@libero.it

**MONFORTE D'ALBA**
**Az Agr Costa di Bussia\***
Tenuta Arnolfo, Loc Bussia
26. Tel: 0173 77017. Fax:
0173 776305. 0800-1800.
18th-century cellars.
Museum. E.F.TF.WS.b.
E-mail: sartirano@isiline.it
**Az Agr Elio Grasso**
Località Ginestra 40. Tel:
0173 78491. Fax 0173
789907 (Elio Grasso).
E.F.TF.WS.B.
E-mail: elio.grasso@isiline.it

*Serralunga d'Alba lies in the hills of the beautiful Langhe area and the heart of the DOCG Barolo zone.*

superior wines. Vineyard names like Cerequio, Cannubi, or Brunate on a bottle indicate that the grapes came from one of these sites. *Bricco* is another common label word; it means "top of the slope" and therefore indicates a site where the grapes will be of outstanding quality because of their long exposure to the sun.

La Morra is a small town in the middle of some of the best sites accounting for 40% of the total DOCG area. This is a town that is full of wine activities. The *Cantina Comunale* (see page 19) is an association of local growers where you can taste Nebbiolo, Dolcetto, Barbera, and, above all, Barolo.

One of their best schemes is the *Sentieri del Vino* footpath system for those who want to combine a healthy walk in the vineyards with wine tasting at a local producer's. Visit the Winery and Museo Ratti at the Abbazia dell'Annunziata nearby, which displays a wine artifact and

documentation collection put together by the late Renato Ratti, the man who began the modern codification of the Barolo vineyards according to the quality of the sites.

## Barolo

From La Morra retrace your route to the road to Barolo and its Enoteca, housed in the eponymous castle with a small museum. It displays Barolo from over a hundred producers. From 1250 to 1864 it was the home of the Falletti, and it was the last Marchesa, Giulia, who is credited with the creation of Barolo in the 19th century.

The first reference to "Barolo wine" comes, in fact, from the cargo list of an English merchant in the 18th century when war with France interrupted supplies from Bordeaux. But it was not until the Marchesa Falletti followed the French practice of vinifying the wine so that it would be drier and age longer that Barolo took on its modern form.

Barolo-producing territory is divided, roughly speaking, into two valleys, the valley of Barolo which includes the communes of Barolo, Annunziata and La Morra, and the valley of Serralunga, with the communes of Serralunga d'Alba, Castiglione Falletto and Monforte. Experts admire the Serralunga valley as the source of some of the biggest and most long-lived wines. Some say that Monforte is the top Barolo site of them all.

## Dogliani

From Barolo take the road to Dogliani, whose Bottega del Vino (open weekends only) is devoted to one of Piedmont's most attractive lighter red wines, Dolcetto. The name derives from the sweetness only of the grapes, which used to be prescribed medically as the basis for a purgative diet. Dolcetto the wine is a smooth and very fragrantly aromatic dry red wine which has a slightly bitter aftertaste.

The return journey to Alba takes in typical picturesque villages of the Langhe. Stop at Serralunga d'Alba for its castle. The pink-striped winery down in the valley is Fontanafredda, sited in the old hunting lodge where Victor Emmanuel II, first King of all Italy, kept his mistress "La Bella Rosin".

## Barbaresco

Barolo's lighter cousin, is how Barbaresco is described by those who do not know it. In fact, Barbaresco is often just as robust and often just as full-bodied, despite the fact that its obligatory aging in barrel is one year less. As usual, individual styles of winemaking confound most generalizations.

But Barbaresco is much smaller in vineyard area than Barolo, and much more difficult to find outside its production zone. Angelo Gaja has made it famous, not least because his indisputably good wines are also some of Italy's most expensive.

By way of compensation, the wines of the local co-operative, Produttori del Barbaresco, are some of the best value and finest quality of any co-operative in Italy. One of the best places to taste Barbaresco is the Enoteca (see page 18), which is sited in the deconsecrated church of San Donato in the main square of Barbaresco itself.

### The "Four Wines" of Neive

Close to Barbaresco is the hilltop town of Neive, where high-quality Barbaresco is produced. Its ancient Town Hall is the site of the Bottega dei Quattro Vini, an Enoteca run by an association of 29 local producers.

The Four Wines have now grown into ten, reflecting the growth of popularity of new wine styles in Piedmont and the general development in sophistication of wine tourism and wine production.

To the original quartet of Barbera, Dolcetto, Moscato and Barbaresco, have been added Arneis (a local rediscovery), Freisa (ditto), Chardonnay (international style), Sauvignon (ditto), Nebbiolo (declassified Barbaresco), Passito wines (very fashionable), together with sales of grappa, mushrooms, truffles and handmade confectionery.

## LA MORRA

**Az Agr Poderi Marcarini** Piazza Martiri 2. Tel: 0173 50222. Fax: 0173 509035. (Manuel Marchetti). 0800-1200, 1400-1800. E.Sp.TF.WS.B. E-mail: marcarini@ marcarini.it www.marcarini.it

**Az Agr Renato Ratti** Fraz Annunziata 7. Tel: 0173 50185. Fax: 0173 509373. (Pietro Ratti, Massimo Martinelli). Mon-Fri 0800-1200, 1400-1700. Museum. E.F.TF.WS.B.

**Az Agr Roberto Voerzio** Loc Cerreto. Tel/Fax: 0173 509196. (Roberto Voerzio). 1130-1800. F.TF.WS.B.

**Cantina Comunale di La Morra** Via Carlo Alberto 2. Tel: 0173 509204. Fax: 0173 509043. 1000-1230, 1430-1830. Closed Tue. Video show. E.F.TP.WS.

## NEIVE

**Bottega dei Quattro Vini** Piazza Italia. Tel: 0173 677014. Mon 1600-1900, Wed-Fri 1500-1900, Sat, Sun 1030-1300, 1430-1900. E.F.TP.WS.b.

## SERRALUNGA D'ALBA

**Fontanafredda** Via Alba 15. Tel: 0173 613161. Fax: 0173 613451. Sat, Sun. E.F.G.Sp.TP.WS.B. E-mail: info@fontanafredda.it www.fontanafredda.it

## VERDUNO

**Castello di Verduno\*** Via Umberto 19, 12060 Verduno (CN). Tel: 0172 470284. Fax: 0172 470298. (Gabriella Burlotto). 0900-1200, 1400-1900. *Agriturismo.* E.F.TF./TP.WS.b. www.castellodiverduno.com

## CINZANO

The visit to Cinzano lasts about an hour and a half; it guides the visitor through the history and production of Cinzano sparkling wines and vermouth. The setting is the ex-hunting lodge of Carlo Alberto of Savoia. The visit begins in the sparkling wine cellars and proceeds to the vermouth plant where the hundred herbs and spices used for flavoring perfume the air.

The UDV Glass Collection in the villa comprises more than 140 rare glasses and the Historical Archives contain a fascinating collection of posters from the early part of the century.

**CINZANO MUSEUM AND UDV GLASS COLLECTION\*** Strada Statale 63, 12069 S Vittoria d'Alba (CN). Tel: 0172 477111. Fax: 0172 478002. (Mathilde Elbaz). Mon-Fri a.m. only. Admission free. E.F.G.TF.WS.B. E-mail: santa.vittoria@udv.com

# Vercelli, Carema and Novara

The wines of Asti and Alba are so sumptuous that it is often forgotten that other parts of Piedmont are important for wine production, too.

The distinctive terraces with their stone *topioni* pillars signal the vineyards of the most northerly of Piedmont's Nebbiolo-based wines. Carema is a long-lived wine that has acquired something of a cult following among Italian wine lovers. The local co-operative that is responsible for almost the entire production also runs a Bottega del Vino exclusively to exhibit its Carema wines.

From Carema, continue south on the SS26 to Ivrea, the home town of Olivetti, which has a 14th-century castle and a good museum. A few miles before Ivrea at Borgofranco d'Ivrea look for the centuries-old *balmetti*, over 130 cellar-caves, still in use today.

### Erbaluce di Caluso

South of Ivrea lies the town of Caluso and the zone of the curiously named white wine, Erbaluce di Caluso (loosely translated as "green light of Caluso"). Erbaluce is a traditional Piedmontese grape that has been rediscovered and found to be very suitable for the techniques of modern vinification. Unusually, it can be used for Spumante, for still wines and for a highly prized *passito* wine (see Glossary) made from dried grapes. The ancient name for this wine is *vin greco* (Greek wine): wine was introduced to Italy by the Greeks, and *greco* is a term generally used in Italy for bunches of grapes that grow in two clusters rather than one.

Caluso is west of the Dora Baltea river which passes through Ivrea. If at Ivrea the traveller turns off the SS26 and goes east of the river on the SS228, the next important stop is the castle of Roppolo on the banks of Lake Viverone.

*A medieval watchtower guards vineyards overlooking the town of Gattinara.*

The Enoteca Regionale della Serra (see page 19) in this castle is probably better known to the tourists who come to vacation by the lake than to Italians. Its history, though, is intimately connected with wine – and is reflected in the emblems on the coat of arms of one of its first lords.

The story goes that one Carlo Beccaria, servant to Lothario I, alerted his master to a poisoned chalice that he was just about to drink. Thankful for his escape, Lothario ennobled his servant, and gave him the castle of Roppolo and the right to display his own coat of arms, which is still in evidence at the castle today: three chalices full of red wine on a silver ground. Carlo Beccaria then changed his name to Carlo Bicchiero (*bicchiere* meaning glass).

**CAREMA**
**Cantina Produttori Nebbiolo di Carema** Via Nazionale 28. Tel/Fax: 0125 811160. (Clerin Muggiani). 0900-1200, 1430-1900. E.F.T.F.WS. (B for groups). E-mail: cantinacarema@libero.it

**GATTINARA**
**ER di Gattinara e delle Terre del Nebbiolo del Nord Piemonte** C.so Valsesia 112. Tel/Fax: 0163 834070. 1000-1230, 1600-1930. Closed Mon. E.F.T.F./TP.WS. E-mail: fizzcom@tiscalinet.it www.gattinaradocg.it

Some of the historical associations of this castle are less pleasant, however: it is said to have the ghost of the knight Bernardo di Mazzei who was walled up alive in the castle in the 15th century.

The Enoteca specializes in the wines of the area around Vercelli and Novara: principally the Nebbiolo-based wines from around Gattinara, but Erbaluce from Caluso as well. It is also a hotel and restaurant, and outdoor concerts are held here in the summer.

**Towards Milan**

Taking the motorway E13 at Santhià and heading east, the traveller begins to encounter the rice fields that were originally planted to form a quickly floodable defense for Milan. Pasta as a food is a relatively recent addition to the northern Italian diet; risotto is more traditional here.

Exit on the SS299 at Agognate and the line of wine towns begins with Fara, then Sizzano, Ghemme and finally Gattinara. Lessona is a few miles to the east, Boca a few miles to the west. All of these towns give their names to Nebbiolo-based wines which have the potential to age well and are much lighter than their better-known southern Piedmontese cousins, Barolo and Barbaresco. The Nebbiolo in this area is called Spanna, and this is also the name used for wines that are not generally of the standard of those named after their towns of origin.

Of all these wines Gattinara seems to be the one with the most potential. History relates that viticulture began in the area with the Romans and that Cardinal Mercurino Arborio, the native of Gattinara who became Chancellor to Emperor Charles V, served Gattinara wine at court. Even 20th-century experts agreed that Gattinara was an exceptional wine –

*The spire of San Gaudenzio in Novara resembles Turin's more famous Mole Antonelliana.*

until about 20 years ago, that is, when overproduction and bad cellar practices gave the wine a reputation as lean, unbalanced and tannic. Giving it the DOCG classification recently was the necessary impulse to change direction. Only about half a million bottles are produced every year by a very small band of growers. It is in their interest to upgrade the wine's image and quality. This is now being done: a visit to the Bottega del Vino in Gattinara itself is recommended.

**GHEMME**
**Antichi Vigneti di Cantalupo*** Via M Buonarroti 5. Tel: 0163 840041. Fax: 0163 841595. (Alberto or Giulio Arlunno). 0800-1200, 1400-1800. E.F.TP.WS.B. E-mail: cantalupovigneti@ tiscalinet.it www.cantalupovigneti.com

# Acqui, Ovada and Gavi

**GAVI**
**Az Vit Castellari Bergaglio***
Fraz Rovereto. Tel: 0143
644000. Fax: 0143 644900.
0900-1230, 1400-1800.
E.TP.WS.B. E-mail:
gavi@castellaribergaglio.it
www.castellaribergaglio.it **[1]**
**Tenuta La Giustiniana***
Fraz Rovereto 5. Tel: 0143
682132. Fax: 0143 682085.
E.F.TF.WS.b. E-mail:
lagiustiniana@libarnanet.it **[2]**
**Az Agr La Chiara*** Loc
Vallegge 24/2. Tel/Fax: 0143
642293. E.F.TF.WS.b. **[3]**

**TAGLIOLO MONFERRATO**
**Az Agr Castello di
Tagliolo*** Via Castello 1. Tel:
0143 89195. Fax: 0143 896387.
0800-1800. E.F.G.TF.WS. (B for
groups). E-mail:
castelloditagliolo@tin.it **[4]**

In the borderlands where Lombardy,
Emilia Romagna, Piedmont and
Liguria intersect there are three
distinct wine areas.

## Acqui Terme and Ovada
A bare 18km (11 miles) separates these
two towns, one a spa in the plain, the
other a border town in the hills. Both
have a Dolcetto with their town names
as a *denominazione*, though it is the
Dolcetto d'Ovada that is attracting
attention in the wine world at the
moment. At last, in Ovada at least, this
grape seems capable of producing rich,
chocolatey wines with a good structure.

Acqui Terme, by contrast, is also
well known for the sweet sparkling
dessert wine that has become popular
in North America, Brachetto d'Acqui.

Acqui Terme has been famous since
Roman times for its therapeutic waters.
Pliny the Elder was amused by the
contradictory name for the local wines,
*vinum aquense*, or "water wines."
However, the town's coat of arms is an
aqueduct with a bunch of grapes above
it, and Acqui is still known both for its
spring waters and its wine. Palazzo
Robellini in the town is the site of the
Enoteca Regionale, which specializes in
the wines of this area. Acqui is worth
visiting anyway for its cathedral, its
castle and its museum of archeology.

## Gavi
Moving east from Ovada you come to
the place of a wine legend – Gavi.

Gavi, the wine, shot to fame some
20 years ago as the local white wine,
made from the Cortese grape. Called
Gavi if it was within the larger
*denominazione* area and Gavi di Gavi if
it was in the smaller *classico* area, it was
suddenly hailed by an influential
journalist as Italy's answer to white
Burgundy. It was, in any case, the most
serious Piedmontese white wine that
had appeared for a long time. Prices
went sky high and restaurants began to
demand a Gavi on their list at any cost.

Since then, the bubble has burst and
Gavi is being re-evaluated. But,
ironically enough, the wine itself has
never been better than it is now. It may
be comparable to a Mâcon – it has that
steely fruitiness and moderate aging
ability. But Puligny-Montrachet, it isn't.
It can take a dose of new oak, it can be
made into a sparkling wine, but neither
of these treatments are necessary.
Enjoy it as it is, a superior white wine
without being a Fine Wine.

Gavi the town is charming. It is
dominated by an imposing castle and
has a network of narrow, winding
streets at the foot of the castle hill.

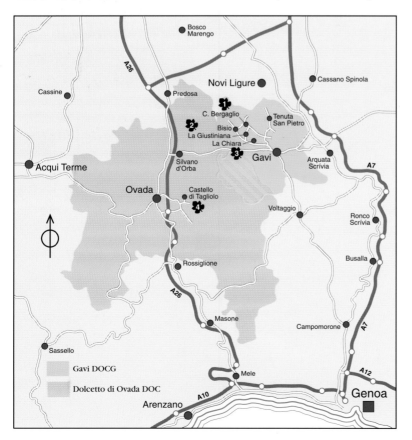

# Oltrepò Pavese

The *Milanesi* drink the wines of Oltrepò Pavese. Indeed, the villas and castles of this charming countryside of hilltop towns and villages are often owned by families from Lombardy's capital city.

As a consequence, the wines find a ready local market and are rarely seen outside the area. Don't be surprised to find that the young wines often have a slight sparkle to them, both the whites and the reds. This is quite deliberate; the food of Milan with the sticky delights of dishes such as *ossobuco* needs a wine with the freshness of youth and a refreshing sparkle to counteract its richness. Throw away all traditional Anglo-Saxon prejudices about what red wine should be like (old, full-bodied and complex, served at room temperature and made of Cabernet grapes) and you will find that what the local salami needs is a young, slightly sparkling, cool cellar-temperature easy-drinking wine, such as Barbera or Bonarda.

There is a well-developed *Strada del Vino* system to follow, and local producers are used to receiving visitors. Montelio at

*These rolling, vine-clad hills are typical of Oltrepò Pavese – the land "on the other side of the river Po."*

Codevilla organize day tours which take in visits to their vineyards and cellars, lunch in a local restaurant, a visit to historic monuments and the opportunity to buy local salami and almond cakes.

The Fugazza sisters at the castle of Luzzano are one of the region's best producers, and offer *agriturismo* opportunities and organized tours of the area with detailed itineraries. Each area has its own wine specialty. Rovescala is well known for its Bonarda. Santa Maria della Versa is famous for its sparkling wines, particularly from the highly regarded local co-operative winery. Canneto is the place of origin of two rare and colorfully named wines, Sangue di Giuda (Judas' Blood) and Battafuoco (Sparks of Fire). Recent efforts to bring international standards into the area have met with success with wines such as Vercesi del Castellazzo's excellent Pinot Nero. Whatever the wine, the vineyards are a picture.

**CASTEGGIO**
**Tenuta Pegazzera\*** Via Vigorelli 151. Tel/Fax: 0383 804646. Mon-Fri 0900-1200, 1400-1700; Sat 0900-1200. Sun by appointment only. E.F.WS.B. (TP for groups).

**CODEVILLA**
**Az Agr Montelio\*** Via Domenico Mazza 1. Tel: 0383 373090. Fax: 0383 373083. 0830-1200, 1430-1800. E.TP.WS.B.

**MONTÙ BECCARIA**
**Az Agr Vercesi del Castellazzo\*** Via Aureliano 36. Tel/Fax: 0385 262098. 0930-1230, 1430-1830. E.F.TF.WS.b. (TP.B. for groups).

**ROVESCALA**
**Az Agr Martilde\*** Fraz Croce 4/A/1. Tel/Fax: 0385 756280. E.TP.WS.B. E-mail: martilde@martilde.it www.martilde.it
**Castello di Luzzano\***
*See page 74 for details.*

**S MARIA DELLA VERSA**
**Fattoria Gambero** Tel: 02 5454213. Fax: 02 5454576. F.G.TF.

**S GIULETTA**
**Le Buone Terre di Castello Az Agr Marchesi\*** Casa G Pietro, Fraz Castello. Tel: 0383 899733. Fax: 0383 814063. 1000-1200, 1500-1900. Organic wine. Museum. Restaurant. F.TF.WS.B. (TP for groups). E-mail: marchesi.daniele@tin.it
**Az Agr Isimbarda\*** Cascina Isimbarda. Tel: 0383 899256. Fax: 0383 814077. Mon-Fri 0830-1230, 1400-1800; Sat 0830-1230. F.TF.WS.b.

# Liguria

*Vineyards surround the villages in the coastal hills of Liguria. Very little wine is exported, and the region's vineyard area has been in slow decline for some years.*

**CASTELNUOVO MAGRA**
**Az Agr Ottaviano Lambruschi** Via Olmarello 28. Tel/Fax: 0187 674261. (Fabio Lambruschi). E.TF.WS.b.
**ER Liguria e della Lunigiana** Palazzo Ingolotti-Cornelio. Tel: 0187 693801. Fax: 0187 670102. Open summer Tue-Sun 0900-1200, 1600-2000; winter Fri-Sun 1600-1900. Wide selection of Ligurian wines. E.F.G.b.

**CHIAVARI**
**Enoteca Bisson** Corso Gianelli 28r. Tel: 0185 314462. E.F.G.TF.WS.EP. E-mail: ggcava@tin.it www.enotecabisson.it

**IMPERIA**
**Enoteca Fratelli Lupi** Via Monte 13, Loc Oneglia. Tel: 0183 291610.

**MANAROLA**
**Cooperativa Agricoltura di Riomaggiore Manarola Corniglia Vernazza e Monterosso** Loc Groppo. Tel: 0187 920435. Fax: 0187 920076. E.F.TF.WS.

**Via dell'Amore**
The beautiful walk from town to town on the coast linking the Cinque Terre is subject to a small entry charge (5,000 Lire – $2.40 – in 2001).

The English Romantic poet Shelley set the example. English travellers have been attracted to the steeply sloping bay of the Italian Riviera for generations. Indeed, their old villas give the area a feeling of faded gentility even today.

Most wine produced in Liguria is for local consumption – and for the descendants of those pioneering travellers, who are now more likely to be making just a brief trip to Portofino. The peasant wine producer is a dying breed; working the steep slopes of the vineyards is difficult, and only a part-time activity for most of the vine-growers who remain.

Liguria's interest for the wine connoisseur lies in the tips at either end of its half-moon shape.

Soon after crossing the border from France near Ventimiglia, a left turn to the town of Dolceacqua brings one to the vineyards of Liguria's only serious red wine, the Rossese di Dolceacqua. Dolceacqua, with its ruined medieval castle and picturesque charm, is typical of the villages of the Valle di Nervia.

At the other tip of the crescent is the delightful area of the Cinque Terre. Only the first of these five villages, Monterosso al Mare, is readily accessible by car. But to reach the others it is a pleasure to walk the cliff path through the olive groves and the vineyards of Liguria's most famous white wine, Cinque Terre. This dry wine goes well with the local fish, but the most prized version is the dessert wine, Schiacchetrà.

# Food of North-West Italy

## Aosta

This is not an olive oil-producing region, but the butter and cheeses are very good.
*Cotoletta alla Valdostana:* veal fried with ham topped with fontina cheese.
*Carbonade:* meat stew with onions and red wine.
*Fonduta:* Alpine fondue.

## Liguria

Extra-virgin olive oil is the traditional all-purpose condiment, fish the traditional main course.
*Pesto:* ground mixture of basil, garlic, oil and pine nuts, a sauce for pasta, especially with trenette (pasta).
*Torta Pasqualina:* a savory Easter dish made of puff pastry filled with ricotta and chard or spinach mixed with eggs.
Fish: *baccalà* (salt cod), *bianchetti* (whitebait), *triglie* (red mullet).
*Farinata:* type of pizza bread made with olive oil and chickpeas.

## Piedmont

The produce of the *contadino* (peasant farmer), such as corn, hazelnuts, apples, rabbits, pigs and oxen inspires the traditional dishes. In the rice-growing area of Novara soups and risottos are traditional.
*Bagna cauda:* fresh vegetables accompanied by a dip made with olive oil, anchovies and much garlic.
*Vitello tonnato:* cold roast veal with a creamy tuna fish sauce.
*Brasato al Barolo:* beef braised in Barolo.
*Finanziera:* lights and brains in a wine and cream sauce.
*Fritto misto:* mixed fried meats, brains and semolina.
*Bollito misto:* mixed boiled meats.
*Bonet:* chocolate pudding.
*Carne cruda all'Albese:* thinly sliced raw meat dressed with oil, lemon and thin slices of parmesan.
*Gianduja:* hazelnut chocolate.

*A Piedmontese trifolau or truffle hunter with his sharp-nosed hound – and a stick to make sure the dog isn't too successful.*

### TRUFFLES

The famous *tartufo bianco d'Alba* (*tuber magnatum pico*) is the finest Italian truffle and to be distinguished from the more common black truffle (*tuber unicatum*) found all over Italy. The Alba truffle season runs from October to December and the truffles themselves are found in the hills of the provinces of Asti and Alba by the *trifolau*, or truffle-hunters, who use dogs to find their precious walnut-sized produce in pre-dawn excursions to secret locations.

Fortunes can be made by the lucky discoverer of good-sized truffles in good condition, which are sold privately for handfuls of cash in brief early morning encounters in the arcades of Asti, Alba, Moncalvo and Nizza Monferrato. Prices, up to more than $300 per 100g (3.5 ounces), depend on truffle size and the season. Members of the public can buy in the shops, or on the web. More information: www.albatartufi.com

**FOR FURTHER INFORMATION**

**Assessorato al Turismo** (Piedmontese Tourist Board) Via Magenta 12, 10128 Torino. Tel: 011 43211. Booklets include the excellent *Our Piedmont: short combinable itineraries for a long and unforgettable vacation* (suggestions from members of *Le Donne del Vino del Piemonte* – the Women of Wine in Piedmont). E-mail: regione.turismo@ regione.piemonte

**Azienda Promozione Turistica** Viale Mazzini 45, 19124 La Spezia. Tel: 0187 770900. Fax 0187 770908. Information on the Cinque Terre area in Liguria. E-mail: info@aptcinqueterre.sp.it www.aptcinqueterre.sp.it

*Continued from page 23*

**MOASCA**
**Cascina La Ghersa-Pietro Barbero\*** Via San Giuseppe 19. Tel: 0141 856012. Fax: 0141 856484. (Massimo Pastura Barbero). 0830-1200, 1400-1700. E.F.TF.WS.b. E-mail: info@pietrobarbero.it www.pietrobarbero.it

**ROCCHETTA TANARO**
**Braida\*** Via Roma 94. Tel: 0141 644113. Fax: 0141 644584. 0900-1200, 1500-1800. E.F.G.TF.WS.B. E-mail: info@braida.it www.braida.it

**Cantine dei Marchesi Incisa della Rocchetta\*** La Corte Chiusa, Via Roma 66. Tel: 0141 644647. Fax: 0141 644942. Sat-Mon 1000-1200, 1500-1800. Guest rooms. E.F.G.TF.WS.b. E-mail: marchesi.incisa@ lacortechiusa.it www.lacortechiusa.it

# North Central Italy

Three distinct wine-producing areas make up north central Italy: the slopes and hills of the Adige and Isarca valleys which lead into Austria, the Valtellina that skirts the southern border with Switzerland, and the hills that are strung along the line between Bergamo and Lake Garda. Two regions of Italy are involved: Lombardy and Trentino-Alto Adige.

Lombardy is the industrial powerhouse of Italy, and alone is responsible for about 20 per cent of the gross national product. Milan is such a cosmopolitan city that it stands apart from the other widely differing principal cities of Bergamo, Brescia, Mantua and Pavia. Indeed, it is difficult to find a common characteristic for the Lombardi, a fact that is reflected in the wine production, too.

Many excellent wines come from the hills above Bergamo, from Franciacorta west of Brescia, from the Valtellina, and from the western banks of Lake Garda. If any wine is a leader in these areas at the moment, it is probably sparkling Franciacorta.

Further east, Trentino-Alto Adige is a very divided area. In 1918 what was part of the Austro-Hungarian Tyrol was given to Italy, and renamed Alto Adige. Later Mussolini tried his best to Italianize the region by settling industrial workers from the South in the area, and incidentally promoting the wine of Santa Maddalena to the official rank of third-best wine in Italy (the other two were more obvious choices then: Barolo and Barbaresco).

The Alto Adige retained its independent spirit, however, and although German and Italian are the dual official languages of the area, German is more commonly used.

In Alto Adige the vast majority of the wine produced is DOC, a high proportion for Italy, which in fact reflects the economic reality that it makes little sense in this area of mountainous labor-intensive wine production to centralize the wines to make a mass market product. This is also the reason why the co-operatives of both Trentino and Alto Adige are among Italy's finest. With so much effort going into pendulous viticulture in steep vineyards, the wine had better be good.

Some of the best wines in Italy are now coming from the mountain slopes of the Adige valley, and the chorus of approval for Pinot Nero has been loud recently. The Valtellina, a valley lying just south of Switzerland, has been wrestling with a legacy of old-fashioned high-alcohol wine styles. The flagship wine, Sfursat, is a raisiny wine made in the same way as Verona's Amarone – by leaving the grapes to dry and concentrate in sugar before pressing. Only now are the leading producers finding out how to produce the elegance that modern consumers demand.

Franciacorta is another matter. Sparkling Franciacorta is now DOCG, and very proud of it, too. The leading producers, Ca' del Bosco and Bellavista particularly, have long made superb sparkling wines, and the Italians themselves can't get enough of it.

Franciacorta is also a naturally attractive area full of country villas, lakes and soft hills. It has also adopted wine tourism with enthusiasm; so a positive experience is guaranteed.

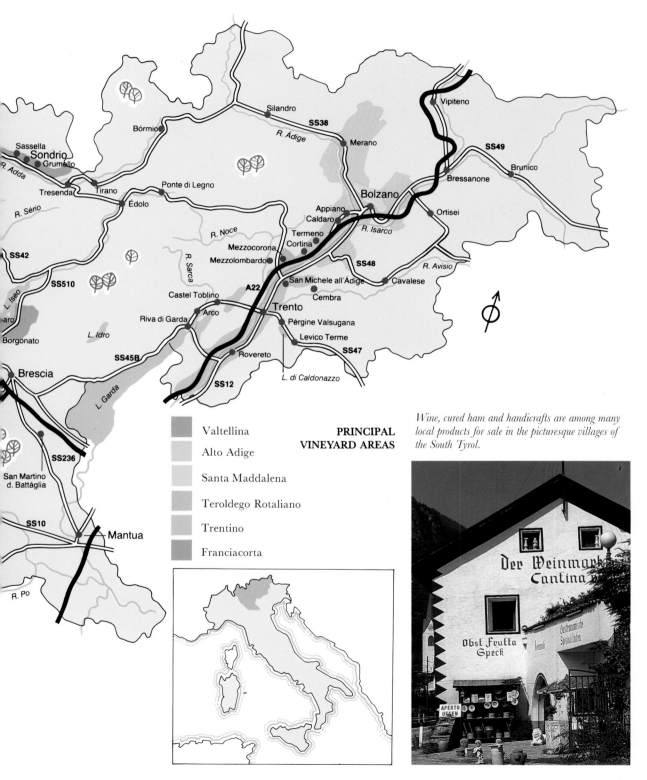

Silandro
**SS38**
Bórmio
*R. Ádige*
Vipiteno
Merano
**SS49**
Bressanone
Brunico
Sassella
Sondrio
Grumello
*R. Adda*
Tirano
Ponte di Legno
Bolzano
Tresenda
*R. Sério*
Édolo
Appiano
Caldaro
Ortisei
*R. Isarco*
Termeno
Cortina
**SS42**
*R. Noce*
Mezzocorona
*R. Sarca*
Mezzolombardo
**SS48**
San Michele all'Ádige
Cavalese
*R. Avisio*
**SS510**
*L. Iseo*
Castel Toblino
**A22**
Cembra
Trento
-aro
Arco
Riva di Garda
Pérgine Valsugana
Borgonato
*L. Idro*
Levico Terme
Rovereto
**SS47**
Brescia
*L. Garda*
**SS45B**
**SS12**
*L. di Caldonazzo*
**SS236**
San Martino
d. Battáglia
**SS10**
Mantua
*R. Po*

**PRINCIPAL
VINEYARD AREAS**

Valtellina

Alto Adige

Santa Maddalena

Teroldego Rotaliano

Trentino

Franciacorta

*Wine, cured ham and handicrafts are among many local products for sale in the picturesque villages of the South Tyrol.*

# South Tyrol – *the* Weinstrasse

*Caldaro is typical of the picturesque towns along the South Tyrol's Weinstrasse. Weinverkauf signs outside shops and wine producers' premises indicate that wine is for sale.*

## The wines

Most of the production is in the hands of co-operatives, necessarily so in this area where average vineyard holdings are so small in size. To their credit, it is the leading co-operatives just as much as the individual producers who are in the vanguard of wine development in this area.

It is the bigger red wines of South Tyrol, varietals made from Pinot Noir and Cabernet, that are attracting the most attention in the wine world at the moment. Low yields from high-altitude vineyards and vinification using *barriques* are the characteristics of the new blockbuster red wines.

At the same time the whites are being made with good fruit and length, Chardonnay and Sauvignon are just as popular here as native varietals such as Gewürztraminer. But the wines will never be cheap – the intensive labor involved in mountain viticulture ensures that.

### CORTACCIA
**Tiefenbrunner**
Schlosskellerei Turmhof, Via Castello 4. Tel: 0471 880122. Fax: 0471 880433. (Christof Tiefenbrunner). 1000-2000. E.G.TP.WS.B. E-mail: info@ tiefenbrunner.com

### MAGRÈ
**Alois Lageder Tenuta Löwengang** Tel: 0471 809500. Fax: 0471 809550. (Alois Lageder). Mon-Fri 1000-1300, 1500-1900; Sat 1000-1300, 1500-1700. E.G.TP.WS.B.EP. E-mail: info@lageder.com www.lageder.com

### NALLES
**Castel Schwanburg** Via Schwanburg 16. Tel: 0471 678622. Fax: 0471 678430. (Dieter Rudolph). 0800-1200, 1400-1800. F.G.TP.WS.B.

### TERMENO
**Vigneti-Cantina Vini Josef Hofstätter** Piazza Municipio 5. Tel: 0471 860161. Fax: 0471 860789. E.G.TF.WS. E-mail: info@hofstatter.com www.hofstatter.com

### WINE MUSEUM
**Südtiroler Weinmuseum** Goldgasse 1, Caldaro. Tel: 0471 963168. Apr 1 to Nov 11, Mon-Sat 0930-1200, 1400-1800. Sun and holidays 1000-1200. Charge for entry. G. E-mail: volkskundemuseum@ provinz.bz.it www.provinz.bz.it/ volkskundemuseum

# Franciacorta

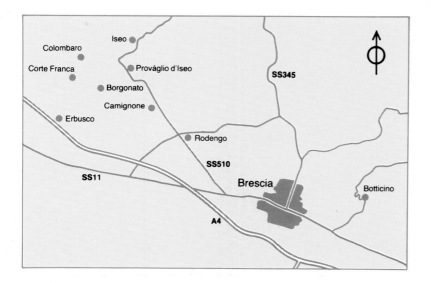

## BERGAMO

### GRUMELLO DEL MONTE
**Carlozadra\*** Via Gandossi 13. Tel: 035 830244. Fax: 035 4420417. Closed Jan. E.G.TP.WS.EP. E-mail: carlozadra@tiscalinet.it

## FRANCIACORTA

### BORGONATO
**F.lli Berlucchi\*** Via Broletto 2. Tel: 030 984451. Fax: 030 9828209. 0830-1230, 1330-1730. Historic cellars. E.F.WS.B. E-mail: info@berlucchifranciacorta.it www.berlucchifranciacorta.it
**Berlucchi Guido & C** Piazza Durante 4. Tel: 030 984381. Fax: 030 984293. E.F.TF.WS.B.

### CAPRIOLO
**Az Agr Ricci Curbastro\*** Via Adro 37, Villa Evelina. Tel: 030 736094. Fax: 030 7460558. 0830-1200, 1430-1900. Agricultural life museum. *Agriturismo.* E.F.Sp.TP.WS.b. E-mail: agrit.riccicur@imp.it www.riccicurbastro.com

The area between Bergamo and Lake Garda does not seem an obvious choice for the wine lover. The principal town of the area, Brescia, is better known for its steel mills and armaments factories than for its wines. But it is difficult to find a corner of Italy without sights to see and wine to discover; and this is no exception.

## Bergamo
The principal DOC is Valcalepio, which comes from an area east of Bergamo, once the ancient domains of the Calepio family. The reds, made from Merlot and Cabernet Sauvignon, are more interesting than the whites, mostly Pinot Bianco and Pinot Grigio, although there are some good sparkling wines in the area.

Bergamo itself has a delightful medieval old town, the Città Alta. Don't miss the Colleoni Chapel at Santa Maria Maggiore and the Accademia Carrara museum of art.

## Franciacorta
The Franciacorta area, just to the west of Brescia, has become famous as Italy's premier bottle-fermented sparkling wine area, while at the same time improving the quality of Terre di Franciacorta, its still red and white wines. The first of its type to gain the prestigious DOCG appellation, Franciacorta is now very much a brand in its own right, in proud distinction to Italy's otherwise blanket brand of Talento.

No one is completely sure about the origin of the name Franciacorta. Some say it comes from the time when French troops settled in the area in the 16th century; others that it dates from the time when tax exemption was granted to the local monasteries. Whatever lies in its name, this is an area of gentle hills south of Lake Iseo full of villas that were built as the country mansions of the Brescian and Bergamasc nobility.

Franciacorta is just the other side of the Oglio river to Valcalepio. Start at Capriolo, a little hilltop town with medieval streets and some fine town houses. Its name derives from the roe deer which used to be common in the area. Go on to Paratico with its castle ruins and local legend that Dante composed part of the *Purgatorio* here.

Clusane, on Lake Iseo, declares itself *il paese della tinca al forno* ("the land of baked tench," fish from the lake, usually served with polenta).

Turning back from the lake towards the vineyards again, go towards Corte Franca. A neat inversion of Franciacorta, Corte Franca as a name only dates back to 1928, and reflects the common origin of the four villages of the new borough as rural domains, free from feudal dues after the drainage of the farmland by monks from San Pietro in Lamosa. (The monastery itself is at Provaglio d'Iseo – it suffered from neglect after disestablishment in 1817, but has now been restored.)

Borgonato, the first village, has its history linked to the Lana family who constructed two *palazzi*, now owned by

**ERBUSCO**
**Az Agr Bellavista\*** Via
Bellavista 5. Tel: 030
7762000. Fax: 030 7760386.
Mon-Fri after 1000. Closed
harvest time. E.F.G.TF.B.
E-mail: bellavista@
terramoretti.it
www.terramoretti.it
**Enoteca Le Cantine di
Franciacorta\*** Via Iseo 56.
Tel: 030 7751116. Fax: 030
7751126. Wines at direct-
from-the-cellar prices.
E.F.TF.WS.
E-mail: cantine@
cantinefranciacorta.com
www.cantinefranciacorta.com
**Ca' del Bosco** Via Case
Sparse 20. Tel: 030 7766111.
Fax: 030 7268425. 0900-
1200, 1400-1800. E.F.TF.B.
E-mail: cadelbosco@
cadelbosco.com
www.cadelbosco.it
**Az Agr Cavalleri** Via
Provinciale 96. Tel: 030
7760217. Fax: 030 7267350.
Mon-Fri 0900-1200, 1400-
1700; Sat 0900-1200.
E.TF.WS.B.
E-mail: cavalleri@cavalleri.it
www.cavalleri.it

**GARDA**

**CASTREZZONE DI
MUSCOLINE**
**Az Agr La Guarda\*** Via
Zanardelli 50. Tel/Fax: 0365
372948. E.F.TP.WS. (B for
groups).

**UGANA DI SIRMIONE**
**Az Agr Ca' dei Frati\*** Via
Frati 22. Tel/Fax: 030
919468. 0800-1200, 1400-
1900. E.F.G.TF.WS.b.
E-mail: info@cadeifrati.it
www.cadeifrati.it

**PUEGNAGO**
**Az Agr Masserino\*** Via
Masserino 2. Tel/Fax: 0365
651757. E.G.WS. (TP.B. for
groups).

*Borgonato, a medieval village with the two Berlucchi
wine companies within its confines.*

two branches of the Berlucchi family.
Colombaro, nearby, has clearly visible
origins as a fortified village.

Adro, a small town at the foot of
Monte Alto, with many fine old
*palazzi*, is the next stop. One
kilometer (half a mile) outside the
town, the church of Santa Maria in
Favento is rich in votive frescoes.

The modern center of sparkling
Franciacorta wine is Erbusco. The
church of Santa Maria Assunta has
magnificent frescoes, and Villa Lechi,
one of the many noble villas of the
area, is unusually grand. Bellavista and
Cà del Bosco, the two producers with
the finest reputations for Franciacorta
sparkling wines, are based in this area.

Castle enthusiasts might like to visit
Passirano. Its well preserved medieval
fortress was built as a defense against
Hungarian invaders in the 10th century.

## Lake Garda

The city of Brescia is surrounded by
steep slopes, with the DOC wines
Cellatica to the west and Botticino to the
east. Neither denomination is of much
more than local interest. The hinterland
of Lake Garda on the Brescian shore,
from Salò southwards to Sirmione, is not
as well known as the opposite bank on
the Veronese shore at Bardolino, at least
in wine terms. But there are experts who
say that the vineyards on the Brescian
side are actually superior in quality.

Whatever the reality, the one wine
from this part of Lake Garda to make
an international impression is Lugana,
a superior white wine made from the
Trebbiano grape variety, here believed
to be closer to Verdicchio in type.

# Trentino

With so many tourists passing through from Austria on their way south, and so many passing through from Italy on their way north, Trentino is well organized for wine tourism (see page 45 for details of useful publications).

Trento, the scene of the Council of Trent (1545-63), is a good starting point for your tour. Visit the former palace of the Prince Bishops at the Castello del Buonconsiglio, and the Duomo.

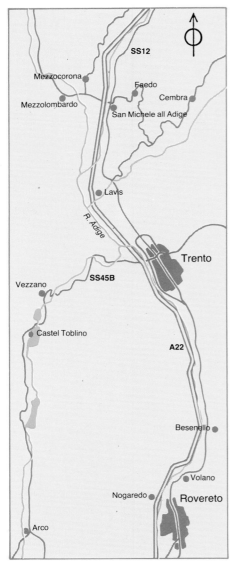

## Principal wines

Dry sparkling wines are a specialty of the Trentino wineries. The best of Italian *metodo classico* wines, Ferrari, is made here. Chardonnay is the up-and-coming white, but made in the fresh Italian fashion rather than aged in oak. Other whites to look out for are Pinot Bianco and Pinot Grigio, Riesling and Traminer. A curiosity is the Vino Santo, produced only in the Sarca valley from Nosiola grapes dried on racks and pressed about Eastertime.

Teroldego and Marzemino are the most famous Trentino reds. Caldaro, Lagrein and Casteller are lighter reds. The international trio of Cabernet Sauvignon, Cabernet Franc and Pinot Nero are increasingly popular; Trentino seems to bring out their aromatic qualities very successfully.

## Cembra and Teroldego

From Trento go north to Lavis on the SS12 and stop at the Cantina La Vis to visit their *Vinoteca* visitor center for a tasting orientation of wines of the Trento hills and Cembra valley.

After Lavis turn east to Cembra for a pretty route up the valley, whose steep right bank is covered with terraces of vines. Cembra's co-operative, its Cantina Sociale, is the highest in Europe, and specializes in Caldaro and Müller-Thurgau.

Descending the valley again and taking the road to San Michele all'Adige via Faedo, the vines are trained in the centuries-old *pergola trentina* fashion that is unique to Trentino.

San Michele has the well-known Istituto Agrario Provinciale and Experimental Wine School in the buildings of an old monastery, where wines may be tasted. The folk museum here is also worth a visit.

**BORGHETTO ALL'ADIGE**
**Az Agr Marchese Carlo Guerrieri Gonzaga***
Tenuta S Leonardo. Tel: 0464 689004. Fax: 0464 682200. (Luigino Tinelli). 0800-1200, 1330-1730. Museum. E.F.TF.WS.B. E-mail: info@sanleonardo.it www.sanleonardo.it

**CIVEZZANO**
**Az Agr Maso Cantanghel***
Via Madonnina 33. Tel/Fax: 0461 859050. (Piero Zabini). 1000-1800. Historic cellars. Restaurant. F.G.TF.WS.b.

**LAVIS**
**Cantina La Vis Scarl***
Via Carmine 7. Tel: 0461 246325. Fax: 0461 240718. (Rosario Pilati). 0900-1200, 1500-1900. Visitor center. E.G.TF./TP.WS.b.ER. E-mail: cantlavis@tin.it

**MARANO D'ISERA**
**Az Agr de Tarczal*** Via G B Mori 4. Tel: 0464 409134. Fax: 0464 409086. (Ruggero de Tarczal). 0800-1200, 1400-1800. E.F.G.TF.WS.B. (TP for groups). E-mail: tarczal@tin.it www.detarczal.it

**MEZZOCORONA**
**Cantina Rotari** Via del Teroldego 1. Tel: 0461 616300. Fax: 0461 616304. (Sabrina Cattani). Mon-Sat 0830-1230, 1400-1800. Guided Tour. E.F.G.TF.b. E-mail: visite@mezzacorona.it www.mezzacorona.it

**ROVERETO**
**Az Agr Letrari*** Via Monte Baldo 13/15. Tel: 0464 480200. Fax: 0464 401451. (Lucia & Paolo Emilio Letrari). 0800-1230, 1330-1900. 16th-century cellars. E.F.G.TF.WS.b. E-mail: pletrari@tin.it www.letrari.com

Crossing to the other bank of the Adige brings one to the plains of Mezzocorona and Mezzolombardo. Visit the Rotari cellars for a guided tour of a stunning modern winery and a glass of Rotari sparkling wine to finish. Return to Trento via Sorni.

## Casteller and Marzemino

Wherever you go in Trentino, fortresses and vineyards line the route. There is a "Wine and Castles" route in the Rovereto area and Rovereto castle itself has an impressive First World War Museum.

Marzemino, the red wine celebrated in Mozart's opera *Don Giovanni*, comes from Isera and the valley of Vallagarina.

Further south, Avio is well known for the quality of its Casteller wine, a light red made from Lambrusco, Merlot and Schiava, taking its name from the Casteller hill just to the south of Trento at Mattarello.

A steep mountain road west from Trento leads to the attractive Sarca Valley also known as the Valley of the Lakes. Castel Toblino is a romantic lakeside castle surrounded by vineyards, and further down the valley in Arco there is an ancient palazzo. Tourist wine stalls, *punti di vendita*, increase in frequency nearer to Lake Garda.

*Vineyards in the hills of Trentino blaze gold in autumn.*

**ROVERETO**
**Az Agr Conti Bossi Fedrigotti*** Via Unione 43. Tel: 0464 439250. Fax: 0464 439631. (Rosanna Grigoletto). 0800-1200, 1400-1800. E.G.TP.WS.B. E-mail: info@fedrigotti.it www.fedrigotti.it

**S MICHELE ALL' ADIGE Istituto Agrario San Michele all'Adige*** Via E Mach 1. Tel: 0461 615111. Fax: 0461 650872. E.F.G.TP.WS.B. E-mail: walter.ecchi@ismaa.it www.ismaa.it

***For further addresses, see page 45.***

# Valtellina

**CHIURO**
**Nino Negri*** Via Ghibellini
3. Tel: 0342 482521. Fax:
0342 482235. 0800-1200,
1400-1800. E.G.TP.WS.B.
E-mail: negri@giv.it
www.giv.it

**TIRANO**
**Conti Sertoli Salis/Salis
1637*** Via Salis 3. Tel: 0342
710404. Fax: 0342 710428.
0930-1130, 1500-1800.
Historic 17th-century palazzo.
E.G.TE./TP.WS.B.
E-mail: info@sertolisalis.com
www.sertolisalis.com

The "powerful wines and terrible
mountains" of the Valtellina were
noted by Leonardo da Vinci in his
travels. Both are much in evidence
today. The dominant grape here is the
same as for Barolo, the Nebbiolo (here
called Chiavennasca), but it produces
rich, balanced wines once famous for
their alcoholic content, best in the
Superiore version (two years' aging) or
the Riserva (four years' aging). An
excellent heavier red is the Sfursat, a
raisiny *passito* wine made like Amarone
from partially dried grapes.

### The wine route from Como
From the northern tip of Lake Como
the main road to Sondrio (SS38)
crosses the Adda after Morbengo, and
the regular pattern of stone-terraced
vineyards soon becomes apparent.
There are vineyards on both sides of
the Adda up to a height of 1200
meters (4000 ft) but the best are those
on the northern bank of the river –
they get more sun. The mountains
shelter both banks from violent
extremes of temperature.

### Valtellina's sub-regions
Just before Sondrio is the first of the
four Valtellina Superiore sub-regions,
Sassella. Visit the 15th-century church
of Madonna della Sassella surrounded
by vineyards. The wine, like all
Valtellina Superiore wines, is best after
three to five years' aging, and goes well
with roasts and strong cheeses.

After the provincial capital, Sondrio,
is the sub-region of Grumello, named
after the medieval castle, whose wine is
said to have a slight almond taste from
the traditional secondary blending
grape, the Brugnola.

Next along the main road is the
sub-region of Inferno, so called
because the hill terraces become so hot
in the summer. The wine is very long-
lived and takes longer to become ready
for drinking than its lighter cousins.

Tresenda marks the limit of the sub-
region of Valgella wine, almost all of
which is exported to Switzerland, the
traditional market for Valtellina wines in
general. Of all the Valtellina wines,
Sassella is said to be the best-structured
and the most refined; but, as usual,
much depends on vintage and producer.

*The town of Bórmio in the Valtellina. Well known
as a skiing resort, it is also the home of a herbal
digestif called Braulio. The onion-shaped dome of
the church indicates Austro-Hungarian influence.*

# Food of North Central Italy

## FOOD SPECIALTIES

### *Törggelen* in the Alto Adige

*Törggelen* is a dialect word that came from the medieval word for the place where wine was served, and before that, from the Latin *torculum* meaning wine press.

Today, *törggelen* describes the very pleasant habit of late autumn trips into the countryside, where the colors of autumn trees and the last of the sun's warmth can be enjoyed at an outdoor table at the same time as the first of the new season's wine is ready. Roast chestnuts, homemade sausage with *sauerkraut* and *speck* (mountain-cured ham) are the normal accompaniments, served in the characteristic hillside *Weinstuben*.

### Local cuisine

In the past Trentino and Alto Adige had similar cooking traditions based on shared Habsburg and Slavonic influences. Now the Trentino has become more typically Italian regional, whereas Alto Adige has been at pains to preserve its own particular traditions. Trentino cooking does exist, but only in the home; it is not a restaurant culture.

Some dishes are common to the two regions. Soups are encountered more frequently than pasta, for example *canederli trentini* (*Südtiroler Knödel* in Alto Adige), a broth with *gnocchi* of speck, cheese or liver, with or without broth.

### Lombard dishes

Lombardy has given us some of the better-known Italian dishes: *Risotto alla milanese* – risotto with saffron; *Cotoletta milanese* – similar to *Wienerschnitzel*; *Ossobuco*; and *panettone* – the traditional Christmas cake.

### Foods from Brescia

Naturally, the best food of Lakes Iseo and Garda is the fish from the lakes and the olive oil from the lakeside.

Rovato is noted for its meat. The plains of Brescia are a great source of cheese and butter. Some of the more noted cheeses are: Grana Padano, similar to parmesan, but not so expensive; Gorgonzola; and Taleggio, a semi-soft cheese from the town of the same name.

Specific dishes include: *Risotto alla pitocca* (chicken risotto); *Minestra mariconda* (pasta in broth); *Tinca all'Iseana* (tench roasted in oil, butter and laurel, coated with breadcrumbs, cheese, rosemary and parsley).

### Valtellina meats and cheeses

The most famous product of the Valtellina is an international favorite: *bresaola*, cured and dried beef. There is a version made from cured goat's meat, *violino*, so called because of the traditional method of carving it in a way that recalls the playing of a violin.

In the province of Sondrio as a whole, specialties include: cheeses such as Bitto, Formaggelle and Stracchino; dishes based on mushrooms; and the inevitable corn dish, *polenta*, a staple of northern Italy, and particularly of Lombardy and the Veneto.

### Grappa

Common to all the mountainous regions of northern Italy, grappa varies in quality considerably and can equally be nectar or fire-water. The producers of Trentino make a soft aromatic version of grappa using the gentle but laborious "Tullio Zadra method." This involves distilling in a *bain-marie* (gentler) and discontinuously (more control), to make refined grappas with elegant aromas. (See also pages 136-7.)

**FOR FURTHER INFORMATION**

**Alto Adige Promozione Turismo** Piazza Parrocchia 11, 39100 Bolzano. Tel: 0471 413808. Fax: 0471 413899. A wealth of information on wine touring in South Tyrol – hotels, itineraries and wineries.

**Camera di Commercio di Trento** Via del Suffragio 3, 38100 Trento. Tel: 0461 235858. Fax: 0461 239853. Map *Trentino DOC, Spumante, Grappa, Vino* and brochure *Itinerari Enoturistici* with wine routes and details of producers.

**APT Rovereto e Vallagarina** Via Dante 63, 38068 Rovereto (TN). Tel: 0464 430363. Fax: 0464 435528. Booklet *Passeggiate tra Vini e Castelli* (Wines and Castles Visits). E-mail: rovereto@apt.rovereto.tn.it www.apt.rovereto.tn.it

**Promozione Franciacorta** Via Brescia 87, 25050 Rodengo Saiano. Tel: 030 6811004. Fax: 030 6811917. *Franciacorta Itineraries* (also in English).

*Continued from page 43*

**TRENTO**
**Cavit*** Via del Ponte 31, Loc Ravina. Tel: 0461 381711. Fax: 0461 912700. 0800-1200, 1300-1700. E.G.TF.WS.B. E-mail: cavit@cavit.it www.cavit.it
**Ferrari*** Via del Ponte di Ravina 15. Tel: 0461 972311. Fax: 0461 913008. (Andreas Kössler). 0900-1200, 1500-1800. Closed weekends. E.F.G.Sp.TF.WS.B.EP.ER. E-mail: info@cantineferrari.it www.cantineferrari.it

# The Veneto

Once the site of fierce fighting in the *Risorgimento* and World War I, the Veneto is a peaceful region, and its plains and foothills, decorated by villas and cypresses, are redolent of prosperity. Many towns proclaim peace on their statues of the Lion of Saint Mark: *Pax Tibi Marce Evangelista Meus*.

Set within the natural boundaries of the Dolomites in the north, the Venetian lagoon in the east, and Lake Garda in the west, it is easy to see why the Veneto has always been popular with the tourist. Its cities are rich in art and culture. Verona is famous for the opera festival held every year in its Roman amphitheater, and for the Romanesque church of San Zeno with its marvelous medieval bronze doors; Vicenza is the city of the great Renaissance architect Palladio (1501-80); Padua has the basilica of Sant'Antonio, and Giotto's masterly fresco series in the Scrovegni Chapel; and Venice, of course, is unique.

*The Lion of St Mark in Venice is both the symbol of the Evangelist and of the power of Venice's trading empire. Similar statues can still be found in towns throughout the old Venetian territories. The Latin motto translates as "Peace be unto you Mark, My Evangelist."*

While the Veneto does not produce anything like the volume of wine that comes from the southern regions of Italy, its wines are the most widely available of all Italian wines abroad.

Soave and Valpolicella, Bianco di Custoza and Prosecco, for example, are all instantly recognizable names, and the wines themselves are getting better and better as producers

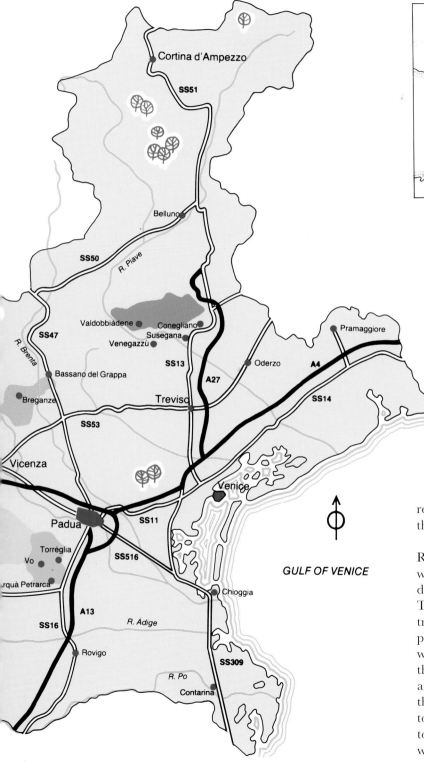

**PRINCIPAL VINEYARD AREAS**

Prosecco di Conegliano Valdobbiadene

Breganze

Bardolino

Bianco di Custoza

Valpolicella

Soave

Colli Berici

Colli Euganei

recognize the need for lower yields in the vineyards.

But, with the exception of the best Recioto and Amarone wines, few wines from the Veneto can be described as anything but "everyday." This is part of their charm, too. The traveller can easily grasp the very pleasant and unpretentious reality of wine drinking here, enjoying some of the most delightful quaffing wines anywhere in Italy. And, as always, there are still the individual producers to discover who prove the exception to the rule and make outstanding wines by any standards.

47

# Verona and Soave

*The medieval castle of Soave has a grand total of 24 towers.*

**GAMBELLARA**
**Az Agr La Biancara***
Contrà La Biancara 8.
Tel/Fax: 0444 444244.
(Angiolino Maule). TF.WS.b.
**Casa Vinicola Zonin**
Via Borgolecco 9. Tel: 0444
640111. Fax: 0444 640202.
Mon-Fri 0900-1200, 1400-
1700. E.F.G.WS.B.
E-mail: zonin@zonin.it
www.zonin.it

**MONTEBELLO**
**Az Vin Dal Maso**
**Luigino*** Via Selva 62. Tel:
0444 649104. Fax: 0444
440099. (Luigino Dal Maso).
E.F.TF.WS. E-mail:
dalmasovini@infinito.it

**MONTEFORTE**
**Az Agr Prà** Via della
Fontana 31. Tel: 045
7612125. Fax: 045 7610326.
(Graziano Prà). 0900-1200,
1600-1900. F.TF.WS.b.

Verona is a charming city, particularly rich in Roman remains, Gothic churches and Renaissance palaces. Despite the almost uninterrupted occupation by tourists all year round, its people are invariably courteous.

Verona's importance stems from its location. At the foot of the Adige valley it has always been a natural meeting place for the Germanic peoples from the north and the Italians. Indeed, any foreigner in Verona is automatically assumed to be a *tedesco* (German) in much the same way as foreigners in Florence used automatically to be *inglesi*.

In wine terms, Verona can claim to be the center of the Italian export trade through the specialist wine trade fair, Vinitaly, which takes place every April. Its most famous wines, Soave, Bardolino and Valpolicella, created the first wave of enthusiasm for Italian wines abroad in the 1960s and 1970s but subsequent overproduction damaged their reputation to such an extent that it is only now that they are regaining their respect in overseas markets.

Verona's local wines are not natural blockbusters in taste terms – they are the very opposite of New World brashness, which is one reason why it has been so difficult for them to regain international attention. But all of the wines have found ways to attract new interest. Soave has benefited from a realization that lower yields are essential for concentrating flavors, while the dessert version, Recioto di Soave, currently the Veneto's only DOCG, has found a place as one of Italy's greatest sweet wines.

It has been found that Valpolicella can be made much richer in taste if it is given a secondary fermentation on the lees of Amarone. Bianco di Custoza has a wide variety of permitted grape varieties in its formula. Therefore, increasing the percentage of an aromatic grape such as Sauvignon, for example, makes for a more interesting white wine. Non-traditional grapes, such as Cabernet Sauvignon or Chardonnay, are now also being fully exploited.

## Verona's *Osterie*

Verona is rich in restaurants and *trattorie*, from the heights of the Michelin-starred Il Desco downwards. But a simple snack and local color comes from the various *osterie* that can provide interesting wines by the glass. The Bottega del Vino is the best – its Victorian Gothic Revival splendor is matched by a superb wine list.

## Soave

The quickest way to Soave from Verona is by the motorway (Direction Venezia). Surprisingly, this route is also the most picturesque, the ordinary road out of Verona being one long piece of ribbon development.

The little town of Soave is instantly recognizable, with its picture-book medieval castle, town walls and gates, all remarkably well preserved thanks to enthusiastic restoration in the last century. The Enoteca in Via Roma and various gift shops attest to its concern for the tourist.

Soave as a wine continues to suffer from its lack of image abroad and could well soon qualify as Italy's best-kept secret. So negative is this image that in a shock decision the best known quality producer on the international stage, Pieropan, decided recently to withdraw all his wines from the official Soave DOC and rely on his personal brand names.

Meanwhile the growers' consortium is busy identifying clones and vineyard sites in a bid to lay the foundations for assured quality production. Greater attention to work in the vineyards and the reduction of yields (grapes per hectare) have done much to revive the fortunes of this wine and tiny vigneron growers such as Gini have a high reputation.

In fact, smaller producers with serious wines, such as Pieropan and Anselmi, have always been admired. But it is significant that the mass market producers, who in the past have so often been criticized for their bland white wines, have now started to gain attention for new Soaves. These wines have more body and character and even benefit from three or four years' aging.

## Gambellara

One more motorway stop, or about 10 more kilometers (6 miles) towards Vicenza is the town of Gambellara, home of the Zonin company, Italy's largest private winemaking concern. The company has vineyards in all the major wine-producing areas of Italy, but naturally, it also produces the white wine called Gambellara, which is very similar to Soave in its make-up. Zonin's most famous version of the wine is an unusual variation of style: *Recioto* (sweet and made from dried grapes) and *Spumante* (sparkling).

**MONTEFORTE (cont)**
**Az Agr Gini\*** Via Matteotti 42. Tel: 045 7611908. Fax: 045 6101610. (Sandro Gini). E.TP.WS.B. E-mail: az.agricolagini@tiscaline.it

**SOAVE**
**Az Agr Pieropan** Via Camuzzoni 3. Tel: 045 6190171. Fax: 045 6190040. (Teresita Pieropan). Mon-Fri 0900-1200, 1400-1800. E.F.TF.WS.b. (TP for groups). E-mail: pieropan@netbusiness.it www.pieropan.it

**VERONA**
**Pasqua Vigneti e Cantine Spa** Via Belviglieri 30. Tel: 045 8402111. Fax: 045 8402121. (Carlo Pasqua). 0900-1230, 1500-1900. E.F.G.Sp.TF./TP.B. E-mail: antonella.f@pasqua.it www.pasqua.it
**Villa Mattarana (Az Agr Zamuner)** Via Mattarana 32/34. Tel: 045 8342168. Fax: 045 8343750. (Gabriella Tomat, Alessandra Zamuner). Tastings of estate-produced wine in historic villa with visit of 16th-century frescoed rooms. E.F.G.TP.WS.B. E-mail: info@villamattarana.it www.villamattarana.it

**WINE BAR**
**La Bottega del Vino** Via Scudo di Francia 3, Verona. Tel: 045 8004535. Fax: 045 8012273. Russian. E-mail: bottega.vino@ifinet.it www.ifinet.it/bottega

*The Roman arena of Verona is part of the rich historic legacy of a city that is home to the wine fair Vinitaly. Verona is also the chief city of the region that produces Bardolino, Soave and Valpolicella.*

# Bardolino

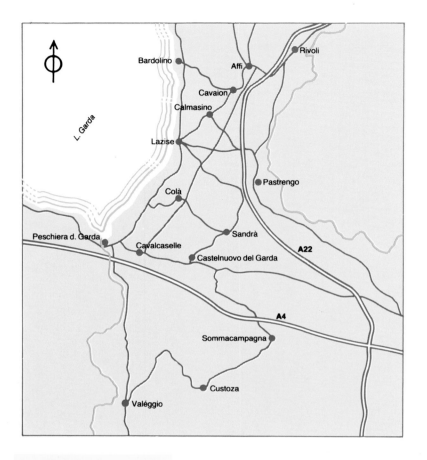

above Bardolino and a drive in the area with a stop for wine tasting makes for a pleasant excursion.

## Verona to Lake Garda

From Verona take the main road to Lake Garda and the town of Peschiera del Garda, an important Austrian stronghold in the years before the great national uprising, the *Risorgimento*. There are remains of the 19th-century fort. To the south lies Bianco di Custoza land, to the north is the territory of Bardolino. The town of Lazise retains its characteristic crenellations, dating from the time when it was the Venetian Republic's main outlet on to Lake Garda. Don't miss Zeni's extensive wine museum and the attractive La Meridiana wine center devoted to Gruppo Italiano Vini's wines from all over Italy.

## Bardolino

Bardolino itself is a small tourist-orientated town of some charm. Do not miss the 11th-century frescoed church of San Severo just by the main road out of Bardolino to Garda.

All of the town's grocery shops and a couple of specialist wine shops sell Bardolino wine, especially that of the most prominent local producer, Azienda Agricola Guerrieri Rizzardi. Countess Rizzardi's villa takes up the southern flank wall of the town and a doorway in this wall leads to the villa's own small museum of winemaking implements and its wineshop. All the Guerrieri Rizzardi wines are estate bottled and the Countess is a proponent of organic cultivation for the vineyards and non-pasteurization for the wines. She has introduced single vineyard versions of all her wines and the quality is consistently high.

**BARDOLINO**
**Az Agr Guerrieri Rizzardi*** Piazza Guerrieri 1. Tel: 045 7210028. Fax: 045 7210704. Mon-Fri 0800-1200, 1430-1730; Sat 0830-1230. E.G.WS. E-mail: mail@guerrieri-rizzardi.com www.guerrieri-rizzardi.com
**Az Agr F.illi Zeni*** Via Costabella 9. Tel: 045 7210022. Fax: 045 6212702. Museum open mid Mar to end Oct 0900-1300, 1400-1800. E.F.G.T.F.WS. E-mail: zeni@zeni.it www.zeni.it

Bardolino is a very ancient wine, but not a pretentious one; it is a light, fruity red with a characteristic cherry-stone taste. Normally a bright garnet color, it is also made in the rosé Chiaretto version that is a perfect summer day's picnic wine.

The signposts for the Bardolino *Strada del Vino* will take you to producers who sell to the public, advertising the fact with their *punto di vendita* signs. Of course, the fact that there is a steady tourist traffic in the area means that the actual quality of the wine can be variable. In fact, the myth of the "peasant who makes wonderful wine just like they used to in the old days" is largely just that. Nevertheless, there are some charming little towns in the soft hills

## The hills of Bardolino

From Bardolino the *Strada del Vino* leads the traveller to Affi, Cavaion, Calmasino, Pastrengo, Sandrà, Colà, Castelnuovo del Garda, and back to Peschiera. These small villages in the range of hills between Lake Garda and the Adige valley are the heartland of Bardolino and have numerous *punti di vendita* for both wine and olive oil.

An interesting detour is from Affi to Rivoli Veronese, the site of a Napoleonic victory in 1797 and now a monument and museum. The castle just outside the village looks down the valley of the Adige, the invasion route from the north.

## OLIVE OIL

The pale yellow extra-virgin olive oil of Lake Garda is, as might be expected, the most perfect olive oil for fish. Lighter and milder than Tuscan olive oil, and definitely not peppery at all, Lake Garda oil is soft and fruity.

The Olive Oil Route signposts indicate a trail along the shore of the Lake, the *Riviera degli Olivi*. Locals swear that the oil is a paradigm of the organic because the microclimate of Lake Garda does not support parasites on the olive fruit, which in other regions might have to be destroyed with chemical sprays.

### OLIVE OIL PRODUCER

**Frantoio Olive Calmasino** Via Monte Baldo 14, Calmasino. Tel: 045 7235006. Mon-Fri 0800-1230, 1400-1800. B.

### OLIVE OIL MUSEUM

**Museo dell'Olio** Oleificio Cisano di Bardolino. Mon-Sat 0830-1230, 1500-1900. Closed Wed p.m. Sun 0900-1230.

### DOLCE

**Az Agr Armani Albino*** Loc Ceradello 401. Tel: 045 7290033. Fax: 045 7290023. 0800-1800. E.TF./TP.WS.B. E-mail:info@ albinoarmani.com www.albinoarmani.com

### LAZISE

**La Meridiana** Via Gardesana. Tel: 045 7580034. Fax: 045 6479073. (Dario Bianchi). Mon-Fri 1000-1230, 1400-1830; Sat 0900-1300. E.F.G.TP.WS. (B for groups).

*The wine town of Bardolino has a maze of narrow streets. The town is pleasantly placed on the shores of Lake Garda: its delicatessens are well stocked with local wines.*

# Custoza

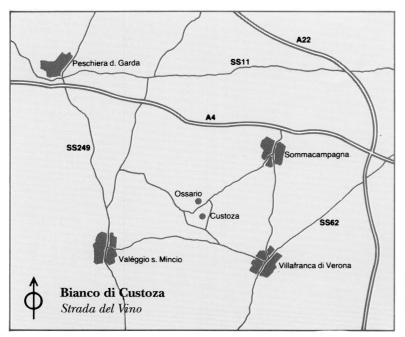

**CUSTOZA**
**Az Agr Cavalchina\*** Loc
Cavalchina, 37060. Tel: 045
516002. Fax: 045 516257.
0800-1200, 1400-1800.
Closed Aug. E.TF.WS.b.
E-mail: cavalchina@
cavalchina.com
www.cavalchina.com

**S BENEDETTO DI
LUGANA**
**Azienda Vitivinicola
Zenato Snc\*** Via S
Benedetto 8. Tel: 045
7550300. Fax: 045 6400449.
0900-1200, 1500-1800.
Closed Aug.
E.F.G.Sp.TF.WS.B.
E-mail: info@zenato.it
www.zenato.it

**SOMMACAMPAGNA**
**Le Vigne di San Pietro\***
Via S Pietro 23. Tel: 045
510016. Fax: 045 8960701.
0900-1200, 1500-1900.
E.F.G.Portuguese.TF.WS.B.
E-mail: carlo@nerozzi.org
www.levignedisanpietro.com

Bianco di Custoza takes its name from the historic town of Custoza about 18km (11 miles) south-west of Verona. As a wine it is enjoying considerable success as an alternative to Soave, partly because it has none of Soave's image problems, but mostly because the permitted *uvaggio*, the blend of grapes, includes aromatic varieties, such as Sauvignon, which can be used to make more interesting wines.

At its best this is a light, fragrant and fruity white wine to be drunk within 18 months or so of production. As with the whole area around Lake Garda, viticulture has ancient traditions here, and probably early origins. Wine production here can be traced back to the 1st century AD.

Of all the wine roads near Verona, these are the most clearly marked, an unusual pleasure. It is easy to follow the main *Strada del Vino* with its *punto di vendita* signs, and there are several large roadside billboards which advertise the route and its points of interest.

## Custoza – the wine route

The starting point for the traveller from Verona is a turning off the motorway about 10km (6 miles) west of Verona, to the town of Sommacampagna. Here one picks up signs for the *Strada del Vino* and finds several *punti di vendita*.

Sommacampagna itself is a noted center for wine production; records referring to the medieval town of Summacampania (it is more like a village today), prove that vineyards flourished here in AD 938.

## Custoza – historic town

Custoza is a small town situated on two hills, each dominated by a particular building. On the highest hill is the Ossario di Custoza, a monument and an ossuary.

The other hill of Custoza is topped by the Villa Pignatti Morano, a grand building restored in the 1930s but retaining in its walls the pockmarks of 19th-century battles. Once past the

### The Ossario di Custoza

This ossuary (literally a bone house, or burial vault) contains the remains of the Austrian and Piedmontese dead of the two battles at Custoza during the troubles of 1848 and the final stages of the *Risorgimento*.

The monument is an imposing needle-shaped structure built at the end of the 19th century. It is open to the public and, on a fine day, is a wonderful vantage point, with views over the immense plain of the Mincio river and hills around the south of Lake Garda.

You can see the hillsides of Bianco di Custoza production lying in a semicircle to the north of the town.

hilltop villa, the *Strada del Vino* forks, left to Villafranca, right to Valéggio sul Mincio. On the way down the hill to Villafranca there is a *punto di vendita* with demijohns of wine displayed outside. This is an attractively wooded area with winding country roads.

Valéggio is dominated by a hilltop medieval castle and has a botanical park in the grounds of the Villa Segurtà. The town itself is tiny but a real gastronomic center by virtue of its own pasta specialty, *tortellini di Valeggio* (delicious meat-filled little pasta parcels) and the restaurants down by the river in the medieval Borgo Antico. From Valéggio the *Strada del Vino* goes to Peschiera del Garda, where the Bianco di Custoza zone overlaps with Bardolino.

**VALEGGIO SUL MINCIO**
**Az Agr Corte Gardoni**
Via Gardoni 5. Tel: 045 7950382. Fax: 045 6370270. 0800-1200, 1330-1830. E.G.TF.WS.b.

*Villa Pignatti Morano is the first sight of Custoza for the traveller approaching from Villafranca.*

# Valpolicella

The Masi winery, one of the top producers of Valpolicella, is set in gently rolling countryside, surrounded by vineyards and cherry trees.

Valpolicella is produced on the north bank of the Adige in the foothills of the Lessini mountains. The area to the west of Verona from Pedemonte to Sant'Ambrògio is the Classico area, but the Valpolicella of the Pantena valley is more than acceptable.

The whole Valpolicella region is well orientated to the wine tourist with numerous trattorias, restaurants and hotels. The main roads are jammed with traffic, but only a little effort is needed to find real countryside as well.

## Valpolicella

Valpolicella, the wine, can be a delight, full of fragrance and flavor. At its best it is a bright, fruity, medium-weight red wine, with a dry finish and a pleasantly bitter cherry-stone aftertaste.

The secret of Valpolicella lies in its grapes, its vinification and its site. The role that each of its constituent grapes plays has been the subject of much research, but basically the two grapes that give weight to the wine are Corvina (now successfully vinified by some growers as a mono-varietal) and Rondinella. Molinara adds a certain spiciness and the other two, Negrara and Rossignola, are traditional, but added in tiny quantities.

The wine has always been made for drinking two or three years after the vintage. Recently, however, some producers have been making longer-lived versions. Masi's Campo Fiorin for example, is made by re-fermenting the wine in what is called the *ripasso* ("passed over again") method on the base of Amarone pressings (the rich pomace left after dried Amarone grapes have been finally crushed).

Producers are basically in agreement that the vanilla wood tastes of new oak overwhelm Valpolicella, but the fact that foreign markets love oak means that experiments continue in the reconciliation of the two tastes.

The denomination Valpolicella Classico Superiore has become shorthand for a richer *ripasso*-style wine

## Out of Verona

Romano Dal Forno is an up-and-coming winemaker based east of Verona who is attracting much praise from the wine critics for his Valpolicella and Amarone. However, he is the exception that proves the rule. Most of the well-known producers are to be found to the north-west of Verona between Pedemonte and Sant'Ambrògio.

You can make an interesting excursion, combining the pleasure of wine travelling with the sight of magnificent mountain scenery, by driving up the Valpantena from Verona and then descending into the Valpolicella.

From Verona take the road to Grezzana, due north of the city. The Cantina Sociale of Valpantena has signs of the Consorzio for Valpolicella indicating the zone of production. The bishop in their logo is San Zeno, patron saint of Verona.

Just before Grezzana on the left of the road is the imposing Palladian Villa Arvedi, often used for official wine presentations. This area is where Bertani's Valpolicella Valpantena, a long-lived version of this famous wine, is produced.

## Valpolicella Classico

By following the winding road up past the marble quarries of the Valpantena, you will eventually emerge into mountain landscape. At Fosse the descent begins into the Progno valley and the Valpolicella whose territory is indicated by vineyards and cherry trees (which have the added function of binding the earth of the vineyard terraces with their roots).

From the attractive town of Fumane, take another winding road to Marano, up through the olive tree and vine plantations. There are several *punto di vendita* signs from now on, but *vino contadino* (homemade wine) can be a trap: it is rarely good quality unless, as does happen, the *contadino* has bought his wine from the local co-operative.

**CELLORE D'ILLASI**
**Az Agr Romano Dal Forno** Loc Lodoletta 4. Tel/Fax: 045 7834923. (Romano Dal Forno). 0800-1200, 1500-1900. F.TF.B. E-mail: az.dalforno@tiscalinet.it

**FUMANE**
**Allegrini** Via Giare 7. Tel: 045 7701138. Fax: 045 7701774. 0900-1230, 1430-1830. E.F.G.TP.WS.B. E-mail: info@allegrini.it www.allegrini.it

**GARGAGNAGO**
**Serègo Alighieri** Via Stazione 2. Tel: 045 7703622. Fax: 045 7703523. (Stefania Perazzolo). 1000-1800. Residence-style holiday accommodation on estate at La Foresteria. E.F.G.TF./TP.WS.B. E-mail: serego@easynet.it www.seregoalighieri.it
**Masi Agricola** Book cellar visits through Serègo Alighieri (above). Tastings available at Serègo Alighieri shop.

All the wineries on the official Valpolicella Classico wine road: www.valpolicella.it/consorzio/info/strada.htm

**NEGRAR**
**Guerrieri Rizzardi\*** Villa Rizzardi Poiega. Tel: 045 7210028. Fax: 045 7210704. (Sig.na Elena). Tue, Thu, Sat 1500-1900. 18th-century garden. E.F.G.TP.WS.B.
**Cav G B Bertani** Loc Novare, Arbizzano. Tel: 045 6011211. Fax: 045 6011222. Mon-Sat 0930-1230, 1500-1800. E.G.TP.WS.B. E-mail: upr@bertani.net

**PEDEMONTE**
**Bolla\*** Via Alberto Bolla 3. Tel: 045 8670911. Fax: 045 8670912. (Chiara Adria). Mon-Thu 0830-1300, 1400-1700, Fri 0830-1300. E.G.WS.B. (TF first two wines). E-mail: bolla@bolla.it www.bolla.it
**Santa Sofia\*** Via Ca' Dede' 61. Tel: 045 7701074. Fax: 045 7703222. (Patrizia or Luciano Begnoni). 0900-1200, 1430-1800. E.TF.WS.b. E-mail: santasof@tin.it www.santasofia.com
**Tedeschi\*** Via G Verdi 4. Tel: 045 7701487. Fax: 045 7704239. (Antonietta Tedeschi). 0800-1200, 1400-1800. E.F.TP.WS.b. E-mail: tedeschi@tedeschiwines.com www.tedeschiwines.com

**S FLORIANO**
**Brigaldara\*** Tel: 045 7701055. Fax: 045 6834525. (Stefano Cesari). E.F.TF.WS.B. E-mail: brigaldara@c-point.it www.valpolicella.it/brigaldara

*The gentle arc of hills near Fumane, the heart of the Valpolicella, where vines and cherry trees intermingle.*

## RECIOTO AND AMARONE

Recioto is a sweet red wine, not unlike a young Port. Amarone is a rich raisiny wine with an attractive bitter twist to the finish. These are the prestige wines of the Valpolicella. The start of the process is the same for both wines.

Selected grapes, mostly Corvina, are picked when fully ripe and laid out on wicker racks in drying lofts. The microclimate creates ideal conditions for the wind to dry these grapes naturally until their sugars are concentrated and they have sufficiently shrivelled in size to produce long-lived sipping wines (*vini da meditazione*, the Italians call them).

Complete fermentation of the sugar-rich must that is the eventual result of pressing the dried grapes leads to a raisiny wine with a dry finish, Amarone (literally "the big bitter one"); while prematurely arrested fermentation leaves a sweet dessert wine, Recioto. Both wines are wonderful with cheese.

### San Floriano and San Giorgio

At the end of the valley you come to San Floriano. The Romanesque church at the crossroads is one of the most important in the Veneto.

Here one can either turn left to Pedemonte, glimpsing the rustic Palladian Villa Serègo (not open to the public), now the headquarters of the Santa Sofia wine company, or right to Sant'Ambrògio, an important center for Classico wines

Just above Sant'Ambrògio in the hills is the village of San Giorgio, with an important Romanesque church and a delightful *trattoria*. Don't miss the Serègo Alighieri estate, owned by direct descendants of Dante since the 14th century and now one of Valpolicella's leading producers.

The most attractive winery-villas are Villa Rizzardi Poiega with its famous 18th-century gardens and, surely the most romantically photogenic of them all, the Bertani-owned villa at Novare near Arbizzano.

# Vicenza and Padua

The two towns of Padua and Vicenza are often passed over by the tourist in search of the more famous delights of Venice in the east and Verona to the west. Giotto's Cappella degli Scrovegni in Padua and Palladio's Teatro Olimpico in Vicenza are my personal favorite buildings in these two towns. The wine lover has then only to go into the hills to the south to find the old country estates of the urban nobility, as well as two modern wine routes.

## Padua – the Colli Euganei
There are no fewer than 13 DOC wines in this area, ranging from the ubiquitous Cabernet and Chardonnay to the highly perfumed Moscato Fior d'Arancio. This is said to have been the cause of the great poet Petrarch's conversion to wine in 1370 when he arrived at the town subsequently called Arqua Petrarca in his honor.

## Vicenza – the Colli Berici
The origins of viticulture in this area go back to at least 3000 BC. More recently, this area was the first to provide wines for the city of Venice in the times of the Republic. The countryside is dotted with numerous Palladian villas, including La Rotonda, the most famous of them all, Villa Pagafetta Camerini and Villa Valmarana ai Nani, just to name a few of the most important.

Colli Berici's most typical wine is the Tocai Rosso, a light and fruity red that, despite the name, has nothing to do with its more famous Hungarian namesake. It is light enough to accompany Vicenza's most famous gastronomic dish, *baccalà*, a stew of dried stockfish whose origins date back to Venetian trading with the Hanseatic League of the Baltic Sea.

*Vicenza, city of the great Renaissance architect Palladio.*

### Breganze: the *Strada del Vino*
Just north of Vicenza, near some of the finest Venetian villas (don't miss the frescoed Castello di Thiene), is the ancient town of Breganze. This is the center of a DOC wine zone with a signposted *Strada del Vino* system.

The leading producer responsible for the fame of Breganze abroad is Fausto Maculan, whose dessert wine Torcolato is a rival to the finest French Sauternes. Breganze has a lively wine festival every year in May.

**BREGANZE**
**Az Agr Maculan\*** Via Castelletto 3, 36042. Tel: 0445 873733. Fax: 0445 300149. E.F.TF./TP.WS.b. E-mail: maculan@metics.net www.netics.net/maculan
**Az Agr Villa Magna\*** Via Repubblica 26, 35066 Sandrigo (VI). Tel/Fax: 0444 659219. E.F.TF./TP.WS.b.

***For further addresses, see page 61.***

# Treviso - the Wine Roads

**PIEVE DI SOLIGO**
**Case Bianche-Col
Sandago*** Via Chisini 79.
Tel: 0438 841608. Fax: 0438
980110. (Lionello Lot).
0800-1200, 1330-1800.
E.F.G.TF.WS.b. E-mail:
info@martinozanetti.it
www.martinozanetti.it

**SUSEGANA**
**Conte Collalto*** Via
XXIV Maggio 1. Tel: 0438
738241. Fax: 0438 73538.
(Adriano Cenedese). Mon-
Fri 0800-1200, 1400-1800;
Sat 0800-1200. E.G.TP.WS.B.
E-mail: collalto@collalto.it
www.collalto.it

**S STEFANO DI
VALDOBBIADENE**
**Bisol Desiderio & Figli***
Via Fol 33. Tel: 0423
900138. Fax: 0423 900577.
(Elena Verri). 0800-1230,
1400-1800; Sat 0900-1200.
E.G.TF.WS.B.
E-mail: bisol@bisol.it
www.bisol.it

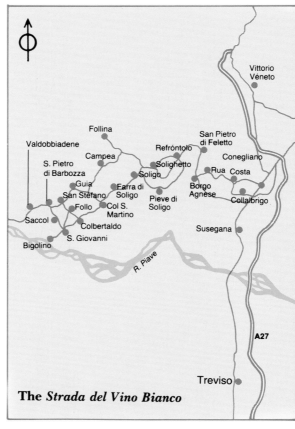

The *Strada del Vino Bianco*

In the soft hills between Conegliano and Valdobbiadene white wine means Prosecco. Some 3000 hectares (7500 acres) of vineyards produce this favorite aperitif of the Veneto, most often found as a dry but intensely aromatic sparkling wine. It is just as delicious in its still or sweet forms and delightful mixed with peach juice in the famous Venetian cocktail, the Bellini. While Prosecco will never have the status of a Fine Wine, it is quite impossible not to like it, and there are serious producers who make notably better versions than the mass-produced brands can provide. Look for *DOC Prosecco di Conegliano-Valdobbiadene* on the label rather than the wider appellation of DOC Prosecco. The Prosecco area actually extends far beyond the

Conegliano/Valdobbiadene hills, but the product from the plains is not as good. The sub-zone of *Superiore di Cartizze* (of only about 100 hectares/250 acres) produces an expensive *cru* version of the wine, but, as usual, the quality of the producer is a better guarantee than the denomination.

### The *Strada del Vino Bianco*
Back in 1966 the *Strada del Vino Prosecco*, which is the more accurate name of the *Strada del Vino Bianco*, was the first to be created in Italy. This area, at the foot of the Venetian pre-Alps, has always been a tourist area. Signposted *mescite* or *botteghe* lie along the route and serve typical regional food and wine. Conegliano, the start of the route, has a special place in the Italian wine world:

**VALDOBBIADENE**
**Canevel Spumanti** Via
Roccat e Ferrari 17. Tel:
0423 975940. Fax: 0423
975961. 0830-1230, 1400-
1800. E.F.G.Sp.TF.WS.B.
E-mail:
canevel@tiscalinet.it
www.canevel.it
**Nino Franco Spumanti***
Via Garibaldi 167. Tel:
0423 972051. Fax: 0423
975977. (Primo or Annalisa
Franco). 0800-1200, 1400-
1800. E.F.TF.WS.B.
E-mail: info@ninofranco.it
www.ninofranco.it

together with San Michele all'Adige in Trentino and Asti in Piedmont, it is one of Italy's major winemaking schools.

The *Strada del Vino Bianco* begins in Conegliano's medieval castle – also the site of the town museum. The route goes west to Rua di Feletto with the remains of its ancient monastery. (Turn off at the Osteria della Guizza and go through Collalbrigo and Parè to Barriera and the Museo dell'Uomo if you want a detour through the hills to the country life museum.) Continue to San Pietro di Feletto with its views over the hills at the Pieve (an ancient frescoed church built on a pagan site). Refrontolo looks out over the Piave valley and the hills of Montello and Grappa, all resonant names in Italy's World War I battle history.

By contrast the Mulinetto (little mill) della Croda in the nearby valley 3km (2 miles) away is a delightful place for a picnic. This area is known as the Isola del Marzemino, and produces a rare red dessert wine from the Marzemino grape; the producer Le Case Bianche is one of its few exponents. Further on towards Valdobbiadene, Pieve di Soligo is the busy capital town of the Piave area, and Col San Martino has the little frescoed church of San Vigilio with views over the Sernaglia plain below. The 12th-century Abbey of Follina is worth visiting. The Cartizze area, Prosecco's top *cru* zone, lies to the west of the road from Fol to Santo Stefano.

It is in the area from here to Valdobbiadene that most of the visitable Prosecco producers can be found.

*Valdobbiadene, at the end of the Strada del Vino Bianco, lies on the slopes of the Venetian pre-Alps. This is the zone of Superiore di Cartizze, a much-prized Prosecco.*

**VENEGAZZU DEL MONTELLO**
**Conte Loredan Gasparini\*** Via Martignago Alto 24A. Tel: 0423 870024. Fax: 0423 620898. (Elfi Barzan). 0900-1200, 1400-1800. E.F.G.TF.WS.B. E-mail: info@venegazzu.com www.venegazzu.com
**Enoteca Vic Tesser Vini** Via Spineda 8. Tel/Fax: 0423 871400. (Vic Tesser). 0800-1230, 1400-1900. E.TF.WS. E-mail: vitesser@tin.it

Once south of the river, there are several possibilities for wine tourism. The Montello area has some interesting stops, including the Venegazzù company, famous for its pioneering Cabernet-based wines, and nearby Vic Tesser's wine shop.

Travelling west, there is the wonderful Palladian villa at Maser, worth visiting not only for its fabulous frescoes and the beauty of its setting, but also because the owners are re-establishing its winery and replanting its vineyards to bring the agricultural side of the estate to the fore again.

The charming hill town of Asolo, with its connections with Browning and Eleanora Duse is on everyone's itinerary, but go to Bassano del Grappa, too; you may be surprised at how much you like Italy's smartest aromatic fire-water (see pages 136-137).

### Treviso

Treviso should not be missed. Only a few miles north of Venice, the bastions, canals and churches of the old town are a delight. The one-way system for traffic is incomprehensible to all but the locals, so park when you can.

### Strada dei Vini del Piave: the wines

As is normal in north-east Italy the vineyards are planted with a mixture of indigenous vines – such as Verduzzo (white) and Raboso del Piave (red) – and French imports that date back to the 19th century and have become assimilated into local winemaking. These are the familiar names of Cabernet and Merlot. As always in the north-east there is a fair amount of Tocai – the white workhorse grape of the Veneto and Friuli.

The universal red is Merlot. This is an extremely easy grape to grow and vinify. It can be grown happily in the plains on

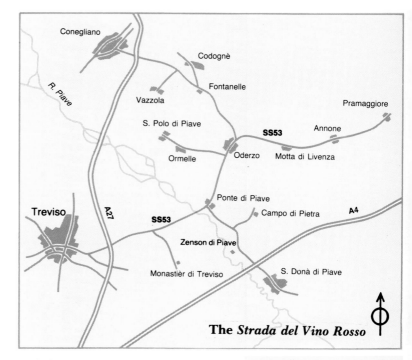

The *Strada del Vino Rosso*

an industrial scale, and the wine itself is smooth and easy to drink. Pinot Nero is rare, Pinot Bianco and Pinot Grigio make good dry white wines, and Chardonnay is ever more popular.

### Strada dei Vini del Piave: the route

From Treviso head towards Roncade, whose splendid moated castle houses a well-respected winery; go to Monastier to see the superb Benedictine monastery and cross the river at Ponte di Piave. The Piave has strong associations with World War I and near Fossalta at Fagarè the Military Memorial commemorates the battle of June 1918.

From Oderzo go to San Polo di Piave. This is a famous fishery, whose gastronomic specialty is eel and red prawns in a garlic sauce. An idea of the antiquity of this tradition can be seen in the nearby church of San Giorgio at Ormelle, where a medieval fresco shows a Last Supper with red prawns.

**MASER**
**Az Agr Villa di Maser\***
Via Cornuda 1. Tel: 0423 923004. Fax: 0423 923002. Villa and winery. Open summer Tue, Sat, Sun 1500-1800; winter Sat, Sun 1430-1700. E.F.G.WS.b. E-mail: villadimaser@tvol.it
www.tvol.it/villadimaser/

**PIAVON DI ODERZO**
**Agricola Rechsteiner\*** Via Frassené 2. Tel: 0422 752074. Fax: 0422 752155. (Dr Hans Onno Stepski Doliwa). 0830-1230, 1430-1830. E.G.TF.WS.b. E-mail: rechsteiner@rechsteiner.it

**RONCADE**
**Az Agr Castello di Roncade\*** Via Roma 141. Tel: 0422 708736. Fax: 0422 840964. (Barone Vincenzo Ciani Bassetti). E.F.G.TP.WS.B. E-mail: vcianib@tin.it
www.castellodironcade.com

*Treviso's picturesque Old Town is intersected by numerous canals.*

## FOOD OF THE VENETO

Much of the food of the Veneto seems very familiar to city dwellers in the USA and England. This is the home of the fashionable *polenta*, *radicchio* and monkfish that we have all learned to order at our local Italian eateries. *Polenta* usually accompanies strong meats, such as rabbit, guinea fowl or pheasant, served with rich sauces.

Another universal dish of the Veneto is *risi bisi*, a risotto made with rice and peas, again of peasant origin. Nearly all traditional first courses are equally filling: *pasta e fagioli* (bean and pasta soup), for example, and *zuppa di trippa* (tripe soup). A legacy of pre-refrigerator days is the specialty of Vicenza, *baccalà alla vicentina*, salt cod simmered in milk and onions with the possible addition of tomatoes.

"The Rose of Chioggia" is another name for the *radicchio* plant that is used for many purposes near Treviso: in salads, grilled with pasta and even as a flavoring for grappa.

By the Adriatic they are especially proud of their seafood. Some of the more usual fish dishes are:

*Zuppa di pesce*: fish soup.
*Insalata di mare*: mixed salad of seafood.
*Seppie alla Veneziana*: squid stewed in its own ink and served with pasta or with *polenta*.
*Coda di Rospo*: monkfish tail, usually grilled.

Strangely, the Venetians are not known so much for particular fish dishes, as for *Fegato alla Veneziana*, calves' liver cooked in butter with onions.

**PRAMAGGIORE**
**ER del Veneto** Via Cavalieri di Vittorio Veneto 13. Tel: 0421 799036. Fax: 0421 799275. Mon-Fri 0830-1230, 1400-1800. Closed Apr-May. TP.WS.

*Continued from page 57*
**COLLI EUGANEI**
**Az Agr Conte Emo Capodilista\*** Via Montecchia 16, 35030 Selvazzano Dentro (PD). Tel: 049 637294. Fax: 049 8055826. (Conte Giordano Emo Capodilista). Mar-Nov 0900-1200, 1430-1930. 16th-century villa. Museum. E.F.G.TP.WS.B. www.ware.it/Agritour/MTV/ Veneto/Padova/LaMontecchia
**Az Agr Dominio di Bagnoli\*** Piazza Marconi 63, 350923 Bagnoli di Sopra (PD). Tel: 049 5380008. Fax: 049 5380021. (Michela Borella). E.TP.WS.B.

# Friuli-Venezia Giulia

The inhabitants of Friuli are a mixture of Slav, Latin and Teutonic traces who live peacefully in a border region which has often been the site of bitter fighting. The signs of this past are all around: Roman Aquileia, the Venetian Republic's fortress town of Palmanova; Trieste, the port of the Austro-Hungarian Empire; and the World War I battlefields at Redipúglia. But despite mass emigration after World War II and the earthquake of 1976, Friuli is one of Italy's most prosperous regions. Friuli produces an annual total of 1.1 million hectoliters (about 29 million gallons) of wine, about half are whites (mostly Tocai Friulano, Pinot Grigio, Sauvignon, Pinot Bianco and Chardonnay); the rest are reds (Merlot, Cabernet, and Refosco dal Peduncolo Rosso) and sparkling wines. The northern half is mountainous and unsuited to winemaking. In the South, however, there is an ancient tradition of viticulture which is epitomized by Friuli's most famous wine, Picolit. This is one of the great wines of the 19th century that is still produced today. The white wines of Friuli are considered by many experts to be the best in Italy.

*The 4th-century mosaic floor of the ancient basilica in Aquileia is one of the glories of Friuli. It was rediscovered by accident in 1909.*

Although the wine industry here is small, the focus is on quality. New grapes, such as Cabernet, Sauvignon and Riesling, were introduced in the 19th century and today Friuli's wines have a reputation for excellence.

There are eight distinct DOC regions: Grave, Collio, Colli Orientali, Annia, Latisana, Aquileia, Isonzo, and Carso. Most of them produce the same wide range of wines, but there are exceptions – for example, Picolit is mainly produced in Colli Orientali.

Friuli's major problem in wine terms is the sheer number of varietals each producer cultivates. A single producer with perhaps ten hectares (25 acres) will make just as many varietal wines from individual grape varieties. And yet it is inconceivable that every producer will own ideal vineyard sites for each type of wine. Having said that, it remains true that Friuli is Italy's third most important wine region, in terms of quality, after Piedmont and Tuscany. The wine is almost all high quality, and at a commensurate price.

Paluzza

Pontebba

Tarvisio

Ampezzo

Tolmezzo

**A23**

Longarone

Gemona
di Friuli

Tarcento

Nímis

Attimis

COLLI ORIENTALI
DEL FRIULI

SLOVENIA

Maniago

San Daniele
del Friuli

**A23**

Tavagnacco

Spilimbergo

Dignano

Cividale

San Foca

FRIULI GRAVE

Campofórmido

**Udine**

Rosazzo

Dolegna

Polcenigo

COLLIO

Plessiva

Oslávia

**Pordenone**

Manzano

SS13

Sacile

Codróipo

Mortegliano

Cormons

Monte
Calvario

**Gorizia**

**A28**

San Vito al
Tagliamento

Palmanova

FRIULI ISONZO

Brugnera

Rivignano

Romans

Sagrado

**A4**

Pasiano di
Pordenone

**A4**

FRIULI
AQUILEIA

Cervignano

Monfalcone

Latisana

FRIULI
ANNIA

Sistiana

CARSO

Aquiléia

FRIULI
LATISANA

VENETO

Lignano
Sabbiadoro

Grado

**Trieste**

Tagliamento

# Udine, Grave and Colli Orientali

*Grapes are harvested for Collavini, producers of the best-selling sparkling wine Il Grigio.*

## GRAVE

### ONTAGNANO
**Az Agr Di Lenardo***
Piazza Battisti 1. Tel: 0432 928633. Fax: 0432 923375. 0900-1200, 1400-1800. E.T.P.WS.B.
E-mail: info@dilenardo.it
www.dilenardo.it

### PRATA PORDENONE
**Az Agr Vigneti Le Monde***
Via Garibaldi 2, Loc Le Monde. Tel: 0434 622087.
Fax: 0434 626096. 0900-1900. E.F.TF.WS.B.
E-mail: pemonde@icl.it
www.vignetilemonde.com

### VALERIANO
**Az Agr Vicentini Orgnani***
Via Sottoplovia 2.
Tel/Fax: 0432 950107.
Mon-Fri 0830-1230, 1400-1800; Sat 0900-1200.
E.F.TP.WS.B. E-mail:
vicentiniorgnani@libero.it
www.vicentiniorgnani.com

## Friuli Grave: the wines

The area's name derives from the word *grave*, describing the gravelly nature of its vineyards. This is the big wine-producing area in Friuli (Pordenone has the greatest vineyard area, 5000 hectares), and white wines predominate over reds, but only just. The most common red is the Merlot, a smooth, fruity wine. Tocai Friulano is the most common white and is also the house white of every *trattoria*.

Enter Friuli on the SS13 through the charming riverside town of Sacile and the provincial capital Pordenone: if you can, take the time to see the paintings of Il Pordenone, Friuli's most famous artist, in the Duomo.

The most important factor which influenced the structure of old-established agricultural estates of this area was its annexation to Venice in the 15th century. The Tagliamento river became the eastern border of Venice's land-based territories and the supply of wood, cereals, wine, food and wool to the Serenissima became the purpose of the farming estates. Visit

Vigneti Le Monde, once the home farm of the Villa Giustinian estate, now a wine estate, and Azienda Vistorta, a typical 18th-century estate surrounded by a great park and now the seat of a 20-hectare (50-acre) winery, to get some idea of what these old agricultural complexes were like.

The Venetian Republic was formally brought to an end by Napoleon in a treaty signed just the other side of the Tagliamento at the beautiful Villa Manin, last home of the Venetian Doges.

Other places of interest in the area include Spilimbergo (with one of the finest medieval churches in Friuli), and the hill town of San Daniele, whose *prosciutto crudo* is reckoned to be even finer than the *prosciutto di Parma*.

Udine is a provincial capital with fascinating architecture, including a castle and Venetian Gothic and Renaissance buildings. It also has a wine center, the Casa del Vino, displaying all the wines of Friuli.

## Colli Orientali del Friuli

Some of the finest wines in Friuli are produced in the range of hills that forms an arc to the east of Udine. These same hills begin as Colli Orientali del Friuli (often abbreviated to COF), and become the more famous Collio Goriziano (Collio, for short) once they pass south into the province of Gorizia.

The range of COF wines is wide, 12 whites and eight reds. COF producers feel that they suffer unfairly by comparison with Collio. In some respects they are right. Most of their estates are just the other side of a provincial border to Collio, but very close geographically and producing much the same types of wines. COF also has two unique specialties: Picolit, the legendary, expensive (and not always worth it) dessert wine; and Verduzzo di Ramandolo, another dessert wine, by no means cheap, but a much better bet. COF reds are also usually bigger wines than their Collio counterparts.

From Tarcento, home of the fragrant sweet white wine, Verduzzo di Ramandolo, travel south via Nimis, Attimis, and Cividale, with its 8th-century Tempietto Longobardo, then Rosazzo, with its abbey where mixed cultivation of vines and olives has been recorded since the 12th century.

## COLLI ORIENTALI (COF)

### BUTTRIO
**Conte d'Attimis-Maniago\***
Tenuta Sottomonte di Buttrio, Via Sottomonte 21. Tel: 0432 674027. Fax: 0432 674230. Mon-Fri 0800-1200, 1400-1800; Sat 0800-1200. E.F.TP.WS.b.

**Az Agr Marina Danieli\***
Via Beltrame 77, Caminetto di Buttrio. Tel: 0432 673283. Fax: 0432 674421. *Agriturismo.* E.G.TP.WS.b. E-mail: beutmus@tin.it www.aziendagricolamarina danieli.it

### COLLOREDO DI SOFFUMBERGO
**Az Agr Comelli Paolino\***
Tel: 0432 711226. Fax: 0432 510520. Mon-Fri 1000-1200, 1400-1800. Medieval church on site. E.TF.WS.b. E-mail: comellip@tin.it www.comelli.it

### CORNO DI ROSAZZO
**E Collavini\*** Via della Ribolla Gialla 2, Loc Gramogliano. Tel: 0432 753222. Fax: 0432 759792. 0900-1200, 1500-1700. Museum. E.TF.WS.B. E-mail: collavini@collavini.it www.collavini.it

### MANZANO
**Az Agr Le Vigne di Zamo'\*** Loc Rosazzo. Tel: 0432 759693. Fax: 0432 759884. Romanesque Benedictine Abbey. E.G.TP.WS.B. E-mail: info@levignedizamo.com www.levignedizamo.com

### S GIOVANNI AL NATISONE
**Az Agr Ronco del Gnemiz\***
Via Ronchi 5. Tel/Fax: 0432 756238. 0900-1200, 1500-1800. E.F.G.Sp.TF.WS.B.

*The Piazza della Libertà in Udine has an assembly of statuary dominated by an ornate clock tower dating from 1527.*

# Collio

**CAPRIVA DEL FRIULI**

**Az Agr Castello di Spessa***
Via Spessa 1. Tel: 0481
639914. Fax: 0481 630161.
(Patrizia Stekar).
E.G.Sp.T.P.B.
www.castellospessa.com

**Az Agr Mario Schiopetto***
Via Palazzo Arcivescovile 1.
Tel: 0481 80332. Fax: 0481
808073. (Mariangela
Schiopetto). E.G.B. E-mail:
azienda@schiopetto.it
www.schiopetto.it

**Az Agr Russiz Superiore***
Via Russiz 7. Tel: 0481
99164. Fax: 0481 960270.
(Roberto Felluga). 0800-1200,
1400-1800. E.T.P.B.
E-mail: info@marcofelluga.it
www.marcofelluga.it

**Az Agr Villa Russiz*** Via
Russiz 6. Tel: 0481 80047.
Fax: 0481 809657. (Dr
Gianni Menotti). Mon-Fri
0830-1200, 1400-1800.
Historic cellars. T.F.B. E-mail:
villarussiz@villarussiz.it
www.villarussiz.it

**DOLEGNA DEL COLLIO**

**Az Agr Venica & Venica***
Via Mernico 42. Tel: 0481
61264. Fax: 0481 639906.
(Ornella Venica). 0830-1230,
1430-1830. Accommodation.
E.F.T.P.W.S.B.
E-mail: venica@venica.it
www.venica.it

**GRADISCA D'ISONZO**

**Marco Felluga*** Via
Gorizia 121. Tel: 0481 99164.
Fax: 0481 960270. (Roberto
Felluga). Mon-Fri 0800-1200,
1400-1800. E.G.T.P.B. Also
Trattoria Alle Viole (Tel: 0481
961042).
E-mail: info@marcofelluga.it
www.marcofelluga.it

**Enoteca La Serenissima**
Via Battisti 26. Tel: 0481
99528. Fax: 0481 99598.
1030-1430, 1700-2230.
Closed Mon. E.G.T.P.W.S.E.R.

Most of the old "Garden of the Austro-Hungarian Empire," where Imperial civil servants used to vacation, is now in Slovenia. What remains is a land that produces about 1300 hectoliters (roughly 30,000 gallons) of top quality wine every year.

White wines predominate over reds by four to one. Tocai takes up one third, then, in order of size of production, Pinot Bianco, Pinot Grigio, Sauvignon, Chardonnay, Malvasia Istriana and Collio Bianco. Of the reds the most important are Merlot, Cabernet Franc and Pinot Nero.

Generally, Collio wines are bigger, rounder and fatter in taste than their counterparts from the other areas of Friuli. They are made with a slightly higher alcoholic content and are perfect wines to go with a meal.

A signposted *Strada del Vino* system was set up for the Collio in 1963. It takes in some of the most attractive vineyard-covered hill scenery in Italy, but it is also an area which saw some of the fiercest fighting of World War I – trenches are still visible in the landscape, ammunition and skeletons are still dug up in the course of vineyard cultivation.

**Collio wines: the *Strada del Vino***

The wine route begins in Gorizia at the Ponte del Torrione. Gorizia itself is worth seeing for its castle, cathedral and Museum of Folklore. From Gorizia the route goes to Monte Calvario with its monument to the dead of World War I, and Oslávia, whose cemetery contains the bones of 60,000 Italian dead.

On a hill overlooking Slovenia is San Floriano del Collio. The 15th-century castle at the summit belongs to Count Michele Formentini. Here, in castle buildings that his family has owned since 1520, Count Formentini has created a complex which

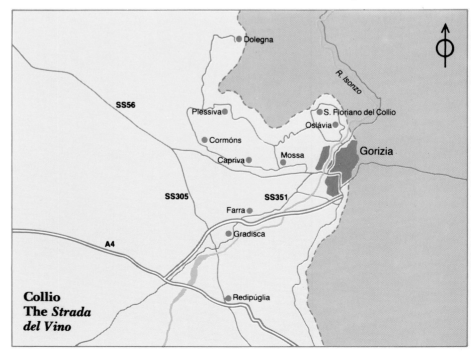

**Collio
The *Strada
del Vino***

combines a hotel furnished with
family antiques, an Enoteca for the
tasting and sale of Collio wines, and
a wine museum which displays
traditional winemaking artifacts. The
whole complex is surrounded by
Formentini vineyards, and a 9-hole
golf course. Times have changed –
Count Formentini has recently sold
off both vineyards and cellars, but the
wines are as good as ever and still
bear the family name on the label.

From San Floriano the road
follows the Slovene border to Plessiva.
Italians can cross the border with
only an identity card.

Incidentally, it may well be
imagined that crossing the border to
Slovenia would lead the wine lover to
cheaper Collio style wines produced
by their Slovene neighbors. In fact,
Slovenian wine can be very good, but
it is not cheap.

From Plessiva go to Dolegna, with
perhaps a tasting at Gianni Venica's
winery. Thence double back to
Cormons. The town is in the heart of
Collio wine production but is famous
for quite another reason. In 1910,
before World War I, it was part of the
Austro-Hungarian Empire and was
graciously granted the status of *città*
by Emperor Franz Joseph. Old
"Ceccho Beppe" ("Blind Jo"), as the
townspeople called him, is still
remembered every year on August 18
by Slovenes, Austrians and Italians
nostalgic for the old empire.

Before returning to Gorizia, visit
the Regional Enoteca in the old
Venetian fortress town of Gradisca
d'Isonzo. Sited in the 15th-century
house of the Provveditori Veneti, the
Enoteca displays wines from Friuli
that have won the annual Gran
Premio Noè competition.

*Villa Russiz is surrounded by
its own vineyards in the midst
of the Collio country. This is
one of the most prestigious
vineyard areas in Friuli.*

**MARIANO DEL FRIULI**
**Az Agr Vie di Romans**
Loc Vie di Romans 1.
Tel/Fax: 0481 69600.
(Gianfranco Gallo). E.TF.B.
E-mail:
viediromans@tiscalinet.it

**S FLORIANO DEL
COLLIO**
**Cantina Formentini** Via
Oslavia. Tel: 0481 884131.
Fax: 0481 884214. (Marco
Del Piccolo). Golf, hotel,
restaurant, winery. TF.WS.B.

# Friuli – the Coastal Plains

The Adriatic coast of Friuli includes the four DOC wine areas of Latisana, Annia, Aquileia and, near Trieste, the Carso. Inland at the foot of the Collio are the DOC lands of the Isonzo river. Each of these areas has its own wine characteristics.

## Latisana

Just over the border from the Veneto in the south-western part of Friuli is Latisana. As a town it is not particularly interesting, but as a DOC winemaking area which includes the flat land bordering the Tagliamento river on the Friuli side it is worthy of some note.

The wines are more honest than exciting, but good examples of standard Friuli favorites, such as the whites Tocai and Pinot Bianco and the red Cabernet, can be found. Two thirds of Latisana wines are red; one third is white.

A route around the vineyards might start at Latisana, go north to Varmo, east to Rivignano and descend again, via Precenicco to the seaside resort of Lignano Sabbiadoro.

## Aquileia

The other side of the lagoon from Lignano is the DOC area of Aquileia. Aquileia itself was founded in 181 BC, and in Roman times became one of the principal towns of north-east Italy.

Aquileia's cathedral has important 4th-century mosaics (see photograph, page 62). Grado, the old port for Aquileia and the town the inhabitants of Aquileia fled to after the collapse of Roman rule, is also worth visiting.

Red wines predominate here. Refosco is a personal favorite, but almost the whole range of Friulan wine types can be found somewhere in the area.

A tour of the wine-producing area might start at Cervignano del Friuli, go north to the Venetian fortress town of Palmanova, go east to San Vito al Torre and descend to Aquileia and Grado via the town of Ruda.

## Carso: *Strada del Terrano*

The Carso is a relatively new DOC area created in 1985. It is named after the particular geological feature, *carsismo*, which means that water has carved out underground caverns and tunnels in the rock. The most obvious effect of this can be seen at San Giovanni al Timavo where the river suddenly bubbles up to the surface after 38km (24 miles) underground.

The two wines of the region are Malvasia Istriana and Terrano, the traditional table wine of Trieste that is reputed to be good for the blood. A *Strada del Vino* system has recently been set up with signposted roads that cover the area bounded by Monrupino, Sgonico and Duino Aurusina.

**LATISANA**
**Az Agr Isola Augusta***
Casali Isola Augusta 4, 33056 Palazzolo della Stella (UD). Tel: 0431 58046. Fax: 0431 589141. (Massimo Bassani). *Agriturismo.* Museum. E.G.TF.WS. E-mail: info@isolaugusta.com www.isolaugusta.com

*Left: A cypress-lined street in old Roman Aquileia.*
*Below: Villa Manin at Passariano (see page 64) once the residence of Venice's last Doge.*

The Carso being an exposed strip of Italy next to Slovenia, much of it is under military jurisdiction, although tension has eased considerably since the brief period in which Slovenia was involved in the Balkan troubles.

### Isonzo: *Strada del Merlot*
The DOC Isonzo area lies in the river valley at the foot of the more famous wine-producing area of the Collio hills. The Isonzo has a 40km (25 mile) *Strada del Merlot* which takes in vineyards not only of the area's best wine, Merlot, but also of the white wines Riesling Italico and Traminer.

It starts at Gradisca d'Isonzo, whose Enoteca Regionale, Enoteca La Serenissima, is a must to visit on the wine tour of Friuli (see pages 66-7), and goes on to Romans, Fratta, Medea, Borgnano, Angoris, Cormons, Brazzano, Mariano, Corona and San Lorenzo Isontino.

Excursions in this area might include the Military Museum at San Michele, near the memorial at Redipuglia, and the fortress town of Palmanova.

**ISONZO**
**Az Agr Luisa\*** Via Campo Sportivo, 34070 Mariano del Friuli (GO). Tel: 0481 69680. Fax: 0481 69607. (Edi Luisa). G.TF.WS. E-mail: azienda@viniluisa.com www.viniluisa.com

**TRIESTE**
The Balkans begin in Trieste. Slovenes, Croats, Serbs, inhabitants of Trieste, even a few regular Italians, and a very few tourists come to this faded city fronted by the mercantile office blocks or palaces of a century ago. It all has a slightly raffish air.

There is one haven for the wine lover, especially on a Friday night. Right in the city center, the Gran Malabar – which is so small that you have to sit outside in the corner of the square with the bar's tables and chairs – has an astonishing range of up-to-the-minute Italian wines. It was here that I tasted my first *barrique*-aged Pinot Grigio. Not bad, either. The salami was good, too.

Ask for Walter, and if you go on Friday nights, there is always a special food and wine pairing evening – one wine and one dish – and Walter's enthusiastic explanatory notes.

**Gran Malabar** Piazza S Giovanni 6, Trieste. Tel: 040 636226. Fri evening tastings with food. E.F.Sp.TP.WS.

# Food of Friuli-Venezia Giulia

**FOR FURTHER INFORMATION**

**Movimento del Turismo del Vino (Friuli-Venezia Giulia)** Via Poscolle 6, 33100 Udine. Tel: 0432 509394. Fax: 0432 510180. The source of much useful information, including booklet *Itinerari del Gusto – Vini, Delizie, Bellezze in Friuli-Venezia Giulia* (also in German). E.TF.WS.B. E-mail: villarussiz@ villarussiz.it www.villarussiz.it

**Consorzio Tutela Denominazione Origine Vini Collio** Via N Sauro 9, 34071 Cormons (GO). Tel: 0481 630303. Fax: 0481 630660. E-mail: info@collio.it www.collio.it

**Consorzio Tutela Vini DOC Friuli Grave** Via Oberdan 26, 33170 Pordenone. Tel: 0434 523654. Fax: 0434 21530. Useful booklet *Le Strade del Vino nel Friuli Occidentale* (also in English and German). E-mail: docgrave@docfriuligrave.com www.docfriuligrave.com

**Consorzio Tutela Denominazione Origine Vini Colli Orientali del Friuli** Via Candotti 1, 33043 Cividale del Friuli (UD). Tel/Fax: 0432 730129. E.G.TF.b. E-mail: info@colliorientali.com www.colliorientali.com

## OSTERIA AND FRASCA

To explore the riches of Friulan cuisine it is essential to discover the *frasca* and the *osteria*.

The *osteria* can be found in most parts of Italy, but perhaps it is here that it comes closest to the original idea of an all-day convivial meeting place where you can have a snack and glass of wine or beer at any time. There is in fact a Committee for the Defense of the Friulan *osteria*.

The *frasca*, or *mescita*, is a more impromptu and seasonal outdoor *osteria*, which mainly occurs in the two to three months around spring. Throughout the wine-producing areas *frasche* will suddenly emerge in the courtyards of farmhouses. A few rickety chairs and tables may be set outside, and you can have a plate of the typical homemade farmhouse salami and cheese products with a glass of the new season's wine for a modest sum.

## FESTIVALS

### Friuli
More formal festivals in Friuli include the following:
*February:* GRADISCA D'ISONZO: exhibition of *barrique* wines.
*End March:* GRADISCA D'ISONZO: week-long festival of wines of the Carso.
*End April:* CASARSA DELLA DELIZIA: festival of wine and Friulan folklore.
*End April:* AQUILEIA: wine festival.
*End April:* BUTTRIO: regional wine exhibition.
*End April:* S. FLORIANO DEL COLLIO: Tasting and Exhibition of Collio Wines.
*End May:* CIVIDALE DEL FRIULI: exhibition of DOC wines.
*End May:* GRADISCA D'ISONZO: exhibition of wines and *Gran Premio Noè*, the most important wine competition of Friuli and the one that decides which wines will be exhibited at the Enoteca Regionale at Gradisca.
*July:* CORMONS: wine festival.

## FOOD OF FRIULI
The Friulan gastronomic tradition is a very varied one. Slav, Italian and Germanic styles are used to prepare the different foods available from the sea, hills and mountains.

The most famous food to come from Friuli is the *prosciutto crudo* of San Daniele. A recipe book published in 1450, written by Mastro Martino, the chef of the Patriarch of Aquileia, reveals how to test the readiness of this ham by plunging a knife into its center. Nothing much has changed except that nowadays they use a fine horsebone for the same purpose. More unusual than the San Daniele ham is that of Sauris, which is another *prosciutto crudo* made from a rare breed of Friulan pig.

The Friulani are fond of soups; *jota* is the traditional soup of Trieste; *pasta con fagioli* soups are common, as is *brovada* (broth).

Rice is normally found in the coastal regions, and is used to make exquisite fish risottos. Other Friulan dishes include: *Cialzon* – each region has its own filling (rarely meat) of this traditional ravioli; *Muset* – the pasta *cotechino* is aged for about a month (hence its name, deriving from *mesetto*), and is often served in soup as a *Brovada di Muset*; and *Gulyas* – a goulash.

*August:* SACILE: wine festival.
*August:* SAN DANIELE DEL FRIULI:
Prosciutto Festival.
*September:* CORMONS,
RASPANOCASSACO, POVOLETTO: Festa
dell'Uva.
*October:* GRADISCA D'ISONZO: regional
exhibition of Grappa.

*November:* S. GIUSEPPE DELLA CHIUSA,
RICMANJE, S. DORLIGO DELLA VALLE:
*Mostra Assaggio del Vino Nuovo,* tasting
of the new season's wine.
*November:* ROMANS D'ISONZO: tasting,
exhibition of Collio and Isonzo wine.
*December:* GRADISCA D'ISONZO:
exhibition of sparkling wines.

*Italians are acknowledged leaders
in the field of bottle and label
design. Heavy opaque bottles with
deep "punts" give a touch of
special elegance to the wine. (The
punt is the indentation in the
center of the base – a feature
associated with Champagne and
other fine wines from France.)*

# The Via Emilia

T he Roman road of the Via Emilia unites the prosperous cities of Emilia Romagna. Every one is worth a visit, for the frescoes, statues and mosaics in their baptisteries and churches. Parma and Modena have very fine medieval and modern buildings; the Teatro Farnese in Parma and the Galleria Estense in Modena are worth seeing. Bologna is famous for its many towers, its university, and, of course, for its wonderful food. Faenza has a museum of the decorated ceramic ware that bears its name, while the ancient mosaics of Ravenna, for a time the capital of the Roman Empire after the fall of Rome, should not be missed on any account. Dante's tomb is also in Ravenna; and Garibaldi's hut in the woods, where he hid before escaping to America, can also be visited. Ferrara bears many reminders of a splendid cultural past when great Renaissance poets and painters came to the court of the Este. But there is also a special ambience to the towns and the countryside. Anyone who has seen *The Garden of the Finzi-Continis* or Bertolucci's *1900* will already have a good idea of the region's atmosphere.

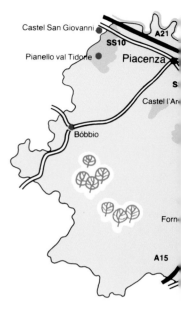

Unfortunately, the region is associated with its great export, the notorious cheap party wine, Lambrusco. But, on its home ground, Lambrusco is in fact quite different. It is a great peasant wine, and it expresses in its instant earthy drinkability the first reason for drinking wine at all – for refreshment.

Wine is produced in all eight provinces of Emilia Romagna. Most comes from the large co-operatives of Forlì, Bologna and Ravenna. But the best wine comes from individual producers.

Of the most commonly found reds, the best are Gutturnio from Colli Piacentini, Lambrusco from Sorbara, and Sangiovese di Romagna. Of the whites, look out for the Sauvignon and the sparkling Malvasia from Colli di Parma, which can be both a dry aperitif wine or an excellent sweet dessert wine. Ortrugo and Pignoletto are the latest discoveries for insiders in the wine world. Albana has long been criticized as an unworthy

DOCG, but is now finding its true vocation as a delicious *passito* wine. These wines are some of Italy's best-kept secrets.

*The wines of Romagna are promoted by the Ente Tutela dei Vini Romagnoli, which uses as its trademark the bearded figure of a* Passatore, *the gentleman bandit of the 18th and 19th centuries, part of the folklore of the once lawless Romagna region.*

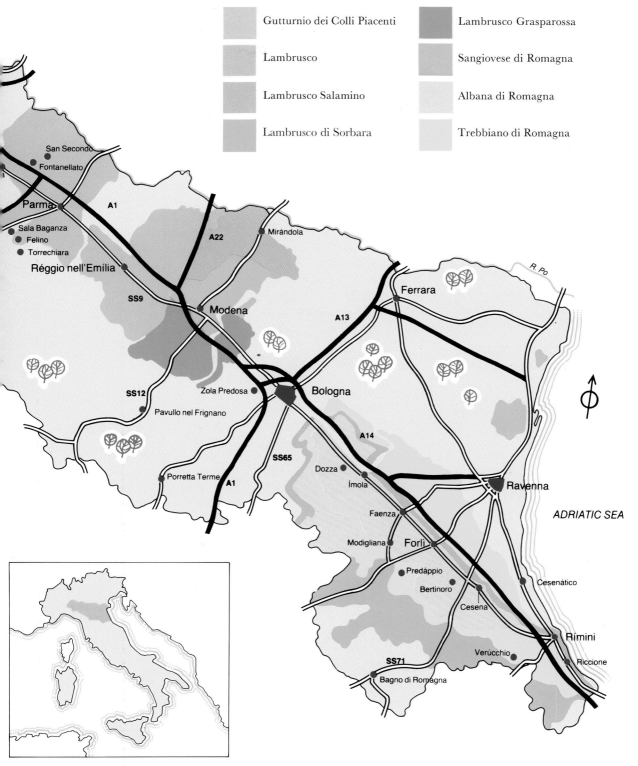

The Via Emilia

PRINCIPAL VINEYARD AREAS

- Gutturnio dei Colli Piacenti
- Lambrusco
- Lambrusco Salamino
- Lambrusco di Sorbara
- Lambrusco Grasparossa
- Sangiovese di Romagna
- Albana di Romagna
- Trebbiano di Romagna

San Secondo
Fontanellato
Parma
A1
A22
Miràndola
Sala Baganza
Felino
Torrechiara
Réggio nell'Emília
SS9
Modena
Ferrara
R. Po
A13
SS12
Zola Predosa
Bologna
Pavullo nel Frignano
A14
SS65
Dozza
Ravenna
Porretta Terme
A1
Ímola
ADRIATIC SEA
Faenza
Modigliana
Forlì
Predáppio
Cesenático
Bertinoro
Cesena
Rimini
Verúcchio
Riccione
SS71
Bagno di Romagna

73

# Wines of the Via Emilia

## PIACENZA

### VAL D'ARDA

**Az Agr Vit Buffalora\***
29020 Rezzano, Carpaneto
Piacentino (PC). Tel/Fax:
0523 850123. (Luigi
Montesissa). 0800-1200,
1400-2000. TP.WS.b.

**Az Agr Luretta** Paolini di
Bradasco 3, 29010
Vernasca (PC). Tel/Fax:
0523 895465. (Carla Asti).
0900-1730. E.F.TP.WS.B.
E-mail: lurettavini@tin.it

**Az Agr Vitivinicola
Pusterla\*** 29010 Vigolo
Marchese (PC). Tel/Fax:
0523 896105. (Giovanna or
Giorgio Freschi or Eugenio
Gandolfi). Mar-Oct 1000-
1900. Historic cellars.
E.F.G.TP.WS.B.

### VAL NURE

**Az Agr La Tosa\*** Loc La
Tosa, 29020 Vigolzone
(PC). Tel: 0523 870727.
Fax: 0523 870358. (Stefano
Pizzamiglio). 0800-1200,
1400-1800. Small museum.
E.F.TF.WS.B.
E-mail: latosa@libero.it

### VAL TIDONE

**Castello di Luzzano\***
Az Agr M & G Fugazza,
27040 Rovescala (PV). Tel:
0523 863277. Fax: 0523
865909. (Giovanna
Fugazza). 0800-1200,
1400-1800. Roman
archeological remains on
site. *Agriturismo* with
restaurant, organized wine
tours. E.F.TF.WS.b. (TP for
groups). E-mail:
info@castelloluzzano.it
www.castelloluzzano.it

The Via Emilia was constructed by the Romans in the late 2nd century BC. It stretches from Piacenza in the north to Rimini on the Adriatic coast. It was, and still is, a great commercial highway.

## Piacenza

The town of Piacenza itself was badly damaged in World War II. Its importance in the wine world lies in the wines produced in the Colli Piacentini hills that line the valleys fanning out to the west and south. Most Colli Piacentini wines – even the reds – can be still, semi-sparkling, sparkling, sweet or dry, depending on how the producer wishes to make them. The locals prefer their wines to have a slight sparkle, *frizzantino*, to accentuate the fruit and freshness of young vintages. Perhaps the most interesting wines for the visitor are the honest, very quaffable reds, Bonarda and Barbera, and the delicate whites Ortrugo and Malvasia.

Gutturnio, a serious wine drinker's red wine, definitely not sparkling, is a blend of Barbera and Bonarda and named after the Roman drinking vessel found near Piacenza in 1878 that has become the symbol of its producers. Just to add to the plethora of wines in this area, many serious producers are now using Chardonnay, Sauvignon, Cabernet and Pinot Noir, the international varieties, with increasing success. The aromatic qualities of Sauvignon and Pinot Noir particularly come out well in an area used to making aromatic wines.

## Piacenza – the wine roads

Visiting producers in the Colli Piacentini means exploring the valleys that lie to the south of the city. From west to east these are:

**Val Tidone:** Go through Borgonovo with its castle to begin the vineyard area leading to Ziano, the capital town of Val Tidone with more than 750 registered wine growers. Go south to the impressive fortress of Olgisio or follow the hills from Vicobarone to Fornello or Luzzano to the west.

**Val Trebbia:** The Trebbia valley has its own tongue-twisting white wine, Trebbianino, and was described by Hemingway as one of the most beautiful valleys in Italy. The main road, the SS45, is the old road to Liguria and is dotted with castles that used to defend it, such as Ancarano, Montechiaro and Bobbio. The basilica of Bobbio is the resting place of Saint Colomba of Ireland.

**Val Nure:** If you have a taste for medieval pastiche, visit Grazzano Visconti to see the Victorian Medieval Gothic village and try the wines in the Enoteca there. The valley has its own sparkling white wine, Valnure, and is the site of several leading wine companies.

**Val d'Arda:** Visit Castell'Arquato to see a delightful medieval fortified town and to taste wines in the regional Enoteca. The Arda valley has a sweet sparkling wine called Monterosso, which, as usual with the local wines of Colli Piacentini, is a variation on the theme of a grape mix using Ortrugo, Malvasia and Trebbiano grapes.

## Parma, Reggio Emilia and Modena

The town of Parma is well worth a visit, but again it is the hills, the Colli di Parma, that provide the wine. This is an area which is attracting increasing interest for its whites, particularly Sauvignon and Malvasia. The *frizzantino* versions are the standard white wine aperitifs in local bars. Reggio Emilia is a surprisingly attractive and unspoiled town, full of wonderfully operatic piazzas and impressive churches. The wines of the area are Lambrusco Reggiano, from the plains, and Bianco di Scandiano, from the hills to the south.

Modena is a busy commercial city that seems to mix a modern sense of purpose with a stately architectural background. This is where the other two Lambrusco wines, Lambrusco Salamino di Santa Croce and Lambrusco di Sorbara, come from.

## Lambrusco

The actual denomination of Lambrusco does not seem to matter for quality purposes, the important point is to find a serious producer. The bubbles are usually the product of tank fermentation, but there are still a few producers who make the costly bottle-fermented version, which can be very good. As usual, good local Lambrusco is the ideal accompaniment to good local foods.

Lambrusco is, of course, always red, and either dry or *amabile* (medium dry). The sweet red, white and rosé versions that can be found in supermarkets are as far away from real Lambrusco as British ice cream is from Italian.

## Colli Bolognesi

Bologna was one of the European Cities of Culture in 2000 and is readily accessible from its growing airport. The National Art Gallery is excellent. But the food is so good that it outshines the wine; to find wine interest, go to the Colli Bolognesi, the hills to the south of the city. Colli Bolognesi wines include Cabernet, Barbera and Merlot reds; and Pignoletto, Sauvignon, Riesling, Chardonnay and Pinot Bianco whites. Pignoletto produced by the Gaggioli company is one of my personal favorites, as is the Cabernet Sauvignon from Terre Rosse.

The wine route in the gentle Colli Bolognesi starts at Zola Predosa, goes on to Bazzano (castle), then to Monteveglio (medieval town complex) and Savigno by the old Roman Via Claudia; then the road loops back towards Bologna via San Chierlo (visit the church of San Biagio in the Poggio district) and the 12th-century Abbey of San Fabiano near Calderino.

## Wines of the Romagna

The principal wines of the Romagna are: Sangiovese di Romagna, a red wine that varies from the alcoholic blockbuster to the light and uncomplicated; Trebbiano di Romagna, a simple white wine; Cagnina and Pagadebit (this last one literally providing big enough crops to "pay the bills"); and the controversial Albana di Romagna.

Albana was the first Italian white wine to gain the prestigious DOCG recognition (see pages 10-11), but no one quite knew why. What has emerged, however, as a result of the stringency of DOCG regulations, is that *passito* Albana di Romagna is an exceptional dessert wine.

## VAL TREBBIA

**Az Agr La Stoppa*** Loc Ancarano, 29029 Rivergaro (PC). Tel: 0523 958159. Fax: 0523 951141. (Angela and Elena Pantaleoni). 0830-1230, 1400-1900. E.F.Sp.TP.WS.b. (B for groups or outside office hours). E-mail: lastoppa@tin.it

**Az Agr Marchese Malaspina*** C.da Borgoratto 26, 29022 Bobbio (PC). Tel: 0523 936048. Fax: 0383 60195. (Obizzo & Currado Malaspina). E.F.TP.WS.B. E-mail: clemalaspina@libero.it

## PARMA

**Az Agr Monte delle Vigne*** Via Costa 27, 43036 Ozzano Taro (PR). Tel/Fax: 0521 809105. (Elisabetta Oppici). 0900-1300, 1500-1900. Also producers of cheese and Parma ham. E.F.TP.WS.B. E-mail: montevigne@libero.it

## REGGIO EMILIA

**Az Agr Venturini-Baldini*** Via F Turati 42, 42020 Roncolo di Quattro Castella (RE). Tel: 0522 887080. Fax: 0522 888141. (Daniela Brindani). 0800-1200, 1400-1800. On Terre di Matilde di Canossa route. E.TF./TP.WS.B. E-mail: info@venturinibaldini.it

*Brisighella, in the Romagna, celebrates its history with a two-week medieval fair each summer.*

## COLLI BOLOGNESI

**Tenuta Bonzara\*** Via San Chierlo 37a, 40050 Monte S Pietro (BO). Tel/Fax: 051 225772. (Francesco Lambertini). 0830-1200, 1400-1800. Agricultural life museum. Restaurant. *Agriturismo.* E.F.TP.WS.B.
E-mail: info@bonzara.it
www.bonzara.it

**Az Agr Gaggioli\*** Vigneto Bagazzana, Via Raibolini 55, 40069 Zola Predosa (BO). Tel/Fax: 051 753489. (Maria Letizia Gaggioli). 0800-1200. E.TP.WS.B.
E-mail: gaggioli@pair.com
www.gaggiolivini.it

**Vigneto delle Terre Rosse\*** Via Predosa 83, 40069 Zola Predosa (BO). Tel/Fax: 051 755845. (Elisabetta Vallania). 0800-1200, 1430-1800. E.F.WS.B.

**Az Agr Vallona\*** S Andrea 203, Loc Fagnano, Castello Serravalle (BO). Tel: 051 6703058. Fax: 051 6703333. (Maurizio Vallona). E.TF.WS.B.

## IMOLA

**Az Agr Tre Monti\*** Via Lola 3, Loc Bergullo, 40026 Imola (BO). Tel: 0542 657116. Fax: 0542 657122. (David Navacchia). 0800-2000. E.TF.WS.b. E-mail: tremonti@tremonti.it
www.tremonti.it

### Imola and Faenza

The little town of Dozza, just outside Imola, is fundamental to any wine tour in Emilia-Romagna. Here, the regional Enoteca, the information center for Emilia-Romagna wines, occupies the old castle whose storerooms provide perfect cellar conditions for wine display. The town has also come to prominence because of the custom of decorating the houses in the narrow town center with pictures painted on to their walls by modern artists.

From Dozza it is only a short distance to Imola, famous for its race-track but relatively undiscovered for its delightful Renaissance and 18th-century architecture.

A detour through the hills goes through the spa town of Riolo Terme to medieval Brisighella. Three outcrops of rock with a clock tower dating back to 1290 and a 14th-century castle dominate the town. The wine route ends in Faenza, with its International Ceramics Museum.

### Forlì

The hills south of Forlì offer two destinations. Modigliana, the home of the Castelluccio winery is reached via Terra del Sole, a fortified complex built by Cosimo de' Medici with some interesting Renaissance *palazzi* and a Museum of Country Life. The other destination is Bertinoro, the "balcony of Romagna," further east towards Cesena, but in the hills overlooking the plain towards Ravenna. It has a medieval center, an Enoteca, and, just outside the town, lies Fattoria Paradiso, providing a unique opportunity to sample wine and admire vintage cars at the same time.

### Ravenna

Surprisingly enough, there are wines produced along the Adriatic coast in the area called Bosco Eliceo around Ravenna. They are difficult to find and the effort is probably better spent feasting the eyes on the glorious mosaics of Ravenna itself in the Basilica of San Vitale and the church of Sant'Apollinare Nuovo.

## DOZZA
**ER Emilia-Romagna\*** Rocca Sforzesca. Tel: 0542 678089. Fax: 0542 678073. Tue-Fri 1000-1200, 1500-1800. Information center for all Emilia-Romagna wines. E. TP.WS.b. E-mail: enoteca@tin.it www.enotecaemiliaromagna.it

## FAENZA
**Fattoria Camerone\*** Via Biancanigo 1485, 48014 Castel Bolognese (RA). Tel: 0546 50434. Fax: 0546 656146. (Dr Giuseppe Marabini). 0800-1200, 1400-2000. E.F.G.TP.WS.B. E-mail: info@fattoriacamerone.it www.fattoriacamerone.it

**Conti Leone\*** Via Pozzo 1, 48018 S Lucia Faenza (RA) Tel: 0546 642149. Fax: 0546 642222. (Leone Conti). 1400-1700. E.TP.WS.B. E-mail: conti.sini@mbox.dinamica.it www.italywines.com

**Az Agr Trerè\*** Via Casale 19, Monticoralli, 48018 Faenza (RA). Tel: 0546 47034. Fax: 0546 47012. (Morena Trerè). 0900-1200, 1430-1830. *Agriturismo.* E.F.TP.WS.b. E-mail: trere@trere.com www.trere.com

## FORLÌ
**Castelluccio\*** Via Tramonto 15, 47015 Modigliana (FO). Tel/Fax: 0546 942486. (Claudio Fiore). Mon-Fri 0800-1700. TP.WS.b. E-mail: ranchidi@castelluccio.it

**Fattoria Paradiso\*** Via Palmeggiana 285. Tel: 0543 445044. Fax: 0543 444224. (Graziella Pezzi). 0900-1200, 1500-1900. *Agriturismo.* E.F.G. Sp.TF.WS.b. (TP for groups). E-mail: fattoriaparadiso@ fattoriaparadiso.com www.fattoriaparadiso.com

*Left: A fruit and vegetable market in one of Bologna's characteristically tall arcades.*

# Food of the Via Emilia

Bologna is Italy's gastronomic capital; all Italians will tell you that their gastronomic dream is to go to one of the better restaurants of Bologna. A simple plateful of *Tortelloni alla Bolognese* served with just a flake of fresh local butter and some freshly grated parmesan, can make the most memorable of meals.

You don't have to be a foodie to realize when you arrive in Bologna that the locals have got it right. Even the pizzas are adorned with fragrant veils of pink Parma ham, or thin shavings of parmesan cheese. And the *tortelloni*, well, even the Italians roll their eyes with anticipated pleasure when you mention that you found the most melting egg pasta. Not to mention the fillet steak with Balsamic Vinegar sauce. Or the delicious apricot sweetness of an Albana *passito* dessert wine. Not for nothing is Bologna La Dotta ("the Learned") also called Bologna La Grassa ("the Fat").

There are four products that the Emilia-Romagnans tempt us with: the wines, of course; parmesan cheese, the finest of all the *grana* cheeses; Parma ham, the sweetest and pinkest of all cured hams; and Balsamic Vinegar, the elixir of Reggio Emilia and Modena.

## Parmesan

Parmigiano-Reggiano is the authentic parmesan cheese. There are other hard cheeses; *grana padano* from near Milan is the nearest competitor, but it is not as good. Parmesan is made in a totally natural and centuries-old way that involves the addition of nothing more than rennet to the milk from cows from a strictly delimited area. The long 18 months' aging and the grazing and micro-organisms specific to the high pastures contribute to the unique taste and cooking qualities of the cheese. Aging can be as long as three years, two is ideal for most purposes.

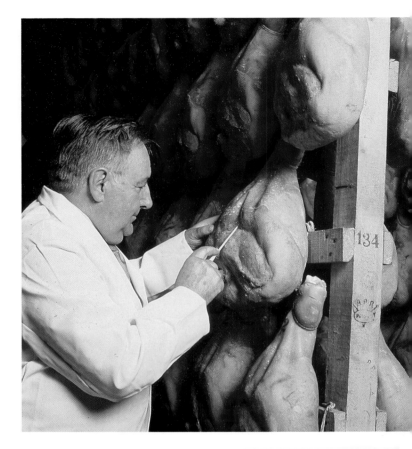

*Parma hams are tested, traditionally with a bone spike, to check for thorough curing. Those that pass the quality control are given the stamp of the Ducal Crown of Parma. Italians regard the Prosciutto di San Daniele, in Friuli, as even better.*

Parmigiano can be bought direct from the makers at any of the small *caseifici* cheese factories in the area (there are several between Reggio Emilia and the hills).

When buying the cheese, examine it carefully. It should be a uniform moist but pale amber colour and should be without any tell-tale signs of dryness, such as white patches or a white rim next to the rind. Taste it – it should dissolve in granular smoothness in the mouth and have a nutty and slightly salty taste.

## Humble pie

There is a phrase in Italian about having to "go to Canossa," which is roughly equivalent to being compelled to "eat humble pie." This recalls the incident in the early 11th century when the Holy Roman Emperor, Henry IV, was forced to humble himself before Pope Gregory VII by going to Canossa and waiting barefoot in the snow for four days before being granted absolution.

The castle at Canossa is now the center of a sign-posted trail (the Percorsi Matildici) in the hills to the south of Reggio Emilia, dotted with hamlets, towers and churches.

## Balsamic Vinegar

Everyone has heard of Balsamic Vinegar, the rich sweet viscous liquid, aged in a series of barrels of differing woods and decreasing size in the vinegar lofts of Modena and Reggio Emilia.

One drop fills the room with perfume; over fifty years old it is used as an after-dinner drink, literally an elixir. This is the stuff of legends; unfortunately, it is rarely the liquid you find, and it really does cost a lot of money. Necessarily so. There are, in fact, two types of Balsamic Vinegar, one rare and expensive and the product of years of careful aging, the other a creation for the mass market.

Unless the Balsamic Vinegar name contains the word *tradizionale*, assume the worst.

Aceto Balsamico Tradizionale di Modena, or di Reggio Emilia, are the genuine products.

**MODENA**
**Az Agr Pedroni\*** Via Risaia 2, 41015 Nonantola. Tel: 059 549019. Fax: 059 548520. 0800-1100, 1700-2000. Restaurant, *aceto balsamico tradizionale*. Wine producer and Balsamic Vinegar maker. E.TF.WS.B. www.acetaiapedroni.com

*Parmigiano-Reggiano (parmesan) cheese is aged for at least 18 months after first being formed.*

## Parma ham

Since Roman times the valleys south-west of Parma have been famous for the production of hams. The wind that dries and sweetens genuine Parma ham blows pure in this region.

The selected hams, from pigs weighing about 150 kilos (330 pounds), have a finished cured weight of about seven kilos (15 pounds). They are salted with the minimum salt possible and hung up for seven to nine months in carefully controlled conditions that include the occasional blast of fresh air.

## Other local foods

*Coppa:* this is a dried and cured meat made from the neck and shoulders of the pig. It is eaten thinly sliced with bread and butter.

*Felino:* reckoned to be the finest salami of Emilia Romagna but hard to locate.

*Zampone di Modena:* pig's feet sausage, can now be bought vacuum-packed in many delicatessens.

*Mortadella:* the huge and soft spiced pink sausage made from pork (all parts), now so famous as to have its cut-price imitations. The genuine product is very good. As is the case with most sausages, it is probably best not to ponder too much on the exact ingredients.

# Tuscany

For many of its visitors, Tuscany is Italy. Indeed this is the geographic and cultural center of Italy and once, from 1864 to 1871, it was the political center too. But most of all Tuscany is Grand Tour country: few cities in the world can compare with Florence for its wealth of art and brilliant architecture; Siena is smaller, but extraordinarily rich in medieval treasures; and the little hilltop town of San Gimignano is a perfectly preserved picture of medieval life. Less obvious are the industries of Tuscany: the marble of Carrara, Prato's textiles, Val d'Elsa furniture, Florentine leather goods, jewelry, and so on. Tourism is still central, of course. The most dynamic wine producers in Tuscany tend to be outsiders, including many foreigners and escapees from Milan, who, having become enchanted with the dream of Tuscan life themselves, are keen to welcome visitors and share the experience. Tourism is such a integral part of Tuscan life anyway that it is no surprise that the *Movimento del Turismo del Vino* was born in Tuscany and finds its keenest exponents here – good news for the wine tourist.

*The dome with a view is a technical and artistic masterpiece by the early Renaissance architect Brunelleschi. It crowns Florence's cathedral.*

Wine tourism in Tuscany is well developed, but is only now just being standardized. There are no fewer than 14 official *Strada del Vino* routes established by the Tuscan Regional Government and the *Movimento per il Turismo del Vino* is at its most active here.

Buying wine by the case from the *fattoria* door is a long-established part of Italian life, but what to do about the casual visitor who would like to taste the wine? This is a new development, and some producers have tried to establish a norm for visitors.

Most Tuscan wineries have evolved a range of solutions. Some have kiosks on the main road selling their wine. A few are happy for anyone to arrive at almost any time. Many provide a very attractive type of tasting and snack service whereby a small group of visitors can book a tasting of the estate's wines with *spuntini*, snacks of local bread, cheese and salami, for a set fee.

If some wineries specify a charge for tasting, this is largely to put off *curiosi* (time-wasters) and to ensure that visitors are serious. It is rarely much more than the cost of the bottles opened and a little bit for the producer's time, and may be forgotten entirely if wine is subsequently purchased. Winemaking is a business, after all.

A15
S62
S63
R. Serchio
S12
A1
S64
S65
S67
La Spezia
S1
Carrara
Massa
A12
Pistoia
A11
CHIANTI RUFINA
Rufina
POMINO
S71
COLLINE LUCCHESI
MONTECARLO
Florence
Lucca
Carmignano
Pontassieve
A11
CARMIGNANO
A12
S12
Empoli
R. Arno
Impruneta
Pisa
S429
Greve
R. Elsa
Certaldo
CHIANTI CLASSICO
S69
Arezzo
R. Era
VERNACCIA DI SAN GIMIGNANO
S. Gimignano
CHIANTI
Livorno
S1
A12
Siena
S222
S71
Montescudaio
R. Cécina
S2
S326
MONTESCUDAIO
S541
VINO NOBILE DI MONTEPULCIANO
Bolgheri
Buonconvento
Montepulciano
BOLGHERI
Montalcino
Pienza
BRUNELLO DI MONTALCINO
A1
S1
S223
S2
Elba
R. Ombrone
Grosseto
ELBA
Scansano
Pitigliano
MORELLINO DI SCANSANO
BIANCO DI PITIGLIANO
Parrina
PARRINA
S1

# From Pisa to Florence

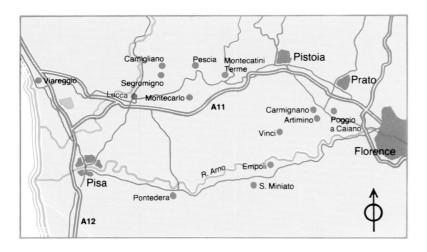

## COLLI FIORENTINI
**Fattoria Montellori*** Via Pistoiese 5, 50054 Fucecchio (FI). Tel: 0571 260641. Fax: 0571 242625. 0900-1200, 1500-1800. E.F.G.TP.WS.b. E-mail: montellori@tin.it www.montellori.com
**Fattoria San Vito in Fior di Selva*** Via S Vito 32, 50050 Malmantile (FI). Tel: 0571 51411. Fax: 0571 51405. 0900-1700. E.F.G.TF./TP.WS.B. E-mail: sanvito@san-vito.com www.san-vito.com

## COLLINE LUCCHESI
**Fattoria Colle Verde*** Loc Castello, 55010 Matraia (LU). Tel: 0583 402310. Fax: 0583 402313. 1000-1200, 1400-1800. E.F.G.S.Sp.TF./TP.WS.b E-mail: info@colleverfe.it www.colleverde.it
**Tenuta Maria Teresa*** 55060 S Martino in Vignale (LU). Tel: 0583 394412. Fax: 0583 394345. Mon-Fri 0900-1200, 1500-1700. E.TF.WS. (B other times).
**Fattoria Maionchi*** 55010 Tofori (LU). Tel: 0583 978194. Fax: 0583 978345. 0900-1200, 1400-1800. E.F.TF.WS.b. E-mail: info@fattoriamaionchi.it www.fattoriamaionchi.it

Despite the growth in direct flights to Florence, for many people Pisa is still the gateway to Tuscany. Towns in between tend to be ignored, which benefits those who do make the effort to visit them.

## Lucca
Driving east on the northern bank of the Arno leads to Lucca. An independent city state up until the creation of the Napoleonic Kingdom of Italy, Lucca retains much physical evidence of its history. A quadrilateral street layout shows its Roman origins: the old Roman amphitheater has been magically transformed into houses, but in exactly the same shape, and the walls that kept the Medici out were always too massive to remove.

The two DOC denominations of the area are Colline Lucchesi, coming from the arc of hills to Lucca's north; and Montecarlo, from the area surrounding the little hilltop medieval village about 15km (10 miles) east of Lucca.

Red Colline Lucchesi and Montecarlo wines are based on Sangiovese, like Chianti. Some are rustic, others modern, barriqued and international in style. The whites allow for exciting grapes to complement the standard Trebbiano (from Semillon to Sauvignon) and the Montecarlo whites have aquired a good reputation. Fattoria del Buonamico has set the example for quality wines that others now follow.

### The wine route
The wine route leaves Lucca going north on the SS12 up the Serchio valley towards Bagni di Lucca, and swings east towards Matraia (Fattoria Colle Verde), Tofori (Fattoria Maionchi), Gragnano and then Montecarlo. There are several imposing villas in the area, particularly Villa Reale at Marlia, Villa Torrigiani at Camigliano and Villa Mansi at Segromigno.

*Lucca retains its medieval street plan, safely protected from development by its massive city walls.*

*The Medicis built the palatial Villa Artimino, one of many princely villas in the Tuscan countryside.*

## Carmignano

Just to the west of Florence, almost the last stretch of real countryside before the suburban sprawl begins, is Monte Albano and the Carmignano area.

Carmignano is a red DOCG wine, and it is almost entirely unknown, even in Italy. It has an illustrious past, having been codified by decree in 1716 when Grand Duke Cosimo III defined its exact production zone, more or less corresponding to the enclosed Medici estate known as the Barco Reale. The link is acknowledged today with the wine called Barco Reale, in effect a second wine to the full-blown Carmignano.

The second boost to Carmignano was the fact that the Medici introduced many experimental vines on their estate, including the all-important Cabernet Sauvignon from France. This enabled modern producers of Carmignano legitimately to build in a certain component of Cabernet in the official DOC for the wine, right from its promulgation in 1975.

Carmignano is in the hands of a very few producers, reflecting its aristocratic past. Visiting the area is an opportunity to see some fine Tuscan villas. Villa Artimino (now a conference center) was built for Cardinal Ferdinando de' Medici in a single year (1594) as a country retreat. There is another, more spectacular, Medici villa open to the public at Poggio a Caiano, where the same Ferdinando's sister-in-law died in mysterious circumstances in 1587.

Carmignano itself is worth a visit to see Pontormo's *Visitation* in the church of San Michele. Nearby Capezzana has the estate of Carmignano's leading producers, the Contini Bonacossi family at Tenuta di Capezzana, who have carried the Cabernet theme of local wines to its logical conclusion with their Ghiaie della Furba, a Bordeaux blend of Cabernet Sauvignon, Cabernet Franc, and Merlot. While in this area, it is worth visiting Vinci, to see the museum dedicated to models of the inventions of the great Leonardo da Vinci, and to visit his birthplace at Anchiano.

### MONTECARLO
**Fattoria del Buonamico\*** Via Prov di Montecarlo 43. Tel: 0583 22038. Fax: 0583 229528. 0830-1230, 1400-1900. E.F.TF.WS. E-mail: buonamico@sole.it www.sole.it

**Fattoria Il Poggio\*** Via S Piero 39. Tel: 0583 22088. Fax: 0583 229554. E.F.G.TF./TP.WS.b. www.websitalia.com/ilpoggio

**Fattoria Michi\*** Via S Martino 34. Tel/Fax: 0583 22011. 0800-1230, 1330-1730. E.TF.WS. (B for food).

### MONTALBANO/CARMIGNANO
**Fattoria di Bacchereto\*** Via Fontemorana 179, 50040 Bacchereto (Prato). Tel/Fax: 055 8717191. Mon-Fri 0800-1230, 1400-1800; Sat 0800-1200. *Agriturismo.* E.F.TF./TP.WS.b. (B for groups and other times).

**Tenuta di Capezzana\*** Via Capezzana 100, 59011 Seano Carmignano (Prato). Tel: 055 8706005 Fax: 055 8706673. Mon-Fri 1500-1700. A.m. visits can be booked. E.F.G.TP.WS.B. E-mail: capezzana@capezzana.it www.capezzana.it

**Fattoria Il Poggiolo\*** 50042 Carmignano (PO). Tel: 055 8711242. Fax: 055 8711252. 0800-1200, 1400-1800. E.TF.WS.B. E-mail: ilpoggiolo@ala.it www.ilpoggiolo.it

**Fattoria Le Poggiola\*** Via Treggiaia 13, 51030 Serravalle Pistoiese (PT). Tel/Fax: 0573 51071. 1500-1900. *Agriturismo.* E.F.TF.WS.b. (TP for groups). E-mail: fattoria@lepoggiola.com www.emmeti.it

# The Coast of Tuscany

The suggestion that good wines can come from Tuscany's coastal hinterland would have seemed ridiculous only a few years ago, if it had not been for Italy's most famous red wine, Sassicaia, which comes from Bolgheri.

## Colline Pisane

The hills south-east of Pisa on the other side of the Arno form one of the seven Chianti zones.

However, the few producers of real quality in the area often make more interesting wines outside the limits of Chianti DOCG regulations than inside.

## Montescudaio

Chianti-formula reds and Trebbiano-based whites have been reinvented with the use of Cabernet, Merlot and Chardonnay as part of the respective blends. The estates of the wine producers lie along the Cecina river and around Casale, Guardistallo and Montescudaio.

## Bolgheri

Why has it taken so long for the success of Sassicaia to be emulated? Cabernet Sauvignon and Merlot seem to flourish in this part of Tuscany and Bordeaux blends (a mixture of the two) are more successful than Sangiovese-based Chianti look-alikes.

The aristocratic estates of the region take in vast areas of scrubby hinterland between the coast and the hills. These used to produce a dull local rosé until Antinori's winemaker, Giacomo Tachis, was brought in to decide what to do with the Cabernet Sauvignon vines brought back from France and planted on the Incisa della Rochetta estate at Bolgheri (closed to the public). The result was Sassicaia, which has been an enormous success.

Of the local estates in the Bolgheri area, probably Podere Grattamacco is the most welcoming and increasingly impressive. An unusual visit in the area might be to the beautifully clean olive oil mill at Fonte di Foiano.

### The south

The coastal hinterland of Southern Tuscany is rich in Etruscan remains. Populonia, now a fishing village, but once Puplona, an important Etruscan trading center, is very impressive. If Etruscan remains fascinate you, then be sure to go to Vetulonia, between Grosseto and Massa Marittima, Tarquinia and Sovana, down near Pitigliano.

Southern Tuscany is the new cutting edge – Tuscany's Medoc, perhaps. Tuscan, Italian, and even international (California's Mondavi) wine companies have raced to snap up land in the area in the last few years. The combination of relatively cheap vineyards and a proven suitability to growing new grape varieties (principally Cabernet, Merlot and Syrah for the reds, Chardonnay and Sauvignon for the whites) as well as the traditional Sangiovese and Trebbiano has been irresistible.

Consequently, areas such as the Val di Cornia, Scansano and the Maremma are now split-personality viticultural zones producing, on the one hand, traditional reds and whites (with some significant nods to modern improved practices in the traditional red Morellino di Scansano and white Bianco di Pitigliano, for example) and, on the other hand, a series of boutique wineries using traditional and/or international grapes to make super premium show wines. Frescobaldi's Luce is the most famous of this latter category. Biondi Santi, the most famous producers from Montalcino, recently bought Graham Greene's Castello di Montepò in the Maremma to make Schidione, a premium wine that has won international acclaim.

*Pitigliano, in the heart of Etruscan Tuscany, is well known for its white wine.*

**MAREMMA**

**Az Agr Erik Banti\*** Loc Fosso dei Molini, 58054 Scansano (GR). Tel: 0564 508006. Fax: 0564 508019. 0830-1230, 1400-1730. E.F.G.Danish.Sp.TF.WS.b. E-mail: info@erikbanti.com www.erikbanti.com

**Tenuta La Parrina\*** Loc Parrina, Albinia, 58010 Grosseto. Tel/Fax: 0564 862636. 0800-1300, 1500-1800. E.F.G.Sp.TF./TP.WS.B. E-mail: parrina@dada.it www.parrina.it

# Rufina

(see page 100).

**NIPOZZANO**
**Castello di Nipozzano\*** Loc Nipozzano. Tel: 055 8311050. Fax: 055 8311325. 1030-1300, 1400-1830. E.F.G. TF.WS.b. (B for large groups). E-mail: info@frescobaldi.it www.frescobaldi.it **[7]**

**POMINO**
**Castello di Pomino\*** Loc Pomino. Tel/Fax: 055 8318810. 0900-1800. Sat 0800-1200. E.TF.WS.b. **[8]** E-mail: info@frescobaldi.it www.frescobaldi.it

**PONTASSIEVE**
**Marchese Gondi Tenuta Bossi\*** Via dello Stracchino 32. Tel: 055 8317830. Fax: 055 8364008. 1400-1800. E.F.TP.WS.b. **[5]**

**Fattoria Castello del Trebbio\*** Via S Brigida 9, Loc S Brigida. Tel: 055 8300051. Fax: 055 8304003. 0900-1200, 1400-1800. E.G. TF.WS. (TP.B. for groups). E-mail: trebbio@tin.it www.vinoturismo.it **[4]**

**Fattoria di Selvapiana\*** Loc Selvapiana 43. Tel: 055 8369848. Fax: 055 8316840. 0900-1900. E.G.TF.WS.b. (B for groups). E-mail: selvapia@centroin.it **[6]**

**RUFINA**
**Az Agr Colognole\*** Via Palagio 15, Loc Colognole. Tel: 055 8319870. Fax: 055 8319605. *Agriturismo.* 0900-1300, 1500-1800. E.F.G.TF.WS.b. E-mail: info@colognole.it www.colognole.it **[1]**

**Fattoria di Basciano\*** Viale Duca della Vittoria 159. Tel: 055 8397034. Fax: 055 8399260. *Agriturismo.* E.F.TF.WS.B. **[2]**

**Fattorie di Galiga e Vetrice\*** Via Vetrice 5. Tel: 055 8397008. Fax: 055 8399041. 0900-1200, 1500-1700. Restaurant. Guest rooms. E.TP.WS.B. E-mail: grati@centroin.it www.grati.it **[3]**

There are seven Chianti denominations. Chianti Classico is the best known, but Chianti Rufina (not to be confused with Ruffino, a producer) has some excellent winemakers and a well-organized *Strada del Vino* system. The Consorzio Chianti Rufina publishes an excellent brochure guide (see page 100).

Rufina is based on the Sieve valley, stretching from Pontassieve, east of Florence, up to Dicomano. The valley is very attractive, but on the whole the towns are not worth visiting. Pontassieve was devastated in World War II, and Rufina has a wine museum in Villa Poggio Reale (opening spring 2001) but is choked with traffic.

The geography of the valley is the key to the quality of Chianti Rufina. High vineyards enclosed in a narrow valley that gets very hot in the day and cools rapidly at night yield grapes that make elegant wine with fragrant bouquets and a capacity for long aging. Chianti Rufina has exactly the same grape composition as the other Chiantis, but if Chianti Classico can be compared to Bordeaux for its rich opulence, Chianti Rufina is more like Burgundy for its elegance.

## The wineries – the Right Bank

Starting at the head of the valley, Fattoria di Colognole has a wonderful view right down the valley from the commanding heights where Marchesa Gabriella Spalletti and her sons are re-establishing the family wine business and making some attractive wines.

Further down the valley, the Grati family have two estates, Galiga and Vetrice, which provide a consistent level of quality Chianti Rufina at the lower end of the market. The tower of the Vetrice villa, typically for a Tuscan property, dates back to the 12th century when it was one of a series of defensive towers in the valley. Back over the hills on steep roads up Monte Romito, Madonna delle Grazie al Sasso is an 11th-century church with panoramic views over the valley.

Down the hill from Santa Brigida you come to one of the most beautiful castles in all Tuscany, Castello del Trebbio. Medieval crenellations, thick walls and a Renaissance courtyard combine with a sense of isolation to produce a very special atmosphere. The castle has a place in Medici history: it was here that the Pazzi Conspiracy was hatched in 1478, after which Giuliano de' Medici was murdered in Florence cathedral on Easter day.

There is a shortcut involving dirt tracks to the next winery, but probably the easiest route is to go right down to Sieci before cutting back up the hill behind the town to Fattoria dei Bossi. This is one of Rufina's up-and-coming estates. The Vin Santo is superb.

## The Left Bank

The other side of the Sieci valley contains the properties of the pioneers of Chianti Rufina. Fattoria di Selvapiana is owned by Francesco Giuntini, whose excellent Riserva Bucerchiale stands out for its quality.

Castello di Nipozzano is part of the Frescobaldi empire. This family traces its winemaking back to AD 1300, and possesses no fewer than 500 hectares of vineyards in Rufina alone. If Chianti Rufina is known at all abroad, it is probably because of the consistent quantity and quality of the Riserva Castello di Nipozzano. Another Frescobaldi fiefdom is Pomino, where Marquess Vittorio degli Albizi planted French grape varieties in the last century.

*Frescobaldi's Castello di Nipozzano offers a panoramic view of the Chianti Rufina district.*

Numbered wineries listed
on opposite page

S67
Dicomano
R. Sieve
Colognole
S556
1
Londa
S. Brigida
Galiga
4
2
3
Rufina
Pomino
8
Sieci
5
S70
S67
6 7
FLORENCE
Pontassieve
Pelago
R. Arno
Vallombrosa

# San Gimignano

The first glimpse of San Gimignano's 13 towers is always an exciting moment as you approach the city through the undulating countryside.

Too many visitors, too many gift shops and too much summer heat can be difficult to cope with, but let the busloads of tourists leave, and it is easy to see why the medieval buildings have become so beloved. The tall towers of the town's feuding families, the narrow streets and courtyards, and the Piazza del Popolo where Dante addressed the Town Council in 1300 (persuading them to change sides in the interminable wars between Siena and Florence) are very romantic.

## Vernaccia di San Gimignano
Vernaccia is Tuscany's own original white wine; all the others are based on Trebbiano, except French derivations, such as Pomino, which therefore do not quite count. Vernaccia, however, is literally the "vernacular" grape variety for the area – it has always been there, and through the centuries it has evolved into something unique.

Vernaccia was the first wine to be granted the DOC qualification in 1966 and it has just been made DOCG. But in a wine world enamored of the big flavors of Chardonnay and spiciness of Sauvignon, its delicacy does not win friends easily.

The problem is that squeaky clean technology combined with high yields in the vineyards renders Vernaccia anonymous and characterless, while a return to the deliberate oxidation of the old-fashioned style in order to find more flavor in the grape is unthinkable.

There are several solutions: dance with the devil and add some Chardonnay to the blend to lift the wine a little; use new-oak *barriques* to add the extra dimension of vanilla and spice; or cut yields drastically and prune hard in the vineyard to get the maximum flavor concentrated in relatively few grapes. Or combine all three solutions.

While the average tourist is happy to buy a souvenir three-bottle pack and not worry overmuch about the quality, there is little incentive for most Vernaccia producers to go to the expense of making a truly fine wine. Nevertheless, there are producers who want to make something world class in San Gimignano and there are good wines to be discovered.

## Visiting the producers
In San Gimignano itself there are numerous souvenir shops that also sell wine. Perhaps it is better to concentrate on the towers, the museum and the wonderful Collegiata Church.

If you walk from the town center down Via San Matteo (incidentally part of the old Pilgrims' Way, the *Via Francigena*, from France to Rome) and just before the town gate turn right into Piazza Sant'Agostino, you will not only have the chance to see some

superbly restored frescoes in the church, you will also be able to buy some of San Gimignano's best wines from the Fattoria di Cusona shop in the square. Cusona itself is some way out of town near Poggibonsi and has, incredible as it may seem, recently celebrated 1000 years of recorded winemaking on the estate.

Other producers are closer. Find Montenidoli and Panizzi by locating the *carabinieri* (police) station first – you want the dirt track down the hill by the side of it.

Montenidoli, run by the irrepressible Fagiuoli family, makes consistently high quality Vernaccia in varying styles, including fashionable (and delicious) barrel-fermented. Panizzi is one of San Gimignano's up-and-coming stars.

Other producers of note near to each other include Casale Falchini, who make a particularly successful Riserva Vigna Solatio and a bottle-fermented sparkling Vernaccia; and Teruzzi & Puthod at Fattoria Ponte a Rondolino, who use computer-controlled equipment, stainless steel halls and new oak to make Vernaccia that has long been held to be among Italy's finest white wines.

*The medieval towers of San Gimignano keep watch.*

**VAL D'ELSA**
**Fattoria Belvedere\*** Loc Belvedere, 53034 Colle Val d'Elsa (SI). Tel: 0577 920009. Fax: 0577 923500. *Agriturismo.* 0900-1200, 1500-1800. E.F.TP.WS.B. E-mail: chiantif@tin.it www.fattoriabelvedere.com
**Fattoria Villa Spoiano\*** Strada Spoiano 2, 50028 Tavarnelle Val d'Elsa (FI). Tel/Fax: 055 8077313. *Agriturismo.* E.F.G.TP.WS.B. E-mail: spoiano@tin.it www.toscanaholidays.com

# Chianti Classico

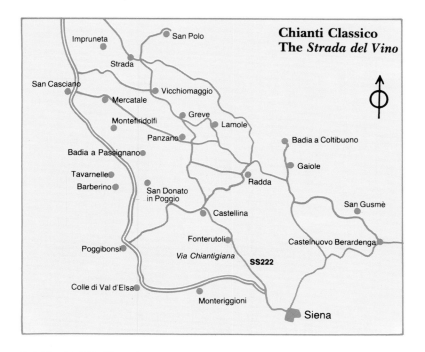

**Chianti Classico
The *Strada del Vino***

Impruneta · San Polo · Strada · San Casciano · Vicchiomaggio · Mercatale · Montefiridolfi · Greve · Lamole · Panzano · Badia a Coltibuono · Badia a Passignano · Gaiole · Tavarnelle · Barberino · San Donato in Poggio · Radda · San Gusmè · Castellina · Fonterutoli · Poggibonsi · Castelnuovo Berardenga · Via Chiantigiana · SS222 · Colle di Val d'Elsa · Monteriggioni · Siena

Chianti Classico is the premier Chianti region. It has always had more stringent regulations than the other six Chianti areas, a fact recognized by the award of its own long-awaited separate DOCG appellation in 1995, finally confirming its distance from the other regions.

For a long time, attention has been focused on the grape mix of Chianti Classico. The original 19th-century formula called for white grapes to be part of the *uvaggio*. This was designed to produce early-drinking, everyday wines, and still holds good today. But when modern producers came to make serious long-lived wines – the Chianti Riservas that are the area's fine wines – they found the white grape rule a handicap.

The solution was to go outside DOCG regulations and produce what came to be called Super Tuscan wines. These could be 100 per cent Sangiovese, or, conforming to international taste, they could have an addition of more than the permitted amount of Cabernet Sauvignon to give the wine greater body.

Traditionally, Chianti is aged in large Slavonian oak barrels that last for years and give very little of their oakiness (because of size and age) to the wine. But modern taste, especially in the export market, required experiments with the vanilla oakiness that comes from using new and almost new French oak *barriques*.

Super Tuscans used to be the excitement of Chianti – the combination of *barriques* and Cabernet was just too seductive, but now the new DOCG regulations finally allow the use of 100 per cent Sangiovese for Chianti Classico, thus removing one of the major incentives to declassify an estate's best wine.

Attention has now moved to the vineyards. What is the ideal density of vines per hectare? What is the optimum yield, balancing quality with quantity? What is the best clone of Sangiovese for which site? All these questions are being addressed by the Chianti 2000 Project overseen by the Consorzio Chianti Classico growers' association.

Of the Super Tuscans, the more successful ones, Antinori's Tignanello or Montevertine's Le Pergole Torte for example, continue to flourish, and, as regulations are continually modified, they too are being drawn into the official classification system as either DOC/G or IGT.

## Chianti Classico touring

Chianti Classico is the most developed part of Italy for wine tourism. Roadside kiosks selling an estate's wine are quite common. Wine shops in the local villages are used to tourists. The facility to stay on a wine estate (*agriturismo*) and to book ahead for meals and snacks with a tasting is widespread. And, for the really enthusiastic, it is quite easy to find courses on Tuscan cooking and wine appreciation organized by the producers themselves. The quickest way to get anywhere in Chianti Classico is to use the fast road that runs from Florence to Siena and to turn off into Chianti at the most appropriate point. Otherwise, a good flavor of the region can be had by following the old main road, the Via Chiantigiana, through the heart of Chianti Classico. You will need a good map of the area; the Consorzio del Marchio Storico (the Chianti Classico growers' association) has its offices in Sant'Andrea in Percussina, near San Casciano, and publishes the best available.

Start at the Consorzio Chianti Classico's offices. These are in the house that was Machiavelli's refuge while he wrote *The Prince* while an exile from Florence. Just opposite is L'Albergaccio, which has been a *taverna* since Machiavelli's day, and is now a trattoria. The owners of the trattoria are also the custodians of the Machiavelli museum. If the trattoria is open, the museum and cellars are open. If not, *pazienza*.

**Enoteca del Chianti Classico** Piazzetta Santa Croce 3. Tel: 055 853297. WS.

**PANZANO**
**Fattoria di Montagliari**
Via di Montagliari 29. Tel: 055 852014. Fax: 055 852804. 0900-1200, 1500-1700. Restaurant 1230-1630, 1830-2130. E.TP.WS.B. E-mail: info@montagliari.it www.montagliari.it

**PANZANO (cont)**
**Enoteca del Chianti**
**Classico** Via G da Verrazzano
8. Tel: 055 852495. WS.

**BARBERINO**
**Fattoria Casa Sola\*** Loc
Cortine. Tel: 055 8075028.
Fax: 055 8059194. *Agriturismo.*
0930-1200, 1500-1900.
E.F.S.TF.WS.b. E-mail:
casasola@chianticlassico.com
**Isole e Olena** Loc Isole 1.
Tel: 055 8072763. Fax: 055
8072236. 0900-1200, 1500-
1800. E.F.G.S.TF.WS.B.
**Castello di Monsanto\***
Via Monsanto 8. Tel: 055
8059000. Fax: 055 8059049.
0800-1230, 1400-1800.
E.F.TP.WS. (B for groups
and guided tastings).
E-mail: monsanto@
castellodimonsanto.it
www.castellodimonsanto.it
**Az Agr Casa Emma\***
S Donato in Poggio. Tel: 055
8072859. Fax: 0571 667707.
0900-1900. E.TF.WS. E-mail:
casaemma@casaemma.com
www.casaemma.com

**CASTELLINA IN CHIANTI**
**Poderi Castellare di**
**Castellina** Loc Castellare.
Tel: 0577 742903. Fax: 0577
742814. 0900-1200, 1500-
1800. E.WS.B. (TP for
groups.) E-mail: isodi@tin.it
www.castellare.it

**VAGLIAGLI**
**Fattoria della Aiola\*** Tel:
0577 322615. Fax: 0577
322509. 0900-1300, 1500-
1900. Hotel. E.F.G.Sp.TF.
WS.b. (TP.B. for groups).

**RADDA IN CHIANTI**
**Podere Capaccia\*** Loc
Capaccia. Tel: 0574 582426.
Fax: 0574 582428. 0900-
1200, 1400-1700.
E.F.G.TF.WS. (TP.B. for
groups). E-mail:
capaccia@chianticlassico.com
www.poderecapaccia.com

*The old hamlet of San Felice has been restored by the wine company and is a working community once more.*

### The wine route – Greve

The first town of note along the Via Chiantigiana is Greve. Piazza Matteotti, the enormous market place that is the heart of the town, is an attractive square with shops under the porticoes that are well used to the tourist and sell wild boar sausages, olive oil and Chianti Classico. The statue is to Giovanni da Verrazzano, the discoverer of New York Bay, who came from the nearby castle.

Just before Greve, if you come from Florence there are several producers' wine kiosks and a little further on, up the hill from its own shop, the castle of Vicchiomaggio. Here Englishman John Matta and his wife Paola produce a wide range of Chianti Classico wines including the superb Vigna Petri, made from 50-year-old vines cultivated in the old-fashioned way, that is in clumps and trained up trees.

Moving on from Greve down the Via Chiantigiana towards Panzano, the next stop might be for lunch or a tasting at Fattoria di Montagliari, where Giovanni Cappelli makes long-lived Vin Santo, excellent Chianti and even some balsamic vinegar. The trattoria attached to his property has the highest recommendation, the owner eats there.

Over the other side of the valley can be glimpsed Villa Vignamaggio, the setting for the Kenneth Branagh film of *Much Ado about Nothing* and, reputedly, the birthplace of the Mona Lisa.

### Panzano to San Donato

Up the hill to Panzano, where the old town has long burst its walls and sprawled out over the top of the hill. The castle was destroyed as long ago as 1260, but the event is commemorated annually every April. The church of San Leolino, just down the hill towards Castellina outside the town, has terracottas by Della Robbia and a wonderful view over the Pesa valley. Below you is the Conca of Panzano, site of some of the most prestigious Chianti Classico vineyards.

Down the hill from Panzano, cross the Pesa and take the sharp right up the other side of the valley to La Piazza (a good trattoria, Osteria alla Piazza) and along a winding dirt track to a T-junction, right to San Donato in Poggio, a typical medieval *borgo* (village) with an attractive Romanesque church on its outskirts, or left towards Castellina past Casa Emma and Fattoria La Ripa.

Just outside San Donato is a pair of contrasting estates. Isole e Olena is one of the innovators in Chianti Classico; here Paolo de Marchi makes his excellent 100 per cent Sangiovese wine Cepparello and experiments with grape varieties as diverse as Syrah and Chardonnay. Further on towards Poggibonsi on the same dirt track is Castello di Monsanto, famous for its long-lived and elegant Chiantis designed to evolve slowly over the years.

However you arrive at Castellina, it quickly becomes obvious that this is a working town in the heart of the wine industry. Greve is positively touristy

compared to Castellina. Have lunch at Trattoria La Torre and watch it fill up with vineyard workers and winery employees sure of getting good food.

Vineyards surround the ruins of the Monastery of San Niccolo just outside the town towards Poggibonsi, where the Castellare estate makes organic wines.

From Castellina the Via Chiantigiana goes south to Fonterutoli, where the Mazzei family make top-class Chiantis. Strike out over the hills to Vagliagli to visit wineries such as Fattoria della Aiola and cut back up to Radda, one of the major centers of Chianti. Dirt tracks are the norm in this area, but do not be alarmed, there is always a stretch of asphalt further on, and the dust and gravel give any trip the status of an adventure.

### Radda

Radda itself is sleepy. The Palazzo del Podestà, with the coats of arms that adorn it, is evocative of medieval times when this was the capital of the *Lega del Chianti* defensive alliance of Radda, Gaiole and Castellina, but one gets the feeling that the last time it was sacked, in 1478, the town expired. There is, however, one good place to stay, the Relais Fattoria Vignale, which

**RADDA IN CHIANTI (cont)**
**Fattoria di Montevertine***
Loc Montevertine. Tel: 0577 738009. Fax: 0577 738265. Mon-Fri 0900-1200, 1400-1700. E.G.TP.B.
**Podere Terreno*** Alla Via di Volpaia. Tel: 0577 738312. Fax: 0577 738600. *Agriturismo.* 1000-1300, 1500-1800. E.F.G.TP.WS.b. E-mail: podereterreno@chiantinet.it www.podereterreno.it

**RADDA IN CHIANTI (cont)**
**Enoteca Vignale** Fattoria Vignale, Via Pianigiani 9. Tel: 0577 738012. Fax: 0577 738730. 0900-1300, 1500-2000. Hotel. E.F.G.Sp.TF.WS. E-mail: vignale@vignale.it www.vignale.it
**Fattoria Castello di Volpaia\*** Loc Volpaia, 53017. Tel: 0577 738066. Fax: 0577 738619. Mar-Oct 1000-1900; Nov-Dec 1000-1800. Olive oil mill. E.F.G.TP.WS.B. E-mail: info@volpaia.com www.volpaia.com/it
**Enoteca Porciatti** Tel: 0577 738055. Mar-Nov. Wines, olive oil and specialty *lardone*. E-mail: casaporciatti@chiantinet.it

**GAIOLE IN CHIANTI**
**Badia a Coltibuono** Loc Badia a Coltibuono. Tel: 0577 744832. Fax: 0577 749235. Tours Mon-Fri. Closed Aug, Nov-Apr. Abbey. E.F.WS at estate shop. (TP for groups of ten or more). E-mail: pr@coltibuono.com www.coltibuono.com
**Barone Ricasoli\*** Cantine del Castello di Brolio. Tel: 0577 7301. Fax: 0577 730225. Mon-Sat 0900-1200, 1300-1900. Sat, Sun 1100-1900 summer only. E.TF.WS.B. E-mail: barone@ricasoli.it
**Riecine** Loc Riecine. Tel/Fax: 0577 749098. 0800-1700. E.G.TF.WS.b. (TP for groups). E-mail: riecine@chiantinet.it www.riecine.com
**Castello di San Polo in Rosso** Tel: 0577 746045. Fax: 0577 746153. 0800-1200, 1300-1700. E.Sp.TF.b. E-mail: info@sanpolo.it www.sanpolo.it
**SM Tenimenti Pile e Lamole e Vistarenni srl\*** Loc Vistarenni. Tel: 0577 738186. Fax: 0577 738549. 0900-1300, 1500-1700. F.TP.WS.B.

combines hotel, wine shop and winery on one site.

The excitement around Radda comes from its wine producers. On one side there is Fattoria di Montevertine, the late Sergio Manetti's great challenge to the received wisdom of Chianti Classico. The estate opted out of the Consorzio Chianti Classico early in its life, when Manetti found that if he belonged to it he was legally obliged to make wine in a way he knew was madness. He knew he should concentrate on the Sangiovese grape and have nothing to do with white grape blends in Chianti for the type of long-lived wines he was aiming at. Time has proved Manetti right and his early bid for independence made his name. His son Martino and son-in-law Klaus carry on the good work.

Another great character of Tuscan winemaking has the estate just up the hill from Montevertine, Podere Capaccia. Giampaolo Pacini is a businessman from Prato, but he was also trained as an enologist. His story is typical of many in Chianti Classico. Seeking the good life in the country he came to Chianti in the 1970s, when many of the smaller hamlets were falling to rack and ruin. He found Capaccia, an abandoned group of houses, decaying after the families who originally lived there left and went to the towns to find more lucrative work.

Slowly, Pacini has rebuilt the main house of the complex and shelters his winery in other partially rebuilt houses. He has also developed gastronomic tourism to its ultimate stage, offering fascinating courses in recreating historical Tuscan cooking, and doing the research himself.

Over the other side of the valley is another medieval complex on a grander scale. This is Castello di Volpaia. The story is familiar; Carlo and Giovanella

Stianti come from Milan and have spent decades restoring much of the village in a hilltop site. One house is for the fermentation tanks, one house contains the aging cellars, one is the offices, another is the olive oil press, yet another is the vinegar plant. Much of the village is in fact a carefully hidden winery. And the church is used for an annual art exhibition of the highest standing.

**Gaiole**
Just down the hill from Volpaia is Podere Terreno, which provides bed, breakfast, dinner and its own wine.

From Radda, take the road east to Badia a Coltibuono, perhaps via Vistarenni in the commune of Gaiole just to taste the wines and admire the impressive Venetian-style villa.

Coltibuono is one of Chianti Classico's great estates and, hidden in the woods on the site of a former monastery, it is in a very tranquil setting. Lorenza de' Medici, wife of the owner and author of many books on Italian cooking, runs courses on Tuscan cuisine here. Naturally, there is a trattoria as part of the complex.

Here, you pick up signs to the *Strada dei Castelli del Chianti*, which makes for less of a wine-intensive tour, but nevertheless leads to properties such as Castello di San Polo in Rosso, which is frescoed church, castle and wine estate rolled into one.

At Coltibuono, stay in Chianti Classico and go on to the castles, or take the road over the hills to Chianti Aretino to visit the more out-of-the-way estates, such as Villa La Selva, whose owner, industrialist Sergio Carpini, is determined to make a showplace for wine.

The next castle is Brolio, back in the commune of Gaiole. This wonderful neo-Gothic pile was built in the last century on the ruins of a more ancient castle by the man who was Italy's second Prime Minister and formulator of the Chianti *cépage*, Baron Bettino Ricasoli. The family have recently taken back control of the estate after a period of sad decline in the hands of a multinational company and the latest vintages are markedly better.

From Brolio it is a short distance to San Felice, which is a sensitively restored medieval village now combining hotel, restaurant and, at 190 hectares, one of Tuscany's biggest wineries. On a clear day you can see the towers of San Gimignano in the far distance in a landscape that cannot have changed much in hundreds of years. It is a magical sight.

**SAN GUSMÉ**
**Agricola San Felice\*** Loc S Felice. Tel: 0577 359087. Fax: 0577 359223. Mon-Fri 0930-1730. E.F.TP.WS.B. E-mail: sanfelice@ agricolasanfelice.it www.agricolasanfelice.it

**SIENA**
**Enoteca Italiana** Fortezza Medicea. Tel: 0577 288497. Fax: 0577 270717. Mon 1200-2000, Tue-Sat 1200-0100. Closed Sun. E.TP. WS.EP. (B for groups). E-mail: enoteca@enoteca-italiana.it www.enoteca-italiana.it

*Left: Siena's Enoteca Permanente is sited in the great Medici fortress. Below: city and cathedral from Siena's bastions.*

# *Montalcino*

South of Siena the countryside changes dramatically. The hills of Chianti with their olive trees, vines and woods give way to the hills of Le Crete Senesi, a beautiful area to travel through, especially before the harvest when the cornfields and sunflowers gild the hills with different shades of yellow, giving the few clumps of cypresses in their midst an almost surreal air.

The SS2 from Siena is part of the old Pilgrims Way to Rome, the Via Francigena, that also runs through the center of San Gimignano.

Buonconvento is the first town of note along the route. Its 14th-century walls are still in good repair. A yellow tourist sign signals the turning to the Abbey of Monte Oliveto Maggiore, where the site and its frescoes make the detour worthwhile.

## The town of Montalcino

Perhaps only Alba, in Piedmont, has such an intense atmosphere of wine as Montalcino. There is a certain mystique about the fabled wine that brings an otherwise sleepy town alive.

There are several wine shops in Montalcino, but the one essential stop for a restorative glass of wine and perhaps a taste of local salami or pecorino cheese is the combined Enoteca and wine bar in the castle.

This was the last fortress of the Sienese Republic to hold out against combined Imperial and Florentine forces from 1555 until 1559. The event is recorded by a plaque on the castle walls which talks of the "Medici Robbers," and even now the Florentines are spoken of with little fondness.

## The great Brunello

The credit for the invention of Brunello goes to the ancestor of its most famous producers, the Biondi Santi family.

It was Clemente Santi who created Brunello in the 1850s when the potential of the Brunello clone of the Sangiovese grape was identified. Franco Biondi Santi and his son Jacopo continue the tradition today. Their wines are famously long lived and famously expensive too.

Brunello has undergone several changes of style since it was first created and along the way has acquired the reputation of being a wine that takes years to come to its peak. However, with the exception of Biondi Santi wines, this is largely a myth. Five to ten years after the vintage is enough.

Aging requirements used to make Brunello a monster despite itself. Many years in old oak dried it out. But since 1998 the obligatory time in barrel has been cut from three and a half years to two years (with four months in bottle for the normal Brunello, and six months for the Riserva). The accent is a modern one based on elegance of structure and fruit in the body, which doesn't mean there is no place for an easier-drinking wine in the Montalcino portfolio.

This is where Rosso di Montalcino comes in. Created DOC in 1984, Rosso is made of Sangiovese but has no obligatory time in wood, new or old. Producers can make it as heavy or as light as they like and the public love it. Rosso di Montalcino is a simpler and fruitier version of Brunello with a bit of structure nevertheless and some of the cachet of its more illustrious cousin.

The other wine of the area is Moscadello, a traditional sweet wine based on a variant of the Moscato grape.

## Visiting the estates

Montalcino's vineyard area can roughly be divided into three sub-zones that produce wines of broadly differing characteristics, although, of course,

### CASTELNUOVO DELL' ABATE

**Tenuta di Collosorbo** Loc Villa A Sesta 25. Tel/Fax: 0577 835534. 0900-1200, 1500-2000. TF./TP.WS.b.

### MONTALCINO

**Altesino\*** Loc Altesino. Tel: 0577 806208. Fax: 0577 806131. 1000-1200, 1400-1900. E.G.Danish.TP.WS.b. E-mail: altesino@iol.it

**Fattoria dei Barbi\*** Loc Podernovi. Tel: 0577 841111. Fax: 0577 841112. Mon-Fri 1000-1300, 1430-1800; Sat, Sun 1430-1800. E.F.TF.WS.b. (G available for guided tours and tastings). E-mail: fattoriadeibarbi@ fattoriadeibarbi.it www.fattoriadeibarbi.IT

**Banfi\*** Castello di Poggio alle Mura. Tel: 0577 816001. Fax: 0577 816021. Glass museum in castle every day. Open winter 1000-1800; open summer 1000-1900. Cellars Mon-Fri office hours. E.F.G.J.Sp.Portuguese. TP.WS.B. E-mail: banfi@banfi.it www.castellobanfi.com

**Tenuta Caparzo\*** Loc Caparzo. Tel: 0577 848390. Fax: 0577 849377. Mon-Fri 1000-1200, 1500-1700. TF.WS. E-mail: caparzo@libero.it www.caparzo.it

**Az Agr Case Basse** c/o Via dei Frassini 39, 20156 Milano. Tel: 02 461544. Fax: 02 48195341). B. E-mail: soldera@tin.it www.soldera.it

**Fattoria Poggio Antico** Loc Poggio Antico. Tel: 0577 848044. Fax: 0577 846563. 0900-2000. E.F.TP.WS.b.

**Tenuta Valdicava\*** Loc Valdicava. Tel: 0577 848261. Fax: 0577 848008. E.TF.B.

such generalizations are easily refuted by an individual winemaker's style.

In general, then, the wines from the north of Montalcino are less full-bodied but more elegant. Wines from the east are bigger, fuller wines as their vineyards are sheltered from any bad weather. Those to the south reflect the warmer weather and are the biggest, most powerful wines of all.

Whatever wineries you visit Brunello provides a consistently high quality wine. Highlights include: Fattoria dei Barbi, which makes its own cheese and salami as well as having its own trattoria; Poggio Antico, which has its own restaurant and

makes top-quality modern Brunellos; Case Basse – a cult wine in Italy; Talenti – one of the magical winemakers of the older generation; and Col d'Orcia, one of the most widely available good-quality wines. Banfi is the biggest producer; American-owned, it provides a wide range of wines in very approachable styles.

Don't miss the Abbey of Sant' Antimo outside Castelnuovo dell'Abate just south of Montalcino, reputedly founded by Charlemagne and restored to magnificence only this century. The new community of monks are famous for Gregorian chant.

**S ANGELO IN COLLE**
**Tenuta Col d'Orcia\*** Tel: 0577 808001. Fax: 0577 844018. 0900-1230, 1430-1800. E.F.G.Sp.T.F.WS.B. E-mail: coldrcia. direzione@tin.it www.coldorcia.it
**Az Agr Talenti di Talenti Riccardo** Podere Pian di Conte 98. Tel: 0577 844064. Fax: 0577 844043. 0800-1300, 1500-1800. E.F.WS.b. E-mail: az_talenti@tin.it

*The countryside around Montalcino is wooded and hilly, with sunflowers in the valley and vineyards on the hillsides.*

# Montepulciano

*The heraldic griffin - symbol of the Consorzio of Vino Nobile producers.*

About half an hour's drive east from Montalcino is its great rival, Montepulciano, the zone of the splendidly named Vino Nobile di Montepulciano.

## Papal Pienza

Pienza is on the way. There is a wine excuse to stop here (a good Enoteca). However, the birthplace of Aeneas Silvio Piccolomini, Pope Pius II, largely rebuilt by him in a felicitous time for architecture (1459-1464), should also be visited for its architectural splendor. In gastronomic terms the town is known for its cheeses, pecorino di Pienza and ricotta.

## Vino Nobile di Montepulciano

The first wine in Italy to be granted the top ranking DOCG status was Vino Nobile di Montepulciano. Exactly why it is called Vino Nobile is uncertain. The wine has always been known for its quality, since at least the 17th century, but more likely the epithet *nobile* refers to the fact that this was the wine produced on the estates of the noble occupants of the grand houses in Montepulciano. Compared with Brunello, it has the advantage of being a more approachable wine ready to drink sooner because of its fewer years of barrel aging.

Vino Nobile is very similar in make-up to Chianti. The major grape is Sangiovese, here called Prugnolo because of its supposed plum-like taste, together with small percentages of Canaiolo, Mammolo, Malvasia and Trebbiano. So, just like Chianti, it varies in style, although, unlike Chianti, it is of a consistently high quality.

Some producers make Vino Nobile with an almost New World richness, full of tight fruit and tannin. Others make a wine of soft aromatic elegance.

Like Brunello, Vino Nobile also has a younger second wine version, Rosso di Montepulciano. This ensures that only the best grapes go into Vino Nobile, but there is no agreement at all about what style the Rosso should have; young and fruity like a Beaujolais Nouveau, or traditionally structured like an everyday Chianti? In any case, only small quantities are produced.

The other wines of the area are Chianti Colli Senesi and Bianco Vergine Valdichiana – honest local wines.

## Montepulciano

The hill town of Montepulciano is about 14km (9 miles) from Pienza. The first feature you see is Sangallo's Renaissance masterpiece, the church of San Biagio, halfway up the slope.

The whole town is something of an architect's dream; it is full of Renaissance palaces from the early 16th century, built for the nobles whose estates provided the Vino Nobile.

Park outside the town at Porta al Prato and begin the climb up the main street, Via Gracciano del Corso. The wine shops begin almost at once. But just at the corner, opposite the stone lion on a pillar, the *Marzocco* that records the town's medieval allegiance to Florence, is the lovely Palazzo Avignonesi, masterpiece attributed to Vignola.

Avignonesi is one of the area's top producers. You can taste the Vino Nobile, the Grifi (Sangiovese and Cabernet), the Merlot, the Marzocco (Chardonnay) and Tuscany's best (and most expensive) Vin Santo in the *palazzo*.

Climbing further up into the town there is a constant succession of delightful buildings, reaching a climax with the stunningly operatic Piazza Grande. The Town Hall, the Palazzo Comunale, is a miniature version of Florence's Palazzo Vecchio, and the cathedral and *palazzi* that form the other three sides of the square are like something out of a stage set; they are a perfectly designed ensemble.

Several of Montepulciano's *palazzi* have ancient cellars dug into the hill of the town. Cantina del Redi has its stunning high-vaulted 15th-century wine cellars in Palazzo Ricci. Don't miss Palazzo Contucci on the edge of Piazza Grande; this is another good wine excuse, for Alamanno Contucci is President of the Vino Nobile Consorzio, and a noted producer himself.

Outside the town of Montepulciano itself the Vino Nobile zone extends over the surrounding hills. There is an interruption for the Val di Chiana (Vino Nobile regulations stipulate a minimum vineyard altitude of 250m/ 820ft) to the east and then an island of Vino Nobile the other side of the valley around the hilltop town of Valiano.

### Il Bravio delle Botti
On the last Sunday in August, the eight *contrade*, or districts, of Montepulciano compete in an energetic wine race. The idea is to race a *botte*, or 80-kg (36-pound) wine barrel, up the main street to the front of the cathedral. Local rivalries are intense and the race is keenly fought before celebrations involving copious quantities of wine.

**MONTEPULCIANO (cont)**
**Az Agr Contucci\*** Via del Teatro 1. Tel: 0578 757006. Fax: 0578 752891. (Alamanno Contucci, Adamo Pallecchi). 0900-1230, 1430-1830. E.F.T.F.WS. (T.P.B. for groups). E-mail: info@contucci.it www.contucci.it
**Fattoria di Gracciano,** Via Umbria 63, Fraz Gracciano. Tel: 0578 708676. Fax: 0578 707097. (Dr Giovanni Folonari). 0900-1200, 1400-1700; Sat 0900-1200. E.F.G.T.F.WS.B. E-mail: w.melloni@tiscalinet.it

The *Strada del Vino Montepulciano* office in Piazza Grande is open every day in the summer and will book winery visits. Tel: 0578 717484. Fax: 0578 752749.

*Palazzo Contucci is one of Montepulciano's many beautiful buildings, a classic example of the Renaissance town palace of a noble family.*

# Food of Tuscany

**FOR FURTHER INFORMATION**
**Consorzio Chianti Rùfina**
Viale Belfiore 9, 50144
Firenze. Tel: 055 3245680.
Fax: 055 3248252. Chianti
Rufina and Pomino Wine
Roads pamphlet. E-mail:
info@chiantirufina.com
www.chiantirufina.com
**Consorzio del Marchio
Storico Chianti Classico**
Via Scopeti 155, S Andrea in
Percussina, 50026 S Casciano
(FI). Tel: 055 82285. Fax: 055
8228173. Essential Chianti
Classico map. E.G. E-mail:
marketing@chianticlassico.com
www.chianticlassico.com
**Consorzio Brunello di
Montalcino** Costa del
Municipio 1, 53024
Montalcino (SI). Tel: 0577
848246. Fax: 0577 849425.
E-mail: consbrun@tin.it
www.consorziobrunello
dimontalcino.it
**Consorzio Morellino di
Scansano** Via Marconi 23,
58054 Scansano (GR). Tel/
Fax: 0564 507710. E-mail:
consorzio_morellino@libero.it
**Consorzio Della
Denominazione San
Gimignano** Via della
Rocca, 53037 San
Gimignano (SI). Tel: 0577
940108. Fax: 0577 942088.
E-mail: vernaccia@iol.it
www.vernaccia.it
**Consorzio del Vino
Nobile di Montepulciano**
Piazza Grande 7, 53045
Montepulciano (SI). Tel: 0578
757812. Fax: 0578 758213.
E-mail: nobile@bccmp.com
www.vinonobiledi
montepulciano.it
**Agenzia per il Turismo
"Costa degli Etruschi"**
Piazza Cavour 6, 57100
Livorno. Tel: 0586 898111
Fax: 0586 896173. Useful
booklet on Livorno, *Discovering
the Local Flavors*. E-mail: info@
livorno.turismo.toscana.it
www.livorno.turismo.toscana.it

### *Agriturismo* – staying on a wine estate

In the main wine-producing areas of Italy there is now a growing demand for houses and apartments to rent for vacations, especially during the summer.

Tuscany is particularly rich in this type of accommodation. Wine producers have converted their villa stable blocks or outlying barns into vacation homes, and some have even converted their own castles or *Fattorie* into hotels.

Such accommodation is very popular, but there is little standardization of facilities.

Many of the estates recommended for their wine in the information panels of this book also offer *agriturismo*. Ask for further details in order to check on exactly the type of accommodation offered, or, if in doubt, book through a reputable travel agent.
E-mail: agriturismo@regione.toscana.it
www.agriturismo.regione.toscana.it

## FOOD SPECIALTIES

Until the quality of the ingredients is appreciated, Tuscan food can seem severe and parsimonious. This is, perhaps, the reason for the fame of *Bistecca alla fiorentina*, a generous rib steak, an island in the sea of soups and beans.

But as good members of this nation of food critics, the Tuscans are fascinated by their food, and their preoccupation is above all with the quality of the raw ingredients.

When the wine estate of Castello della Sala was officially opened to the world's press a few years ago, what really excited the prestigious Antinori company was that they could serve a meal composed of meat, fruit, vegetables and wine, with all the products coming from their own estate. There were no problems about hiring internationally renowned chefs; the food consisted of the freshest ingredients, simply cooked. Typically Tuscan.

### Olive oil

Tuscany is justly famous for its simple foods. The extra-virgin olive oil is so fruity, rich and thick, it is almost a meal in itself. But it is neither as plentiful nor as cheap now as it was before the great frost of 1985 which destroyed so many of Chianti's abundant olive trees. New shoots have now sprung from many of the frost-blasted trees, but it may still be some years before olive oil production recovers fully.

Olive oil is used for cooking, but its main purpose is to bring out the flavor of cooked foods. The *Bistecca* and the *Ribollita*, bean and vegetable soup that is cooked twice, "reboiled," is delicious laced with local olive oil.

Liver is much loved in Tuscany. A favorite dish is *Fegatelli* (or *Fegatini di maiale all'uccelletto*), a type of kebab of pig's liver, bay leaf, and traditional Tuscan unsalted bread. *Crostini di fegatini* is a dish of toasted rounds of Tuscan bread served with a delicious chicken liver and anchovy paste.

### Game and fish

Pasta is not a traditional Tuscan food, but it does appear in dishes which combine the hunter's catch with rich sauces: *Pappardelle sulla lepre*, for example, is wide pasta strips with a hare sauce.

Hunting, once common in the great forests of Tuscany, is still a favorite activity, and hunters may still encounter wild boar in various remote parts of Tuscany. But it is more likely to entail the shooting of *conigli*, rabbits, or *uccelletti*, small birds, which are cooked on a spit and eaten bones and all.

The Tuscan coast provides several fish specialties: *Triglie alla livornese* is red mullet baked with tomatoes, garlic and ginger. *Cèe* or *Cieche alla pisana* are eel fry cooked with olive oil, garlic and sage and served with parmesan. Salt cod, *Baccalà*, is a speciality of Livorno, and is cooked with tomatoes and potatoes.

*Finocchio* – fennel, is baked with butter and parmesan as an accompaniment to roast meats, and is used to great effect to flavor a special type of salami, the *finocchiona*.

## FESTIVALS

*April:* FLORENCE: Easter festival, the "Explosion of the Cart" with fireworks.

*May:* PONTASSIEVE: *Toscanello d'Oro*, an exhibition of Chianti wine.

*July, August*: SIENA: the Palio, the most famous city horse race in Italy.

*August, last Sunday:* MONTEPULCIANO: *Bravio delle Botti*, a costume parade followed by wine-barrel race.

*September, second half:* LUCCA: *Mostra dei Prodotti Tipici*, wine, oil and honey.

*September:* GREVE IN CHIANTI: *Mostra Mercato del Vino Chianti Classico*, the high point of the Chianti-showing calendar.

*September:* AREZZO: Joust of the Saracen, a costume tournament.

### THE GALLO NERO (BLACK COCKEREL)

This emblem of the *Chianti Classico Consorzio* recalls the meeting of two knights who were to have ridden out from Siena and Florence exactly at cockcrow, towards each other, along the Via Chiantigiana. Their meeting point was supposed to establish the future boundary between the warring cities.

The black cockerel of Florence, scrawny and underfed, woke his rider up much earlier than the pampered Sienese cockerel. And consequently the riders met at Fonterutoli, much nearer Siena than Florence.

**Movimento Turismo del Vino Toscana** c/o Sede Legale, Podere Terreno, Alla Via della Volpaia, 53017 Radda in Chianti Siena. Tel: 0577 738312. Fax: 0577 738600. List of all Tuscan members of Movement for Wine Tourism. E-mail: podereterreno@chiantinet.it www.wineday.org

The official website for all 14 Tuscan *Strada del Vino* routes is: www.terreditoscana.regione.toscana.it/stradedelvino/

*The central café and wine shop in Montalcino retains its title of* fiaschetteria *from the days when wine was sold in straw-covered flasks (*fiaschi*).*

# Central Italy

The tourist brochures and guidebooks are full of the phrase *L'Italia ha un cuore verde* (Italy has a green heart), but it is true nevertheless that Umbria as a region is a gentle, green and pleasant land, with enchanting landscapes of green hills and dense forests, and some of the country's most beautiful towns. The smokestacks of industry are confined to the city of Terni. With this exception, Umbria is a jewel of the Middle Ages: Gubbio is the archetypal medieval town; Perugia is a magnificent fortress on a hill; Orvieto's cathedral is one of the wonders of Italy; Spoleto is more cosmopolitan but just as antique. Assisi needs no comment, except perhaps that even if St Francis had not inspired its immense basilica it would still be worth visiting for its hillside setting. Both historically and vinously there is an overlap with the Lazio region, where the cities of Bolsena and Viterbo share an Etruscan heritage with Umbria.

Central Italy is a dynamic winemaking area, with the possible exception of Orvieto, which is a once-famous white wine in need of rediscovery. As is Est! Est!! Est!!! over the border in Lazio – the legend is more important than the wine now (see page 105). But even in these regions it is individual producers who count and excellent wines can be found from the right producer. Other parts of Umbria are most definitely up-and-coming. Just outside Foligno is the town of Montefalco, whose red wines are attracting much interest. Unique to the area is the Sagrantino grape, used to supplement the more usual Sangiovese in Rosso di Montefalco, but also vinified as a red wine in its own right. The taste has been described as reminiscent of blackberries. There is also a *passito* version made with semi-dried grapes which has joined the ranks of Italy's DOCG elite.

South of Perugia, near the famous majolica-producing town of Deruta, is Torgiano. Here, the Lungarotti family have established an Italian institution – the Lungarotti winery, with a hotel, a stunning olive oil museum, and an internationally renowned museum of wine-related artifacts. Torgiano Rosso Riserva is another of the DOCG top wines.

The latest area to gain critical attention is the Colli del Trasimeno DOC to the south-west of Lake Trasimene. Some of the magic of Tuscany seems to be rubbing off onto it.

*Castello della Sala has been restored by Antinori, whose estates produce some of Central Italy's finest wines.*

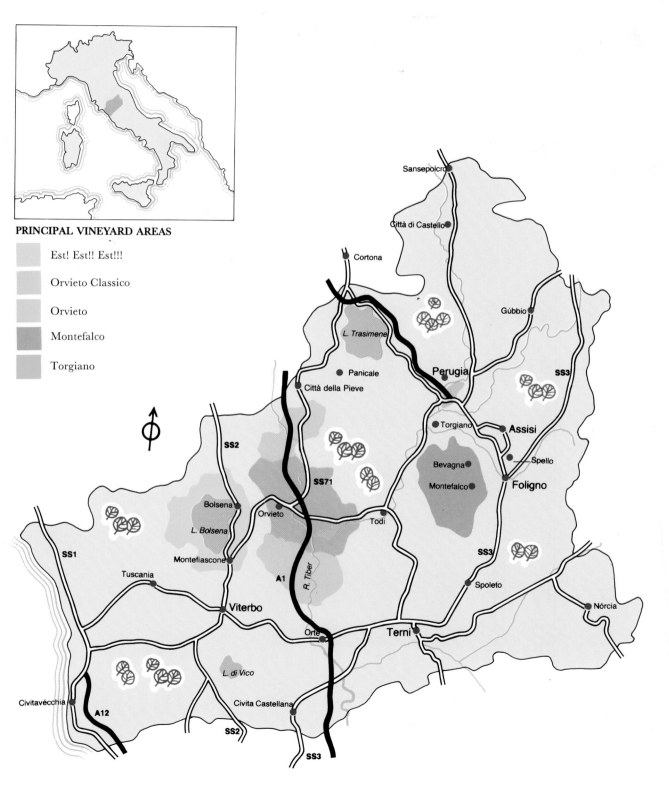

**PRINCIPAL VINEYARD AREAS**

Est! Est!! Est!!!

Orvieto Classico

Orvieto

Montefalco

Torgiano

Sansepolcro

Città di Castello

Cortona

L. Trasimene

Gúbbio

Panicale

Città della Pieve

Perugia

SS3

SS2

Torgiano

Assisi

Spello

SS71

Bevagna

Bolsena

Montefalco

Foligno

L. Bolsena

Orvieto

Todi

Montefiascone

R. Tiber

SS3

Tuscania

A1

Spoleto

SS1

Nórcia

Viterbo

Orte

Terni

Civitavécchia

L. di Vico

A12

Civita Castellana

SS2

SS3

# Orvieto Country

*The façade of the cathedral in Orvieto reflects the Italian sunshine like a gilded wedding cake. Inside there is an elaborate series of frescoes. Outside, shops in the cathedral square sell Orvieto's famous white wines.*

The easiest route to Orvieto from Tuscany is the A1 motorway, the *Autostrada del Sole*.

Various detours are possible, notably to Chiusi for its National Etruscan Museum and to Città della Pieve, the birthplace of the artist Perugino; see his *Adoration of the Magi* in S Maria dei Bianchi.

## Orvieto

The sheer rock face on which Orvieto is built makes it a superb defensive site; it was much favored by the Popes and remained part of the Papal States until 1860. The old town remains largely intact and unspoiled on its table-top position.

The cathedral is unique and though the mosaics on the façade were heavily restored in the 19th century, they follow the original design of the 14th century.

## Orvieto wine

Winemaking in Orvieto goes back at least as far as the Etruscans and may even be reflected in the town's name.

One legend has barbarian invaders foiled in their attempt to carry off chalices by the gold metal inexplicably turning to liquid. "*Aurum vetitum,*" they shrieked, giving the city its name, and ran away.

Another story, no doubt put about by winemakers in the not too distant past, suggests that the *aurum vetitum* was none other than the golden wine that also bears the name Orvieto. It is nonetheless true that the wine, especially the sweeter *abboccato* Orvieto, does have a genuinely golden color.

Orvieto is a wine waiting to be re-invented. Twenty years ago it was the Chianti producers' white wine for the export market, made in a dry *secco* version or, more often, a medium dry *abboccato* version. Now the *secco* is the predominant style, but modern fermentation techniques and commercial necessity often turn it into yet another crisp, light, white with no particular character at all.

The most exciting development recently has been the discovery that Orvieto can be highly successful as a dessert wine, made with grapes affected by noble rot, just like Sauternes. *Muffa nobile*, or noble rot, occurs in the Orvieto region around Lake Corbara where the autumn mists lead to the creation of the *Botrytis cinerea* fungus on the grapes and a consequent shrivelling and concentration of sugars.

Wines such as Antinori's Muffato della Sala, Decugnano dei Barbi's Pourriture Noble and Barberani's Calcaia are proving how successful these luscious dessert wines can be, even if they can only ever be produced in tiny quantities.

Just as interesting is the discovery by Antinori at Castello della Sala that the international grape variety Chardonnay and the local Grechetto can be combined to make a world-class wine, Cervaro della Sala. This is not DOC Orvieto, but it does prove the potential of this part of Umbria.

## Est! Est!! Est!!!

The other wine of note in this area lies in the zone of Montefiascone, between Bolsena and Viterbo. Est! Est!! Est!!! can be pleasant enough, but it is normally of only passing interest. The fascination lies in the origin of its Latin name with its plethora of exclamation marks.

The story behind the wine dates back a thousand years. It is said that a certain German prelate, Bishop Fugger, was journeying south to Rome around the year AD 1000, accompanied by a servant whose task it was to travel ahead of his master to find the best inns with the best wine. Having found a suitable hostelry, the servant would write *Est!* on the door to indicate its suitability, and then hurry on to the next place.

On reaching Montefiascone, the servant was so struck by the quality of the local wine that he wrote not one *Est!* but three on the door, complete with exclamation marks. Apparently his master was equally convinced of the quality of the wine, for he died of drinking too much of it, and was buried in the same place. Until the 17th century, a barrel of wine was emptied on the bishop's grave every anniversary of his death.

### ALLERONA
**Dott Antonino Scambia Tenuta Antica Selva di Meana\*** Loc Poggio Barile. Tel: 0763 624157. Fax: 0763 624285. (Siria Scambia). 0830-1300, 1500-1800. E.F.Sp.TP.WS.b. E-mail: ascambia@tin.it
**Tenuta Poggia del Lupo\*** Loc Buzzaghetto. (Giovanna Ortu). Tel: 0763 628350. Fax: 0763 628005. E.F.TF.WS.B.

### CORBARA
**Az Agr Decugnano dei Barbi\*** Loc Fossatello di Corbara, Orvieto. Tel: 0763 308255. Fax: 0763 308118. (Simone Rocchi). 0800-1200, 1400-1800. Cellars of Etruscan origin. TP.WS.B. E-mail: barbivini@inwind.it
**Barberani Az Agr Vallesanta\*** Loc Cereto, Lago di Corbara, Baschi. Tel: 0763 341820. Fax: 0763 340773. (Dott. Luigi Antonio Barberani). 0800-1300, 1400-1700. E.F.TF.WS. E-mail: barberani@barberani.it www.barberani.it

### ORVIETO SCALO
**Villa Pagliano\*** Loc Castellunchio 67. Tel/Fax: 0763 304051. (Monica or Ernesto Cotti). Open all year, 0900-1200, 1500-1800. Etruscan tomb at gate of villa. E.TF.WS.B. E-mail: villapagliano@libero.it

# Perugia and Montefalco

**MONTEFALCO**
**Az Agr Adanti*** Vocabolo Arquata, Bevagna. Tel: 0742 360295. Fax: 0742 361270. (Alvaro Palini). 0900-1230, 1430-1730. Sat a.m. only. E.F.TF.WS.B. E-mail: info@cantineadanti.com www.cantineadanti.com
**Az Agr Antonelli San Marco*** Loc S Marco 59. Tel: 0742 379158. Fax: 0742 371063. (Filippo Antonelli). All year 0900-1200, 1500-1800. Closed Sun. *Agriturismo.* E.TF.WS.B. E-mail: info@ antonellisanmarco.it www.antonellisanmarco.it
**Val di Maggio A Caprai*** Loc Torre. Tel: 0742 378802. Fax: 0742 378422. (Isabella Preziosi). 0830-1300, 1500-1830. E.TP.WS.B. E-mail: info@arnaldocaprai.it www.arnaldocaprai.it
**Rocca di Fabbri*** Fabbri di Montefalco. Tel: 0742 399379. Fax: 0742 399199. (Simona Vitali). 0830-1230, 1400-1830. Closed Jan. *Osteria.* E.F.TP.WS.B. E-mail: roccafabbri@tin.it www.roccadifabbri.com

Umbria, the green heart of Italy, is a fertile region; but wine has never been a major component of its agriculture. The grape accounts for less than five per cent of its produce: precedence is given to livestock, cereals, and tobacco.

There are two approaches to northern Umbria and the region's capital of Perugia. One way is via Città di Castello and the Tiber Valley; the DOC red and white wine Colli Altotiberini comes from here but is of mainly local interest.

The other way is via Cortona and Lake Trasimene. DOC Colli del Trasimeno is an up-and-coming region. Reflect, as you pass them by, on the village names – Ossaia (ossuary) and Sanguineto (bloody), which indicate the area of Hannibal's victory in 217 BC, at the battle of Lake Trasimene.

## Perugia
Perugia is a great cultural center and combines the rural simplicity of Umbria with the style of a university city. Raphael began his career in Perugia, and the painters Pinturicchio and Perugino also worked here. The Galleria Nazionale dell'Umbria, one of Italy's finest art galleries, is housed in the magnificent Palazzo dei Priori. Don't miss the Archeological Museum and the Etruscan Tomb of the Volumnii just outside the town to the south. For an overview, and tasting, of Umbrian wines, visit the Enoteca Provinciale di Perugia.

## Torgiano
A short distance to the south lies Torgiano, where the world's wine press gather every year for the Banco d'Assaggio National Wine Competition at the Lungarotti estate. Have a glass of wine at the Osteria del Museo and visit the museum itself. Don't miss this wine museum; this is no haphazard collection of old farming implements. Instead, the Lungarotti Museum is in a completely different league. Many of the exhibits would be just as appropriately housed in one of the national art museums.

Don't forget the wine, however. Lungarotti's Vigna Monticchio Rubesco Riserva and Torgiano Riserva are two of Italy's finest reds. The company has long pioneered fine winemaking in an area which is only now emerging from strictly local importance.

## Assisi and Spello
Umbria is full of exquisite medieval sights. Following the Topino valley south from Perugia the first stop is Assisi. It is a tourist trap, but the Basilica of St Francis is wonderfully frescoed, with masterpieces of pictorial narrative by Giotto and many others. It has such atmosphere that the souvenir stalls outside fail to ruin it. And, as with all tourist traps, it is enough to walk away from the main thoroughfares to escape the crowds. Climb up to the

*The pretty hillside wine town of Montefalco, home of Rosso di Montefalco, is surrounded by its vineyards.*

*The Lungarotti wine museum at Torgiano is probably the most important of its kind in Europe. 21 rooms display objects of art and implements of viticulture, ranging from wine presses and wine jars to prints and ceramics by modern and classical artists. Medieval majolica and modern ceramics are impressive, suitably enough for an area of Italy still important today for its artisan-designed ceramics. Engravings and drawings are particularly well represented with artists ranging from Mantegna to Picasso. The collection was started by Maria Grazia Lungarotti, wife of pioneering winemaker Giorgio Lungarotti and founder of the recently opened Olive Oil Museum. For Wine Museum and Olive Oil Museum details, see page 108.*

castle and peer down through the gunports at the town below if the tourists get too much for you.

Spello, some 6km (4 miles) away has everything: a Roman theater, Roman gates, and Perugino and Pinturicchio frescoes. Every year at the feast of Corpus Christi, the streets are decorated with mosaics in petals and seeds.

### Strada del Vino Sagrantino

At the heart of Umbria's claim to world importance on the viticultural scene is a local grape said to have been brought back from Asia Minor by Franciscan monks in the early Middle Ages, the Sagrantino. It produces attractive, brambly red wines that have gained international recognition for the town of Montefalco and its surrounding district. Indeed, Montefalco now hosts the National Center for Passito Wines on the strength of the success of the dessert version of this wine, Sagrantino Passito DOCG. Like the better known Amarone and Recioto of the Veneto, the dessert wine can be either sweet (more traditional) or dry and is made from semi-dried grapes pressed about three months after harvest.

To celebrate this wine the *Strada del Vino Sagrantino* has been set up to take the visitor around the medieval townscapes of its homeland. Stops include Bevagna (don't miss the Romanesque churches in the brooding main square), Montefalco (a superb fresco museum in the ex-church of San Francesco), Gualdo Cattaneo (a fortified village), Giano (the Abbey of San Felice) and Castel Ritaldi (church and castle). This is the land where Saint Francis preached to the animals, where Frederick II Barbarossa practised falconry, and where the Romans built alongside the old Via Flaminia.
The other wines of the area are the usual Central Italian red variation on Sangiovese, called Montefalco Rosso, and usual white variation on Trebbiano, called Montefalco Bianco. The local Grechetto grape, which forms part of the white wine mix, is an interesting nutty-flavored single varietal.

**PERUGIA**
**Enoteca Provinciale di Perugia** Via Ulisse Rocchi 18. Tel: 075 5724824. Mon 1630-2030, Tue-Sat 1030-1430, 1630-2230. Closed Sun. E.F.Sp.TP.WS.b.EP.

**SPELLO**
**Az Agr F.lli Sportoletti Ernesto e Remo*** Via Lombardia 1. Tel: 0742 651461. Fax: 0742 652349. Every day 0900-1230, 1500-1900. E.TF./TP.WS.b. E-mail: office@ sportoletti.com www.sportoletti.com

**TORGIANO**
**Cantine Giorgio Lungarotti*** Via Mario Angeloni 16. Tel: 075 9880348. Fax: 075 9880294. 0800-1300, 1500-1800. D.E.F.G.TP.WS.B. E-mail: lungarotti@lungarotti.it www.lungarotti.it

Strada del Sagrantino route: www.stradadelsagrantino.com

# Food of Central Italy

*Central Italy is proud of an inheritance of celebrated and historic wines. This sign outside a wine shop proclaims the classic regional wines. Produzione propria means that the wine is the shop's own, the produce of its estate.*

## TORGIANO (cont)
**MUSEUM**
**Museo del Vino**
Torgiano. Tel: 075 9880200. 0900-1300, 1500-1900, 1800 in winter. Charge for entry.
**Museo dell'Olivo e dell'Olio** Torgiano. Tel: 075 9880300. Fax: 075 985486. 1000-1300, 1500-1900, 1800 in winter. Charge for entry. E-mail: museoolio@lungarotti.it www.lungarotti.it

## FESTIVALS

*February:* SPELLO: *Festa dell'Olio e Sagra della Bruschetta* olive oil festival and tasting.
*March/April:* TODI: National Antiques Fair.
*April:* GUBBIO (and numerous other Umbrian towns and villages): Good Friday Procession.
*April/May:* NARNI: *Giostra all'Anello,* jousting.
*May:* ASSISI: National Antiques Fair.
*May:* ASSISI: *Calendimaggio,* a medieval fair.
*End May:* GUBBIO: *Palio della Balestra,* medieval crossbow archery.
*May:* GUBBIO: *Festa dei Ceri* race.
*June:* BOLSENA: *Infiorata,* a flower festival on Corpus Christi.
*June:* ORVIETO: Corpus Christi, a medieval procession.
*June:* SPELLO: Corpus Christi flower festival.
*June/July:* SPOLETO: Festival of Two Worlds.
*July:* GRADOLI: Festival of Aleatico, local wine festival.
*August:* CITTÀ DELLA PIEVE/CASTIGLIONE DEL LAGO: *Palio dei Terzieri,* a medieval fair.
*September:* FOLIGNO: *Giostra della Quintana,* a medieval joust.
*October/November:* GUBBIO: truffle festival.
*November:* CITTÀ DI CASTELLO: truffle festival.

## PIZZA A TAGLIO
Hungry tourists looking for a quick snack will appreciate one Umbrian facility, the *pizza a taglio* shops which serve pizza by the wedge, freshly cooked and ready for your mid-morning stroll or pre-dinner *passeggiata.* This custom is not specifically Umbrian, but if you have come from the North the shops may not yet be familiar to you – it is difficult to find them outside the tourist areas further north. The further south you go, the more there are of them.

## FOOD SPECIALTIES

Umbrian cuisine is characterized by the freshness of its ingredients and the immediacy of its cooking methods. With a simplicity and rusticity that befits the land of Saint Francis, the spit, the grill and the wood-burning oven are the traditional cooking methods: *alla brace, alla griglia,* and *al forno di legno* are the signs to look for.

The fruity green olive oil of Umbria is delicious, and probably shares the honors with the olive oil of Tuscany as the best in Italy. Spello, Spoleto, the Valnerina and Amerino valleys are the centers of production. Spello holds a *Sagra della Bruschetta* (*bruschetta* feast) which is a celebration of toasted Umbrian bread rubbed with garlic and sprinkled with extra-virgin olive oil and salt.

*Cinghiale* (wild boar) is often on the menu, as are *piccioni* (pigeons) and *uccelletti* (small birds eaten whole, cooked on a spit with bay leaves and chunks of bread to separate them).

The black truffle of Norcia and Spoleto is a prized ingredient, used especially to flavor omelettes. Cheese and salami, and other pork products from Norcia, are also particularly good. In fact, so famous are the pork butchers of Norcia that the word *Norcineria* is used as a generic term in Italy to denote a high-class *salumeria* (pork butcher).

Lentils from Castelluccio are a prized product. The combination of lentils and pigs' ears in a stew sounds unlikely, but for lovers of comfort food it is unbeatable.

Freshwater fish are represented by trout from the pure waters of Fonti di Clitunno, carp from Lake Trasimene, eels and roach.

Other regional dishes include:
*Cardi alla perugina:* cardoons fried in batter, then cooked in the oven with a *ragù* sauce.
*Palombacce all'uso di Foligno:* casseroled pigeon cooked with its giblets with olives and vegetables.
*Porchetta* sucking pig stuffed with garlic, pepper and rosemary, usually bought from wayside vans and eaten in bread rolls.
*Scottaditto* lamb cutlets, so called because they are meant to be eaten direct from the wood fire, so literally leading to burned fingers.
*Stringozzi* homemade flat pasta, often served with mushrooms or truffles.

**FOR FURTHER INFORMATION**
***Andar per Vigne*** is the title of a useful pamphlet, in English and Italian, produced by the Consorzio Tutela Denominazione Orvieto giving details of wineries in the area open to visitors.

**Consorzio Tutela Denominazione Orvieto Classico e Orvieto** Corso Cavour 36, 05018 Orvieto. Tel: 0763 343790. Fax: 0763 341735. E-mail: consvino@tiscalinet.it www.emmeti.it/ConsOrvieto

Wines and gastronomy of Umbria: www.umbriadoc.com

*The Barberani wine shop in Orvieto's cathedral square displays wines of the region.*

# The Adriatic Coast

The eastern side of the Apennines does not have the same attractions for the traveller as Tuscany or the Veneto, with their obvious cultural delights. It is the motorway-loving vacationers who tend to stay on this coast of Italy. Scan the map and very few towns stand out immediately: Urbino, of course, is known for its Ducal Palace; Ancona, for its port; Loreto, for the Santa Casa; Bari, for its famous church of San Nicola; and Brindisi, for its port and the ferry for Greece.

But there is much more to discover: the hill towns of the Marches, the architectural splendor of Ascoli Piceno, the National Park of Abruzzo, the archeological museum of Chieti, Castel del Monte, the *trulli* of Alberobello and the Baroque palaces of Lecce. The people here are different; they are more relaxed and more friendly, and more insular too. The people of Abruzzo are proud of their reputation as *forti e gentili*, hard of purpose but gentle of manner, and the same attributes apply to the Marchigiani and the Pugliesi as well.

*Harvest time for Verdicchio grapes in the Esino Valley.*

Politically and vinously the Adriatic coast is divided into three main sections: the Marches; Abruzzo/Molise; and Puglia.

The Marches are the home of the most celebrated Adriatic wine: Verdicchio. The amphora, or Lollobrigida-shaped bottle, is a familiar sight on trattoria tables abroad, and this is undoubtedly the best wine to drink with the local fish. Less well known, but perhaps to the connoisseur more interesting, are the two reds of the Marches, Rosso Conero and Rosso Piceno. Other wines of the area are of local interest only. Some producers are making excellent sparkling wines with Verdicchio grapes, and while these are too expensive to compete with other sparkling wines abroad, they are very pleasant to taste during travels in the region.

In Abruzzo there are only three wines: two Montepulciano d'Abruzzos, the red, and the

Cerasuolo (rosé), and Trebbiano d'Abruzzo (white). The rosé and the white can be good, but the red is the most interesting; it is a very drinkable wine that is smooth enough even for those who find most Italian reds somewhat bitter. Molise has two wines almost impossible to find outside the region: Biferno and Pentro. They mirror the wines of Abruzzo in their dependence on the Montepulciano grape for the red and rosé, and on Trebbiano for the white wines.

## Puglia

Puglia is one of Italy's big four regional producers of wine – in quantity, that is. But it is only recently that much quality wine from the area has been exported.

Traditionally, Puglian wine has been used, quite legally, as "blending wine" to give wines from the north of Italy, or indeed from France and Spain, an alcoholic boost and more color in off years. It has also been used as the base wine for Vermouth by such companies as Cinzano and Martini in Piedmont.

Slowly, quality wines are emerging from this anonymous production as local pride, modern technology and demand dictate. There are 19 DOC wines: the ones most commonly found are Castel del Monte, Locorotondo, Martina Franca, and Salice Salentino. Five Roses is a branded rosé.

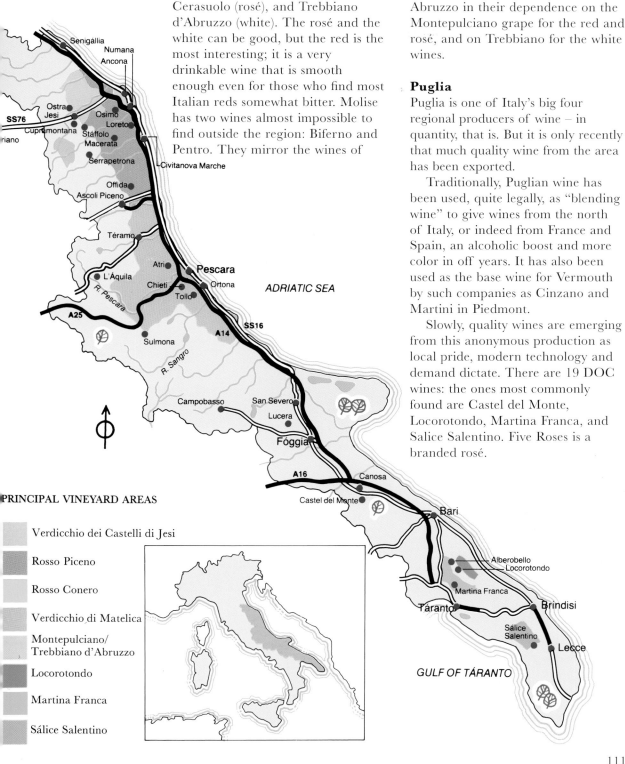

**PRINCIPAL VINEYARD AREAS**

- Verdicchio dei Castelli di Jesi
- Rosso Piceno
- Rosso Conero
- Verdicchio di Matelica
- Montepulciano/ Trebbiano d'Abruzzo
- Locorotondo
- Martina Franca
- Sálice Salentino

# The Marches

## CUPRAMONTANA
**Colonnara, Viticultori in Cupramontana*** Via Mandriole 6. Tel: 0731 780273. Fax: 0731 789610. 0800-1200, 1400-1800. Restaurant. E.F.TF.WS.b. E-mail: info@colonnara.it www.colonnara.it

### MUSEUM
**Museo Internazionale dell'Etichetta** Palazzo Leoni. Tue-Fri 1000-1200; Wed 1600-1800.

## FABRIANO
**Cantine Enzo Mecella** Via Dante 112. Tel: 0732 21680. Fax: 0732 627705. 0830-1230, 1430-1830. E.TF.WS.B. E-mail: enzo.mecella@ fabriano.netuno.it

## LORETO
**Casa Vinicola Garofoli*** Via Arno 9. Tel: 071 7820162. Fax: 071 7821437. 0800-1200, 1430-1830. E.G.WS.B. E-mail: mail@garofolivini.it www.garofolivini.it

## MATELICA
**Az Agr San Biagio*** Via S Biagio 32. Tel: 0737 83997. Fax: 0737 84002. 0900-1200, 1400-1800 E.F.Sp.TP.WS.B. E-mail: azagricolasanbiagio@ libero.it

## NUMANA
**Fattoria Le Terrazze** Via Musone 4. Tel: 071 7390352. Fax: 071 7391285. E.F.Sp.TF.WS.B. E-mail: a.terni@fastnet.it

## OSIMO SCALO
**Umani Ronchi*** SS 16 Km 310,400. Tel: 071 7108019. Fax: 071 7108859. 0830-1230, 1400-1800. Restaurant. E.F.G.Sp.TF.WS.b. E-mail: wine@umanironchi.it www.umanironchi.it

*The Castelli di Jesi hills nourish Verdicchio vineyards and give their name to one of the two versions of the wine.*

The best way to travel along the length of the Adriatic coast is to use the A14 motorway as a vertical axis, and only cut inland as necessary.

## Urbino
Coming south from Romagna, the first detour will be inland to Urbino. The vast hilltop Ducal Palace, now a museum, dates from the mid-15th century, when Federigo da Montefeltro, a great warrior and a notable patron of art, ruled the city.

The wines of the area are the white Bianchello del Metauro and the red Sangiovese dei Colli Pesaresi – both are light wines of local interest.

## Verdicchio
The best known wine of the Marches is Verdicchio. There are, in fact, two Verdicchios; Verdicchio di Matelica is the rarer one and comes from near Fabriano; Verdicchio dei Castelli di Jesi is the well-known one that comes in the amphora-shaped bottle.

Verdicchio has been called variously "the Muscadet of Italy" by admirers of its fresh and steely style and "the Burgundy of Italy" by those who want to invest it with the nobility of oak aging. (Try Umani Ronchi's Le Busche or Garofoli's Serra Fiorese for successful versions of this unusual style). The wine is made from the grape of the same name. As a still wine, it is capable of more character than its nearest rivals, Frascati and Soave. As a sparkling wine, it already has a long tradition; it may have been a French idea at the time of the Napoleonic Kingdom of Italy.

The future of Verdicchio seems more secure with each successive improvement in quality. First, there was cold fermentation, which improved the natural fruitiness of the wine. Then there were decisions to create superior *cuvée* examples of Verdicchio by reducing yields in the vineyards (thereby picking fewer but better quality grapes); making special grape selections from individual vineyards known to be particularly favorably sited; late harvesting (to concentrate the sugars and richness in the grapes naturally); and cold maceration to build structure and depth in the wine. Some even age Verdicchio on the lees (one of the more valid comparisons with Muscadet). The latest move recognizes Verdicchio's aging potential with the creation of the category Verdicchio Riserva for selected Castelli di Jesi wines with at least 12.5 per cent alcohol and 18 months' aging.

Certainly there is no better wine to accompany the local fish and white meats than crisp, fruity Verdicchio.

## The castles of Jesi

The Castelli di Jesi of the Verdicchio wine appellation are the small hill towns surrounding Jesi to the north, south and west. In the times when the Marches were a troubled border area, these satellite fortified towns owed allegiance to Jesi, a garrison town of massive fortifications, now with handicraft and other shops in the alleys of the old fortifications.

Several of the Castelli di Jesi towns are worth visiting. Local food specialties such as *Tagliatelle alla porchetta* are well suited to Verdicchio. Cupramontana is the acknowledged "Capital of Verdicchio" and has an International Museum of Wine Labels. Staffolo has superb views over neighboring hill towns; the church of San Francesco al Musone is reputedly where St Francis halted to pray on his way to Ancona.

North of Jesi there is Morro d'Alba with its own robust red DOC wine, Lacrima di Morro d'Alba. An interesting walk can be had in the 17th-century walkway around the town walls.

## Matelica

Verdicchio's alter ego is well worth visiting on site, not only because of the excellent selection of wines at the Belisario winery's visitor center, but also because of the charming Piersanti art museum in the *centro storico*.

## Rosso Conero and Piceno

There are two important red wines in the Marches, both intended for aging. Rosso Conero comes from Mount Conero just south of Ancona, and is proof of the suitability of the Montepulciano grape, its principal

constituent, to the area. For a prize-winning *barrique* version of this wine try Umani Ronchi's Cùmaro, or, for something more traditional, try Le Terazze's offering. A new *Strada del Vino* route has just been laid out in the Rosso Conero area.

Rosso Piceno Superiore, which can be like a Chianti Riserva, comes from the Tronto valley further down the coast. Don't miss Ascoli Piceno with its wealth of medieval and Renaissance buildings, or the pretty hills around Offida where the Strada del Rosso Piceno leads the traveller past several wineries on the way back to the coast.

*Urbino's Ducal Palace hosts the National Gallery of the Marches.*

**OSTRA VETERE**
**Fratelli Bucci*** Via Cona 30, Pongelli. Tel/Fax: 071 964179. 0900-1900. Sales office, Via Moscova 16, 20121 Milano. Tel: 02 6570558. Fax: 02 6554470. Museum. E.F.T.F.WS.B. E-mail: bucciwines@iol.it www.villabucci.com

***For further addresses, see page 118.***

# Abruzzo and Molise

Until the building of the motorway from Rome, Abruzzo was more or less cut off from the rest of Italy. This was part of its charm, and the reason travellers came to discover the self-reliant Abruzzesi people with their reputation for being *forti e gentili*, or rather rough but honest.

Indeed, once the English gentleman or lady of means had explored the civilizing effects of Venice, Florence and Rome, the Abruzzi, as it was called, was the next stop, to discover some of the worthy values of a sturdy peasantry and some of their folklore (the Procession of the Snake-catchers in Cocullo every May never failed to impress then and still takes place today).

Edward Lear, the Victorian artist, traveller and nonsense rhymer, painted a large series of watercolors of this region he so admired.

Right up to the 1970s this was definitely part of the poor Mezzogiorno, the backward South of Italy. But since the motorway came, the area has gained new wealth, and Abruzzo now has the highest per capita income of the Mezzogiorno.

## Abruzzo's three wines

In wine terms, Abruzzo has the highest percentage of DOC wines in southern Italy, and has no fewer than six *Strada del Vino* routes currently under preparation.

After the complexities of other areas, it is a relief to come across a region where there are only three names to remember.

Montepulciano d'Abruzzo is a smooth red wine with an attractive earthy nose, and is particularly good value; it can be aged for up to about five years. It is made from the

Montepulciano grape (not to be confused with the Tuscan wine Vino Nobile di Montepulciano).

If the skins are extracted from the fermentation process soon after it has begun, a rosé wine results, and Montepulciano d'Abruzzo Cerasuolo takes its name from its cherry-like color. It is a pleasantly dry wine and should be drunk while still young.

The third wine of the region is the white Trebbiano d'Abruzzo. Often the Trebbiano grape produces dull and flat wines. In Abruzzo, however, the whites tend to be more characterful and fuller-bodied. Valentini is the most famous producer.

## The wine roads

Abruzzo has the benefits of mountains, hills and beach resorts all within a short distance of each other. Skiing, sightseeing and swimming are all possible in a single day. It is in the hills just inland from the sea that the vineyards are to be found.

Just over the border from the Marches, the hilly town of Controguerra has panoramic views over the surrounding countryside. This area is Abruzzo's finest, so much so that the producers of the province

of Teramo are currently in the process of applying for a separate denomination in a bid to distance themselves from the mass market wines that come from some of the co-operatives further down the coast. They have their own *Strada del Vino delle Colline Teramane* (Wine Road of the Teramo Hills) with many wineries that welcome visitors.

## Atri to Chieti

On your way southwards on the coastal route, stop at the hill town of Atri. The town has an ancient past. It has a frescoed cathedral built on Roman foundations – indeed the Adriatic Sea may well derive its name from the town's old Roman name, Hadria Picena.

Most of the wine in Abruzzo comes from the province of Chieti. If you have time, try to visit the town for its Roman remains, and for the archeological museum with its prize exhibit, the extraordinary 6th-century BC statue known as the Warrior of Capestrano.

*The town of Celano in Abruzzo with its imposing 15th-century castle bears witness to Abruzzo's military past.*

## Molise

Once considered secondary to the wines of Abruzzo, Molise has recently gained administrative independence. This is remote and attractively rural countryside, and several traditional industries live on here: lace, carpets, ceramics and terracotta, for example.

The two DOC wines of Molise, Pentro d'Isernia and Biferno, can be white (Trebbiano Toscano and Bombino Bianco grapes), red (Montepulciano and Sangiovese grapes), or, more rarely, rosé.

In general, Molise has yet to establish an identity for itself in the Italian wine world. The only member of the Le Città del Vino (Cities of Wine) organization in the area is Campomarino. The town is famous, locally at least, as a center for Biferno Rosso and is reputed to have been founded by the Greek hero Diomedes, one of Ulysses's companions.

**TORANO NUOVO**
**Az Agr Barone Cornacchia*** Le Torri. Tel: 0861 887412. Fax: 0861 88008. (Paola Cornacchia). 0800-1200, 1500-1800. E.F.WS.b.
**Az Agr Pepe*** Via Chiesi 10. Tel/Fax: 0861 856493. (Stefania Pepe). E.F.Sp.TF.WS.B. (TP for full tasting or tasting with typical foods). E-mail: aziendapepe@libero.it www.montepulcianod abruzzo.it

# Puglia

Puglia has always produced vast quantities of wine, up to one fifth of Italian production. Strangely enough, it is is now producing some of Italy's most exciting wines. The new supermarket wines that might be descibed as having "bags of jammy fruit" (reds) or "luscious peachiness" (whites) are now coming from Puglia, often marketed as "made with the help of Australian winemakers." Consequently these wines are largely made to order for the supermarket export trade and not seen in the region at all.

Luckily, there are some producers, Taurino, Leone de Castris and Rivera among them, who produce wines that are internationally famous and can be discovered in Puglia as well.

There are over 20 DOC appellations and several *Vini a Indicazione Geografica Tipica*.

## Puglia's wine roads

Travelling south along the A14 Adriatic motorway one of the first towns encountered is Lucera. Lucera reflects the epochs of Puglia's importance with its Roman amphitheater, Swabian castle and Angevin cathedral. Its wine is a tongue-twister: *Cacc'e mmitte di Lucera* – the dialect name apparently means "drink and pour again."

Puglia is rich in Roman and in early medieval history. Near Canosa is Canne della Battaglia – Cannae, where Hannibal was defeated by the Romans in 216 BC. Canosa itself has two masterpieces of Puglian art in the 11th-century bishop's throne and pulpit in the cathedral.

Rosso Canosa is one of the three local reds: the others are Rosso di Barletta and Rosso di Cerignola. An unusual wine of the area is Moscato di Trani, which is a sweet muscat, excellent with fruit.

*Locorotondo (above) is one of the most splendid "white towns" of the Puglian plains. It produces its own DOC wine, as does its neighbor Martina Franca.*

The finest monument to Puglia's Golden Age is the Castel del Monte, a short distance south-east of Canosa. It was built as a hunting lodge by the Emperor Frederick II around 1240 and has a distinctive octagonal design. Castel del Monte gives its name to the DOC wine whose most famous exponent is the Rivera company in Andria. They are well known for their rosé; their best wine is a Riserva called Il Falcone.

## The *Trulli*

Midway between Bari and Brindisi is Alberobello and the zone of the *trulli*. These conical-roofed peasant dwellings originated as an easy method of house building; the local rocks easily split into thin layers, ideal for dry stone wall construction. In the time of the Bourbon rule, when new houses were taxable, this construction meant they were easily dismantled if necessary. Locorotondo, Ostuni, and Martina Franca are the three local whites.

### Lecce and Táranto
In the heel of Italy is the lovely Baroque town of Lecce. Nearby are the DOC wine areas of Sálice Salentino, Leverano and Alezio. The rosé versions are very successful: Rosa del Golfo from Giuseppe Calò and Five Roses from Leone de Castris especially. Five Roses acquired its name during the war when American soldiers apparently rated it more highly than a well-known Bourbon.

Between Lecce and Táranto is Manduria, home of the Primitivo grape that is perhaps the origin of California's Zinfandel. The wine is a formidably strong red which can be sweet and fortified, too.

Táranto is well worth a visit. It was the most important city in the Greek colony of Magna Graecia and has an important archeological museum.

**ANDRIA**
**Az Vin Rivera\*** SS 98 Km 19,800 Contrada Rivera. Tel: 0883 569501. Fax: 0883 569575. (Carlo de Corato, Leonardo Palumbo). 0900-1700. E.F.Sp.TF.WS.B. E-mail: info@rivera.it www.rivera.it
**Enoteca Pellegrino** Via Firenze 53. Tel: 0883 559727. E.F.G. E-mail: pellegrino@iqsnet.it www.pellegrino-online.com

**GUAGNANO**
**Az Agr Cosimo Taurino** SS605. Tel: 0832 706490. Fax: 0832 706242. (Francesco or Rosanna Taurino). 0800-1300. E.TF.WS.B. E-mail: taurino@tin.it

**SÁLICE SALENTINO**
**Ant Az Agr Vit Conti Leone de Castris\*** Via Senatore de Castris 50. Tel: 0832 731112. Fax: 0832 731114. (Leonardo Pinto). 0830-1230. Museum of winemaking implements. E.F.TF.WS.b. E-mail: leone.de.castris@mail4.clio.it www.leonedecastris.net

*Harvesting in the vineyards around Locorotondo. The local co-operative is responsible for the international fame of its uncomplicated white wine.*

117

# Food of the Adriatic Coast

FOR FURTHER INFORMATION

**Informazioni Accoglienza Turistica** Via B Spaventa 29, Chieti. Tel: 0871 63640. Fax: 0871 63647.

**Abruzzo Promozione Turismo** Ufficio IAT, Via Carducci 17, 64100 Teramo. Tel: 0861 244222. Fax: 0861 244357. www.regione. abruzzo.it/turismo

*Continued from page 113*

**RIPATRANSONE
Tenuta Cocci Grifoni***
Contrada Messieri 12. Tel: 0735 90143. Fax: 0735 90123. 0830-1230, 1500-1900. E.TF.WS.b. E-mail: tenuta.coccigrifoni@tiscalinet.it

**JESI
ER delle Marche** Via Federico Conti 5. Tel: 0731 538250. Fax: 0731 538328. Thu-Sun 1600-2000. TP.WS.

**OFFIDA
Enoteca di Offida** Via Garibaldi 75. Tel: 0736 88005. Mon-Fri 0900-1230, 1500-1900. Sat 0900-1230. TP.WS.ER.

**MATELICA
Belisario Cantina Sociale Matelica*** Via Merloni 12. Tel: 0737 787247. Fax: 0737 787263. Enoteca. 0830-1230, 1530-1930. Closed Sun. E.F.Sp.TF./TP.

## FOOD SPECIALTIES

### The Marches

The cuisine of the Marches is ingenuous and uncomplicated; dishes are cooked in a simple manner, reflecting the naturally healthy Mediterranean diet.

Some specialties:
*Brodetto:* fish stew, traditionally with as many fish as there are apostles.
*Vincisgrassi:* owes its name to an Austrian prince who stopped in Ancona in Napoleonic times, Prince Windisch-Gratz; baked lasagne with chicken liver and white sauce.
*Stoccafisso all'Anconitana:* stewed stockfish.
*Trippa alla canapina*: tripe from Jesi.
Game from Loreto.
Salami from Fabriano.
*Olive ripiene all'ascolana:* large stuffed and deep-fried green olives.

### Abruzzo Molise

The most famous dish of Abruzzo is *Maccheroni alla chitarra*, made by stretching a thin sheet of fresh pasta over a frame with wires like guitar strings that cuts the pasta into strips. The sauce is meat or tomato based.

As in all the Adriatic coastal regions there is a version of *brodetto*, fish soup, adapted to the local catch. Fish is regarded more highly than meat in this region.

The traditional cheese used to flavor pasta dishes is often *pecorino* (sheep's cheese) rather than parmesan. It goes especially well with lamb and vegetable-based sauces.

Some specialties:
*Orecchie di preti:* priests' ears pasta.
*Scripelle imbussi:* pancakes filled with cheese and ham.
*Trippa alla paesana:* tripe with hot peppers and tomatoes.

### Puglia

The cuisine of Puglia is based on simple products and strong flavors. The most famous pasta of Puglia are the ear-shaped *orecchiette*.

The coast provides fresh fish and shellfish: anchovies, mussels, squid and oysters particularly.

Lamb is very important, reflecting the fact that Puglia is the third most important region for sheep farming after Lazio and Sardinia.

Some specialties:
*Annulieddu a lu furnu (Agnello al forno):* baby lamb and potato casserole.
*Calzengfidde:* small *calzone*, or pizza envelope, filled with meat or cheese.
*Ciambotto:* pasta sauce made of tiny fish with onions and tomatoes.
*Cozze gratinate:* baked mussels.
*Melanzane ripiene:* stuffed aubergines.
*Pepperoni arrotolati:* stuffed peppers.
*Zuppa di pesce alla gallipolina:* fish stew with a little tomato and vinegar.

## FESTIVALS

### Marches

*Easter Monday:* SAN MARCELLO: sausage and salami festival.
*May:* MONTECAROTTO: fish and Verdicchio festival.
*First Sunday of June:* SAN MARCELLO: *Palio Sanmarcellese*, folk festival.
*July and August*: NUMANA: Rosso Conero and Verdicchio exhibition.
*First Sunday of August:* STAFFOLO: festival.
*August:* PESARO: Rossini Festival.
*August:* ROSORA: festival of Verdicchio.
*September:* ASCOLI PICENO: *Giostra della Quintana*, medieval joust and Renaissance costume procession.

*Tourism has become important for the trulli – conical-roofed peasant dwellings – in Alberobello at Locorotondo (see pages 116-117).*

*Last Sunday of September:* ARCEVIA: *festa dell'uva (*wine festival). *First Sunday of October:* CUPRAMONTANA: *festa dell'uva* and wine exhibition.

## Abruzzo Molise
*January:* RIVISONDOLI: *Presepe Vivente*, nativity scene.
*Easter:* L'AQUILA: Good Friday Procession.
*Easter Sunday:* SULMONA: *Madonna che scapa in piazza* procession.
*May, first Thursday:* COCULLO: procession of the Serpari in which a statue of St Dominic is paraded adorned with live snakes.
*August:* MONTEPAGANO: wine festival.
*August:* ORTONA: *Rassegna Regionale dei Vin*i, regional wine festival.
*August:* BASCIAMO: *prosciutto* (ham) festival.
*September:* ORTONA: mullet festival.

## Puglia
*May:* BARI: Feast of St Nicholas procession recalls the arrival of the bones of the Saint in 1087.
*September:* MASSAFRA: *Palio della Mezzaluna* celebrates a battle against the Saracens.

# The Mediterranean Coast

The further south you travel the deeper you are in the Mezzogiorno, Italy's most poverty-stricken and depressed region. This is the home of those who have perfected the *arte di arrangiarsi*, the art of getting by, by hook or by crook. It is no accident that Naples, with its high unemployment, has a thriving underground economy. Yet this is a city packed with wonderful churches, Roman, medieval and Baroque, and with a glorious ancient past still manifest in its ruins and museums. (Rome is untypical; ancient, proud and bureaucratic, with great treasures and impossible traffic.)

Four regions are involved. Lazio is divided by Rome, south of which the Mezzogiorno begins. Campania's salvation is the tourism of Naples, Capri, Ischia and the Amalfi coast. Basilicata, in the instep of Italy, is very poor. Calabria's hope and challenge is the tourism the motorways bring.

*The Spanish Steps in Rome, one of countless monuments to the city's Baroque splendor. The English Romantic poet John Keats died in 1821 in a house overlooking the stairway.*

## Lazio

Until the beginning of the present century, Rome was surrounded by deserted and malaria-ridden countryside, except for the Colli Albani hills to the south-east. Here, amidst the summer villas of the Roman aristocracy, the predominantly white wines of the region are produced. Frascati is the most famous, but each hill town has its own wine. Some are DOC: Marino, Montecompatri and Velletri, for example, as well as Frascati. These are clean and simple wines; if they have any striking feature, it is the bitter almond twist to the aftertaste.

Wine is also made north of Rome, around Cervéteri, and between the Colli Albani and the coast, on the plains drained by Mussolini near Aprilia. The Merlot of Aprilia can be very good.

## Campania

The resorts of Capri and Ischia produce their own wines, as much to preserve the typical landscape of these beauty spots as to make a reasonable

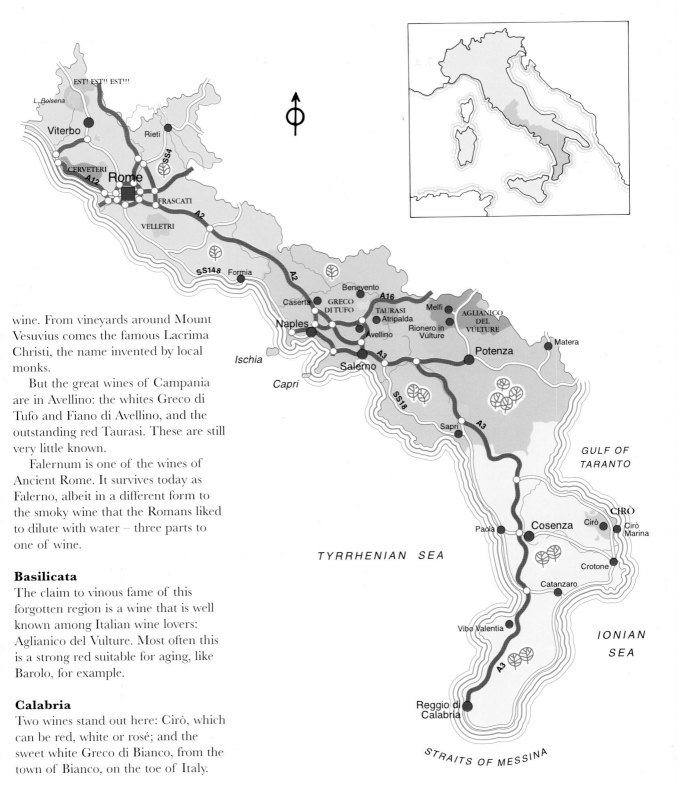

wine. From vineyards around Mount Vesuvius comes the famous Lacrima Christi, the name invented by local monks.

But the great wines of Campania are in Avellino: the whites Greco di Tufo and Fiano di Avellino, and the outstanding red Taurasi. These are still very little known.

Falernum is one of the wines of Ancient Rome. It survives today as Falerno, albeit in a different form to the smoky wine that the Romans liked to dilute with water – three parts to one of wine.

## Basilicata

The claim to vinous fame of this forgotten region is a wine that is well known among Italian wine lovers: Aglianico del Vulture. Most often this is a strong red suitable for aging, like Barolo, for example.

## Calabria

Two wines stand out here: Cirò, which can be red, white or rosé; and the sweet white Greco di Bianco, from the town of Bianco, on the toe of Italy.

# Frascati and the Colli Albani

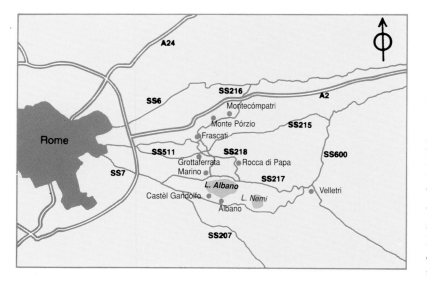

Frascati is the name that everyone recognizes. It is a clean, but slightly rich-tasting pale white, with a touch of almond flavor on the aftertaste. It must be drunk young, no older than two vintages.

### Frascati – the town

Frascati is one of a semicircle of towns around the Colli Albani hills. The hills are, in fact, extinct volcanoes, and the two lakes, Albano and Nemi, are water-filled craters. Lake Nemi was known as the Mirror of Diana in classical times, because of the pagan temple sited on its shores.

The town of Frascati is almost a suburb of Rome, but its splendid villas witness the popularity it enjoyed as a retreat for the Roman aristocracy. Villa Aldobrandini and the monument to Bonnie Prince Charlie in the cathedral of San Pietro are worth seeing.

### Wines of the Colli Albani

Frascati is only one of the wines produced in the Colli Albani area, also south-east of Rome. The others, all whites with pretty similar characteristics, are Marino, Colli Albani, Colli Lanuvini, Montecompatri Colonna, Velletri and Zagarolo. Velletri, unusually, is also made as a quaffable red wine that is usually very good value.

Using the side roads, it is a pleasant drive to turn off the A2 motorway at Monteporzio Catone, where many of the Frascati producers are based, and then follow the roads around the Colli Albani hills to Velletri.

### Grottaferrata and Castel Gandolfo

Grottaferrata has panoramic views and an 11th-century Byzantine abbey. Marino is a little town above the shores of Lake Albano, and its wine is next to Frascati in popularity.

---

## COLONNA
**Pallavicini\*** Via Casilina Km 25,500, Colonna. Tel/Fax: 06 9438816. (Roberta Malatesta). 0830-1300, 1400-1700. Group visits to winery and restaurant. T.P.WS.B. E-mail: saita@ vinipallavicini.com www.vinipallavicini.com

## FRASCATI
**Az Agr Casale Marchese\*** Via di Vermicino 68. Tel/Fax: 06 9408932. (Alessandro Carletti). E.F.T.P.WS.B. E-mail: marchese@ microelettra.it www.casalemarchese.it
**Az Agr L'Olivella** Via di Colle Pisano 5. Tel: 06 9424527. Fax: 06 9425333. (Umberto Notarnicola). Old grotto. E.T.P.WS.B. E-mail: info@racemo.it www.racemo.it

## ARICCIA
**Cantine Volpetti srl\*** Via Nettunense 21 Km 7,800. Tel: 06 9342000. Fax: 06 9342941. (Mauro Volpetti). 0800-1700. E.T.P.WS.B.

The wines of Lazio in general do not have a strong character; they are quite unlike the masculine, opaque reds of Piedmont or the delicate feminine wines of the Veneto. Instead, the whites of Lazio, and its few reds, are often impersonal, despite their attractive drinkability. In other words, they are wines to be enjoyed rather than examined critically.

### Frascati – the wine

For 2000 years the Castelli Romani hills south-east of Rome have been the recreational resort of the Romans. Cicero had a villa at Tuscolo, and tradition has it that Cato lived at Monteporzio Catone. Colli di Tuscolo and Villa di Catone are wine brands that recall this heritage. It is a delightful area, but try to avoid the Roman holidays.

It is still possible to find the traditional rustic *osteria*, where pitchers of local wine can be enjoyed outside at a table sheltered from the sun that Rome seems to bask in for much of the year. What could be better than a glass of cold Frascati and a *panino* of pork and rosemary?

Just around the shores of the lake is Castel Gandolfo, the Pope's famous private residence and ancient site of Alba Longa.

Between the Colli Albani hills and the coast are the plains of Aprilia. Locals claim that the Trebbiano, Merlot and Sangiovese di Aprilia should be excellent, as the climate is similar to California's. My own favorite is the fruity red Merlot.

*Left: An elaborate sculpted fountain at Frascati, near the town hall.*
*Below: Not far from Frascati is the Abbey of San Nilo at Grottaferrata.*

### GROTTAFERRATA
**Az Agr Castel de Paolis***
Via Val de Paolis. Tel: 06 9413648. Fax: 06 94316025. (Giulio Santarelli). Mon-Fri 0900-1300, 1400-1800; Sat, Sun by appointment. E.TP.WS.B. E-mail: info@casteldepaolis.it www.casteldepaolis.it

### MONTEPORZIO CATONE
**Cantine Colli di Catone**
Via Frascati 31-33. Tel: 06 9449113. Fax: 06 9448695. (Carla Pulcini). 0900-1300, 1500-1800. E.TP.WS.B. E-mail: company@ collidicatone.it www.collidicatone.it

**Az Agr Piero Costantini**
Via Frascati – Colonna 29. Tel: 06 9449717. Fax: 06 9448658. (Lorenzo Costantini). E.TP.WS.b. E-mail: villasimone@ pierocostantini.it

**Fontana Candida** Via di Fontana Candida 11. Tel: 06 9420066. Fax: 06 9448591. 0830-1300, 1400-1700. T.F.B. E-mail: fontanacandida@giv.it

**Cantine San Marco** Via di Mola Cavona 26-28, Frascati. Tel: 06 9422689. Fax: 06 9425333. (Umberto Notarnicola). 0900-1230, 1330-1700. E.TP.WS.B. E-mail: info@ sanmarcofrascati.it www.sanmarcofrascati.it

### ROME
**Enoteca Trimani** Via Goito 20. Tel: 06 4469661. Daily 0900-1300, 1600-2000. Marco Trimani is one of the greatest publicists of Italian wine.

### Anagni
On the A2, about 20km (12 miles) before Frosinone, Anagni has a superb Romanesque cathedral as well as Cesanese del Piglio, an unusual red in several styles: dry for long aging; *amabile* (medium-sweet); and *dolce* (sweet). Anagni is also the home of one of Italy's finest red wines, Torre Ercolana, an unusual but highly successful blend of Cabernet, Merlot and Cesanese grapes made on the Colacicchi estate by Marco Trimani, one of the greatest enthusiasts in the Italian wine world and owner of the Enoteca Trimani wine shop and wine bar in the center of Rome.

# Campania

Of all the "emerging" wine regions in the south of Italy, Campania is the furthest forward. The process is familiar: re-evaluate vineyard sites and the potential of local grapes, experiment with international varieties, modernize cellar practices, introduce new equipment in the winery. And then tell the world.

Wine in this land has a very ancient tradition. The Greeks who colonized southern Italy before Roman times were so struck with the vine-growing potential here that they called their colony Enotria, which comes from Greek *oinos*, and also gives us the word "wine." Ischia, whose wine was awarded the first DOC in Campania, was once known as Enaria, "the land of wine."

The Greek tradition lingers today in several wine names: Greco di Tufo, Greco di Somma, Vino Greco; and the major red wine grape of Campania and Basilicata called Aglianico derives from *hellenico*, "the Greek one."

The two islands off the Gulf of Naples, Ischia and Capri, each produce their own red and white wines. On Ischia, the D'Ambra company plays a leading role in preserving the agricultural heritage of the island and makes its Biancolella wine from an authentic *cru* site in an area under constant threat from the pressures of tourism.

Vesuvius is the site of vineyards that grow the Lacryma Christi (meaning "Tear of Christ") del Vesuvio. This red, white and rosé wine is mainly famous for its name, but in the hands of a good producer it is respectable enough.

In the hinterland behind Naples are the best wines of Campania. A turning off the A16 motorway leads to Atripalda, where Mastroberardino has its cellars. If anyone deserves the credit for the fame of the wines of this

area abroad, it is Antonio Mastroberardino, who has put these otherwise obscure wines on the map. Fiano di Avellino and Greco di Tufo are the whites. The red is called Taurasi. It is made of the Aglianico grape and capable of great aging.

*Steeply terraced vineyards and citrus groves on the cliffs near Amalfi, Campania. The wines here are of mainly local interest.*

## PONTE

**Ocone – Agricola del Monte\*** Via Monte CP 56. Tel: 0824 874040. Fax: 0824 874328. (Domenico Ocone). E.F.G.TF.WS.b. E-mail: admocone@tin.it www.oconevini.it

### IN PRAISE OF FALERNUM

The ancient Romans loved the wine Falernum, and it was made to withstand long aging. In fact, the Romans were sophisticated in their treatment of wine, and used both corks and glass bottles. The Emperor Tiberius is said to have had the inventor of an allegedly unbreakable glass put to death, for fear of ruining the economy.

It is unlikely, however, that Roman wine would have been acceptable to modern tastes. For keeping purposes it was often reduced to a concentrated syrupy liquid, and then reconstituted with seawater and flavored with honey and spices.

The new Falerno is made just over the border from Lazio into Campania, where Villa Matilde have made a specialty out of reinterpreting classical Falernum in the light of current winemaking practices. They have now established themselves as one of Campania's top producers, making wines in an extremely modern style.

Other producers have now followed, notably: Feudi di San Gregorio (a real contender for Campania's crown), Terre Dora (more Mastroberardinos), Ocone, Vadiaperti (founded by History Professor Antonio Troisi) and Mustilli. The Mustilli cellars are right in the center of Sant'Agata dei Goti, a wonderful medieval town, and are run by Leonardo Mustilli with the help of his daughter Paola. The company, which has recently launched an *agriturismo* vacation center as well, makes wines only from its own vineyards.

# Basilicata and Calabria

*Vines on bamboo poles in Aglianico vineyards, with Mount Vulture in the background.*

## BASILICATA

**Casa Vinicola D'Angelo**
Via Provinciale 8, 85028
Rionero in Vulture (PZ).
Tel: 0972 721517. Fax:
0972 723495. (Donato
D'Angelo). Near castle of
Emperor Frederick II at
Castelagopesole. E.TF.WS.B.

## CALABRIA

**Librandi** C.da S
Gennaro, SS 106, Cirò
Marina (CZ). Tel: 0962
31518. Fax: 0962 370542.
(Nicodemo Librandi).
0830-1300,1500-1800.
E.F.TF.WS.b. E-mail:
librandi@librandi.it
www.librandi.it
**Az Agr Odoardi** Viale
della Repubblica 143,
87100 Cosenza. Tel: 0984
29961. Fax: 0984 28503.
(Dr Gregorio Odoardi).
E.F.TF.WS.B.
E-mail: odoardi@tin.it

Called Lucania under the pre-war Fascist government, Basilicata only acquired its present name in 1947.

This remote region is movingly described in Carlo Levi's famous autobiographical story *Christ Stopped at Eboli*. Eboli itself is in Campania, but Levi's experience was of Basilicata, where he was "exiled" by the Fascists, and indeed he is buried there. His painting *Lucania 1961* is on display at the Centro Levi in Matera.

Don't miss the Sassi area of Matera where dwellings and churches cut into the rock have been occupied since prehistoric times.

### Basilicata wines

There is one DOCG in the league of great Italian wines: Aglianico del Vulture. This red wine is made in several versions: *Riserva* (five years old), *Vecchio* (three years old), *Spumante* (sparkling), and *Amabile* (a sweet dessert wine).

Aglianico is made in the northern tip of Basilicata in the area around Mount Vulture. Visit Fratelli d'Angelo in Rionero; they are among the best producers of Aglianico.

The deep southern toe of Italy has its economic and social problems. Until recently, emigration from Calabria was the usual course for its young people.

However, the discovery of the spectacular Bronzes of Riace, ancient sculptures found on the seabed off the coast of Calabria, has done much to restore local pride; they are now one of the best reasons to visit the town of Reggio di Calabria.

### Calabrian wines

Most of the Calabrian wines you may find in the area itself are entirely unexceptional. But it is an area that has started to attract interest in the wine world, especially through the work of consultant enologists such as Severino Garofano and Donato Lanati who advise wineries all over Italy. Librandi's Gravello, for example, a blend of the local Gaglioppo grape with Cabernet Sauvignon, is one of the Lanati creations and is regarded as one of southern Italy's best wines.

Cirò has recently acquired a good reputation as an uncomplicated red, white or rosé. It comes from the town on the western coast of Calabria, and can claim to be one of the oldest wines in the world. When southern Italy and Sicily were part of Magna Graecia, the Cremissa wine of this area was, so we are told, awarded to victorious Olympic athletes.

Further down the coast, almost on the toe of Italy, is the town of Bianco. Greco di Bianco and Mantonico di Bianco are two dessert white wines with ancient origins and, supposedly, strong aphrodisiac qualities. Visit the area for its archeological heritage too – nearby Locri has impressive Greek temple remains.

# Food of the Mediterranean Coast

## FOOD SPECIALTIES

### Lazio

Sheep farming was once more important than agriculture to the inhabitants of Lazio. *Abbacchio* is milk-fed spring lamb; *Scottadito* (literally "finger-burner") is grilled cutlets; *Brodetto alla Romana* is a lamb stew with a sauce flavored with lemon and thickened with egg.

Lazio is also the home of several internationally famous dishes: *Spaghetti alla carbonara* – with diced bacon, egg yolk and parmesan; *Spaghetti all' Amatriciana* – with tomatoes, bacon, onion and garlic; *Saltimbocca* – beef rolls with sage and *prosciutto* (raw ham); and *Stracciatella* – consommé, beaten egg and cheese. Rice is not used, except for the curiously named dish *Suppli al telefono*, rice croquettes filled with mozzarella, whose stringiness provides the reference to telephones.

### Campania

Naples is the home of spaghetti and of pizza. Both of these foods are essentially peasant foods and the sauces and toppings tend to be much as they were intended to be: simple. The *spaghetti al pomodoro* tends to have a typical slightly watery sauce.

The best pizzas are cooked in an open wood-fired oven (look for the sign *forno a legno*); a *calzone* is a pizza envelope with a filling rather than a topping; *Pizza alla Napoletana* has a topping of anchovies, tomatoes, and mozzarella flavored with basil and oregano.

### Basilicata: cheese and peppers

From classical times, ancient Lucania has been known for its cheeses: *Provola*, *Caciocavallo* and *Scamorze* are good examples.

The cooking is based very much on local vegetables. Hot and sweet peppers, aubergines, beans, legumes and lentils, which are cooked in olive oil and flavored with herbs – these are the essential ingredients.

### Calabria

The rites of preserving vegetables are still observed in Calabria. Aubergines, olives, tomatoes and mushrooms all benefit from the southern sun.

Fish, especially trout (*trota*) and swordfish (*pesce spada*), and lamb are also popular. Pasta has many shapes, each with its local name.

## FESTIVALS

*February:* NAPLES: feast of San Gennaro; liquefaction of the blood.
*Easter:* CATANZARO, NOCERA TERINESE, PROCIDA: Good Friday processions.
*May:* POTENZA: Cavalcade of the Turks.
*July:* MATERA: Materano Arts Festival.

An Enoteca in Rome displays fine Champagnes as well as Italian wines. Champagne and whisky are both surprisingly popular in Italy, which is the largest market for malt whisky in the world.

# Sicily

*The theater at Taormina is part of Sicily's Ancient Greek heritage.*

Sicily has always been the property of some other nation. Greeks, Phoenicians, Romans, and Goths, then Byzantines, Moors, Normans and Swabians, French, and Spaniards have held sway over the island from one age to another. Even today, the somewhat inward-looking mentality of Sicilians makes it hard to integrate the island with the mainland.

The Temple of Apollo and Artemis in Syracuse is Sicily's history in microcosm: built by the ancient Greeks, subsequently it became a Byzantine church, a Saracen mosque, a Norman church and a Spanish barracks.

Palermo, the capital, has Norman and Baroque monuments, and a medieval palace with glittering mosaic decoration; the northern coast also has Cefalù, a seaside town with a magnificent Norman cathedral. Messina was destroyed in 1908 after an earthquake, and by the Allies in 1943. Taormina's classical remains, clinging to the cliffs beneath Mount Etna, are spectacular. And Agrigento's Temple of Concord is the best preserved Greek temple in Italy.

At last Sicily seems to be fulfilling its wine potential beyond the level of volume production. The reds have always been good, but recent tastings show Sicily is now one of Italy's most interesting regions for white wines, an unimaginable statement ten years ago. Another development is that Sicily is now seriously promoting organized Wine Roads, the *Strada del Vino* system encouraged by the European Community. Seven routes are on offer.

There are 17 Sicilian DOC wines, including the much misunderstood Marsala, with all its variations. Other wines of note are Bianco d'Alcamo, a white wine from the west of Sicily; Cerasuolo di Vittoria, a wine that is undergoing a renaissance of interest in the south of the island; Etna, from the slopes of the volcano; and Faro, from the north-east. Two delicious dessert wines, Malvasia delle Lipari and Moscato di Pantelleria, come from Sicily's islands.

The most widely available and the most reliable wines are the big brands: Corvo (Duca di Salaparuta), Regaleali, Rapitalà, Donnafugata, Cellaro and Settesoli are the names to look for.

But there are some good smaller producers, too. COS, for example, who are leading the rediscovery of Cerasuolo di Vittoria, are fine wine producers at an international level.

There is plenty of potential in Sicily, and it has not all been exploited yet.

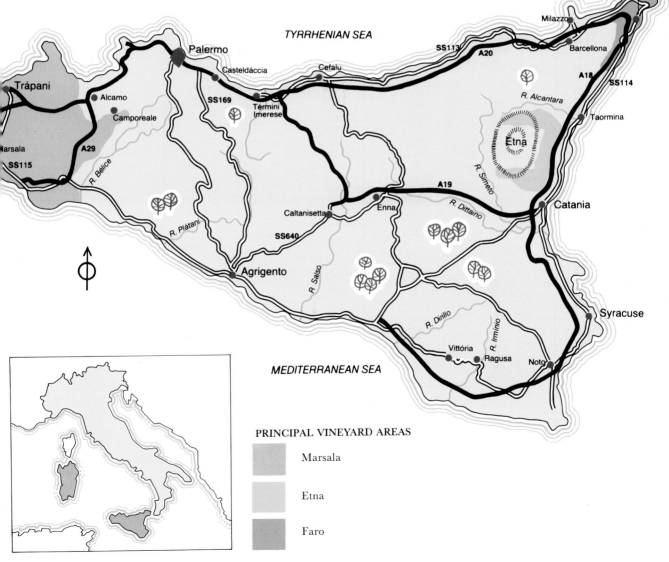

PRINCIPAL VINEYARD AREAS

Marsala

Etna

Faro

# Wines of Sicily

*Dark volcanic soil around Mount Etna, whose lower slopes provide one of the island's most interesting DOC wines.*

**MILAZZO**
**Casa Vinicola Grasso***
Via Albero 5. Tel: 090
9281082. Fax: 090 9224001.
(Alessio Grasso). 0800-1300,
1530-1930. Museum.
T.F.WS. (B for groups.)
E-mail: casavinicolagrasso@
tiscalinet.it

**LINGUAGLOSSA**
**Tenuta Scilio di Valle**
**Galfina** C.da Piano
Arrigo. Tel: 095 932744.
Fax: 095 932822.
E.T.F./TP.WS.B.
E-mail: scilio@dns.omnia.it

Sicily can be divided into four parts for wine touring purposes: the north-east and east coast; the south-east and south coast; the west; and Pantelleria and the islands.

## Milazzo and Etna

Messina, the entry point to Sicily by car, was badly damaged in 1908 and 1943. But here the traveller has the choice of taking a ferry to the Aeolian islands and discovering the marvelous dessert wine from Lipari – Malvasia delle Lipari – or driving along the north coast to Milazzo, with its splendidly-sited 13th-century castle and the Grasso winery.

The third option is to head south on the A18 motorway to Taormina and Mount Etna. Tenuta Scilio and Villagrande are the two producers to

visit in the area. The DOC wine area of Etna is very interesting – high altitude vineyards and indigenous grapes such as Carricante and Nerello Mascalese are a powerful heritage.

Etna has a legendary claim to be the first wine ever created. The young god Bacchus was walking to Sicily, when he stopped to rest on a tree stump, and a mysterious plant grew at his feet. He uprooted it and put it into the hollowed bone of a bird for safe keeping. As he journeyed, it grew so big that he put it in a lion's bone and finally in an ass's bone.

When he reached Nasso, near Taormina, he planted the vine, and it bore fruit. Bacchus picked the grapes and made the first wine. The story has a moral: a little wine makes you light like a bird, more of it makes you feel like a lion, immoderate use makes you an ass.

## Pantelleria

Midway between Sicily and Tunisia is the beautiful island of Pantelleria. It can be reached by air, or by boat from Trapani, Mazara or Porto Empedocle on the Sicilian mainland. Its only main road is a picturesque coastal route.

In wine terms, this island, with its active volcanoes and hot springs, is disproportionately famous for its Moscato wine with its own romantic Greek legend. The goddess Thanit, enamored of Apollo, substituted the wine of Pantelleria for his daily ambrosia, and immediately captured his attention. Indeed, it is the *passito* (sun-dried) grapes that produce the famous dessert Moscato, Passito di Pantelleria, which has discovered a ready export market. In a world looking for ever more variety in its wines, this is something different.

## Moscato and Cerasuolo

Syracuse is the starting point for the third itinerary. The home of Plato and Archimedes, it is a potent reminder of the antiquity of civilization in Sicily. Certainly the city is more interesting from an historical point of view than its eponymous wine, Moscato di Siracusa, which is in any case almost impossible to find. The same applies to the other DOC Moscato of south-east Sicily; visit the town of Noto for its famous Baroque architecture, but do not expect to find much Moscato di Noto wine.

The two Moscatos may lack convincing proponents; Cerasuolo di Vittoria, however, is one of the success stories of modern Sicilian viticulture. The name derives from its cherry-red color, which makes it look like a dark rosé. In fact, the wine has good keeping qualities and, in the hands of producers such as COS, who were founded as recently as 1980,

**RAGUSA**
**Coria Giuseppe & C sas**
Via Monreale 26. Tel/Fax: 0932 229229. Summer Tel/Fax: 0932 850022. (Giuseppe Coria). Own olive oil, honey. E.TF./TP.WS.B. www.space.tin.it/cucina/giucoria

**MILO**
**Az Agr Barone di Villagrande*** Via del Bosco. Tel: 095 7894339. Fax: 095 7894307. (Carlo Nicolosi Asmundo). E.TP. WS.B. www.villagrande.it

**VITTORIA**
**Az Agr COS*** Piazza del Popolo 34. Tel: 0932 864042. Fax: 0932 869700. (Giusto Occhipinti). E.F.TP.WS.B. E-mail: info@cosvittoria.it www.cosvittoria.it

*Moscato grapes laid out to dry in Pantelleria.*

*A market stall in Syracuse in south-east Sicily: shopping for fresh ingredients is a delight.*

**ACATE**
**Valle dell'Acate*** C.da Bidini. Tel: 0932 874166. Fax: 0932 875114. (Gaetana Jacono). 0930-1330, 1500-1730. E.TF.WS.B. (TP for groups). E-mail: valledellacate@tin.it

**VALLELUNGA PRATAMENO**
**Conte Tasca d'Almerita SpA*** Contrada Regaleali. Tel: 0921 544011. Fax: 0921 542783. (Giuseppe Tasca). 0800-1300, 1400-1800. E.F.TP.B. E-mail: info@tascadalmerita.it

**MARSALA**
**Az Ag Vecchio Samperi**
Contrada Fornara Samperi 292. Tel: 0923 962093. Fax: 0923 962910. Museum. E.F.TP.WS.B. E-mail: marcodebartoli@tin.it www.marcodebartoli.com

with the specific aim of re-discovering the glories of Cerasuolo, it is gaining a reputation as a fine wine at an international level. There is a *Strada del Vino* specifically for the Vittoria area, bounded by the Ipari and Dirillo rivers with the sea on one side and the Iblei mountains on the other.

## Agrigento

The temples of Agrigento are a must, but the modern town itself is worth avoiding. Inland, at almost the dead center of the island, is one of Sicily's top producers, Regaleali, a 300-hectare (750-acre) estate owned by the aristocratic Tasca d'Almerita family.

## Western Sicily

Most of the important wine producers in Sicily, those with the famous quality-conscious brands, have their wineries in the north-western part of Sicily. Rapitalà is managed by the French count Hugues de la Gatinais. Corvo is probably the most successful brand; it is an extremely reliable wine found all over the world.

Donnafugata is an upmarket red and white whose name comes from the romantic *donna fugata*, "the woman who fled," a character in Giuseppe di Lampedusa's novel *The Leopard*. The princely villa in the story is on the wine estate.

## The making of Marsala

The story of Marsala dates back to 1773 when John Woodhouse, the son of an English merchant from Liverpool, was driven ashore at Marsala by bad weather on one of his usual trading trips to Italy. It would not have been the first time he had tasted Marsala, but he was sure he could make a profit from shipping it back to England. As was normal at the time, a little spirit was added to preserve the wine on its long voyage back to England, exactly in the same way as Port and Madeira were transported.

Woodhouse's first shipment was of 50 pipes (412 liters each), but he remained in the port of Marsala to hear from his father in Liverpool what he thought of the wine – the response was enthusiastic and Woodhouse set up in business.

The Woodhouse *Baglio*, or factory, still stands by the shore in Marsala, but much changed after two centuries of export trade. Other Englishmen soon followed Woodhouse.

## Nelson's tipple

Originally there were three rival Marsala companies. Woodhouse's company and the wine were given official approval in 1798 when Nelson ordered his Marsala for the fleet after the battle of Aboukir Bay. He described the wine as "good enough to be on the table of any gentleman"; the price was 5d (old pence) per gallon, freight-free to Malta. For a short time Marsala was referred to as "Brontë-Madeira," after the title Duke of Brontë given to Nelson by the Bourbon government.

The other two companies were Ingham Whitaker & Co, founded by the Yorkshireman Benjamin Ingham in 1812, and Florio, founded by Vincenzo Florio in 1832. The busts of the three rivals are in the Florio museum, all three companies having been taken over by Cinzano before World War II.

## Marsala and Garibaldi

Marsala can claim to have influenced the course of history. It was the presence of two English ships in the harbor that prevented the blockading Bourbon fleet from opening fire on Garibaldi as he landed with his famous Thousand volunteers in 1860.

Garibaldi's subsequent visit to the Florio Marsala winery led to a quality of Marsala being named after him; Garibaldi Dolce is still made today, and a plaque commemorating the visit is in the Florio museum.

## Marsala today

The making of *zabaglione* would be impossible without Marsala. And that culinary necessity has kept the Marsala industry alive, sometimes to the detriment of its image. Until recently there was a danger that the real wine would become extinct, since it was disappearing into the sea of new mixed drinks; all sorts of versions were sold in the bottle – egg Marsala is perhaps the most notorious.

Marsala is, in fact, as versatile as sherry; it can be an aperitif or a digestif, it can be a fortified wine, or aged as a solera sherry.

Two other factors have saved it from extinction. Serious producers have realized that serious quality wines have to be made. Foremost among these is Marco de Bartoli, whose Vecchio Samperi is like an oloroso sherry, rich and nutty without being cloying. Secondly, a strict new code of Marsala production was introduced in 1984. Visit the Enoteca in Marsala for a tasting of modern Marsala.

*Palermo is famous for its Baroque buildings and statuary, which includes the delightful 16th-century Pretoria Fountain.*

**MARSALA (cont)**
**Tenuta di Donnafugata\***
Via S Lipari 18. Tel: 0923 724200. Fax: 0923 721130. (Baldo Palermo). 0900-1230, 1500-1730. Historic cellars in Marsala dating back to 1851. E.TP.WS.B. E-mail: donnafug@tin.it www.donnafugata.it
**Cantine Florio** Via Vincenzo Florio 1. Tel: 0923 781111. Fax: 0923 982380. (Signor Parisi). Mon-Thu 0900-1200, 1500-1700; Fri 0800-1200. Museum. E.TF.WS. (B by fax). E-mail: marsala@cantineflorio.com www.cantineflorio.com
**Carlo Pellegrino & C\***
Via del Fante 39. Tel: 0923 951177. Fax: 0923 953542. (Marco de Bartoli or Ute Petersen). 0830-1230, 1400-1730. E.F.G.TF.WS.B. E-mail: info@ carlopellegrino.it www.carlopellegrino.it

# Sardinia

Sardinia is a very separate entity. The fashionable world may alight briefly at the Costa Smeralda on the north-eastern coast, but the Sardinians are still proudly insular, and lack the outward-going nature that gives other Italians of the South such a high profile. Instead, Sardinians are considered almost as mysterious as the neolithic *nuraghi* of their forefathers – round houses that you find throughout Sardinia that are constructed of enormous stones and used variously as fortresses, dwellings and watchtowers.

Viticulture in Sardinia has ancient traditions that go back as far as Phoenician times; these middle eastern traders of biblical times are credited with the introduction of the Nuragus grape to the island. The Spanish domination of Sardinia in the time of the Aragonese kingdom of Naples led to the introduction of Spanish grapes, Cannonau and Monica, in the 17th century. Sardinian agriculture gained most, however, from the period of the Savoy monarchy, in the 18th and 19th centuries, when immigrants from Piedmont, Liguria and Corsica brought with them new methods of winemaking, and new varieties of vine as well.

## Table wines

On the whole, wine production in Sardinia is devoted to table wines of uncertain quality. There are some 39 co-operatives which account for 60 per cent of wine production, but only 4 per cent of all wine produced is DOC. There are few companies that export, and consequently few well-known Sardinian wines.

## Producers

The most widely available Sardinian wines come from the Sella & Mosca company in Alghero, on the north-western coast. They are a legacy of the Piedmontese interest in Sardinia; Emilio Sella and Edgardo Mosca were on a hunting holiday here in 1899 when they realized what ideal vine-growing country it was. Now Sella & Mosca is one of Europe's largest wine estates and a temple to modern technology. Their principal wines are the white Vermentino and Torbato and red Cannonau. The *barrique*-aged red Marchese di Villamarina has recently shown just how well Cabernet Sauvignon adapts to Sardinia.

## Other wines and producers

Other producers of note include Attilio Contini with his long-lived Vernaccia di Oristano, and Argiolas, who produce a famous wine called Turriga. Of the co-operatives, the ones that stand out at the moment are Trexenta (honest Sardinian varietal wines), Santadi (currently regarded as the leader) and Jerzu (with its unique and highly alcoholic red wines).

Wine names to remember are: (reds) Cannonau, Monica di Sardegna, Carignano del Sulcis;

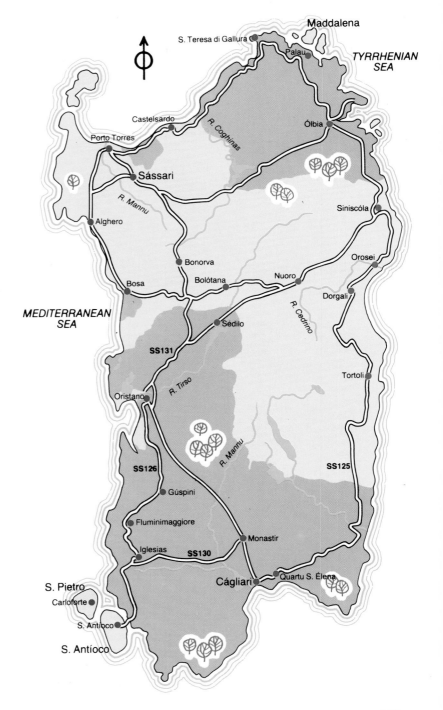

(whites) Malvasia, Moscato (a sweet dessert wine of the Càgliari district), Nuragus, Torbato, and Vernaccia di Oristano (similar to sherry; rich with a nutty aftertaste).

Sardinia vineyard areas

## Sardinian food

The fundamental element in Sardinian food is bread. Bread is baked in a swallowtail shape for baptisms, in garlands for weddings, and brown bread underlines the sadness of funeral feasts.

The most famous product of the Sardinian bakery is *carta da musica*, "music paper," paper-thin circular sheets of unleavened bread. Its origins lie in peasant cooking, when it was necessary for the shepherd to have something that would keep fresh on his long travels.

Another food of the Sardinian shepherd is cheese. *Cacio fiore* is the most traditional. It can be eaten fresh, grated, or aged with black pepper. Ricotta is called here *gentile*.

Cooking meat on a spit, flavored with mint, rosemary, bay leaf and sage, is traditional.

An alternative is *Carne a carraxiu*: sucking pig is encased in a sheep's stomach and covered with herbs. The parcel is placed in a hole in the ground full of embers and a fire is lit on top. *Porcheddu* is the dialect word for *porchetta*, roast sucking pig with rosemary.

*Is malloredus* are Sardinian *gnocchi* (tiny dumplings served as a first course), generally with a tomato or ragù sauce.

Fish is cooked simply. A specialty is the *bottarga* or *buttariga*, smoked mullet or tunny roe.

# *Grappa*

**CANELLI (Asti)**
**Distilleria Bocchino** Via
G B Giuliani 88. Tel: 0141
8101. Fax: 0141 832547.
(Beppe Orsini). 0900-1200,
1500-1900. Museum. Cellars
dug out of tufa rock. Shop.
E.F.G.TP.B.
E-mail: info@bocchino.it
www.bocchino.it

**MONTEGALDA (Vicenza)**
**Distilleria e Fabbrica**
**Liquori Fratelli Brunello**
Via Roi 27. Tel: 0444 737253.
Fax: 0444 737040. All year
(but preferably Sep-Nov).
Guest rooms. E.F.TF.WS.b.
E-mail: paolo.brunello@
vi.nettumo.it
www.brunello.it

**MUSOTTO D'ALBA**
**(Cuneo)**
**Distilleria Santa Teresa**
Corso Canale 105/1. Tel:
0173 33144. (Paolo Marolo).
Office hours. Maximum. 12
visitors at a time. E.F.TF.WS.
E-mail: distilleria@
marolo.com
www.marolo.com

**PERCOTO (Udine)**
**Distilleria Nonino** Via
Aquileia 104. Tel: 0432
676333. Fax: 0432 676038.
Office hours Mon-Fri, Sat
a.m. E.F.G.TF.b.
E-mail: info@nonino.it
www.nonino.it

**PERGOLESE (Trentino)**
**Az Agr F.lli Pisoni*** Tel:
0461 564106. Fax: 0461
563163. (Marco or Elio
Pisoni). 0800-1200, 1330-
1830. Also wine producers.
E.G.TF.WS.
E-mail: grapes@tin.it
www.trentinodoc.it/pisoni

Among the many spirits and digestifs that come from Italy, grappa is one of the most maligned. Mention the equivalent French product, Marc de Bourgogne or Marc de Champagne, and there are instant smiles of recognition. But grappa, unfortunately, has a reputation as tourists' firewater. True, it can be undrinkable and in general it is wise to avoid anything that is very cheap. But it can also be a drink of the highest sophistication. Several different types are available. Grappa is produced throughout the hills and mountains of northern Italy and Tuscany. It is essentially the distillate of grape pressings discarded by the winemaker. Mobile stills used to be trundled from farm to farm at harvest time, transforming the waste of the winemaking process into a high-alcohol spirit, good for keeping the cold out in winter.

Today the traditional homemade grappa of the mountain farmer can still be found, served in the local trattorias in the Alps and the Dolomites. But modern grappa is usually the widely available brands, such as Grappa Julia and Carpenè Malvolti, sold in supermarkets, or the upmarket, luxury product served in smart restaurants.

Improvements in the techniques of vinification have also benefited the world of grappa. Top winemakers have begun to use free-run juice for their wines, the result of soft pneumatic pressing. This leaves a much juicier and more flavorsome pomace for distillation.

Grappa technology has also improved in its own right. Many of the small distillers use discontinuous stills in a *bain marie*, or *bagna maria*, which allow the distillation to take place slowly and give the maximum flavor and sweetness. Logically enough, really fine grappa can only be made from fresh pomace, within 24 hours of the wine being drawn off the remains of the pressed grapes.

The best grappas are not technically grappas at all, being the *distillato di uva*, a distillate of the whole grape, produced with the aim of making a spirit in the first place and never pressed for wine. (The result is technically an acquavit rather than a grappa.)

## Grappa types
There are four types of grappa:
*Grappa giovane* This is young grappa, kept for about six months in stainless steel after distillation, thereby remaining clear in color, and concentrating the natural tastes and fragrances of the distilled grape pressings.
*Grappa invecchiata* Aged grappa, kept for months or years in wood, which gives it an amber color and makes it softer and smoother.
*Single grape variety grappa* The most exclusive variety, made from a single grape variety in order to enhance its particular flavors. The strongly perfumed varieties are very attractive: Grappa di Moscato is a good example.
*Grappa aromatizzata* This is made with a herb or fruit flavoring and was traditionally used for medicinal purposes. Gentian-flavored grappa, they say, is a remedy for insomnia. In Alto Adige, especially, there is a tradition of making fruit-flavored Schnapps.

Grappa is the after-dinner drink of northern Italy and, after a recent revival, Tuscany. Producers can be visited in all those areas, but two in particular are outstanding.

The Nonino company, based in Friuli, were pioneers in the making of both the *distillato di uva* and single grape variety grappas described above. Giannola Nonino saw the possibility of selecting a grape variety for its particular virtues of taste and fragrance. Some of Nonino's finest grappas are aged in cherry wood, a practice that started because cherry trees are plentiful in the area. Now the single-grape, cherry-wood-aged grappas of Nonino in their bulbous bottles are among the most sought after in Italy.

In Piedmont, the Bocchino firm has made grappa for one hundred years.

Antonella Bocchino has rediscovered some of the traditional grape varieties of Piedmont to produce some very special single-grape grappas. Neiret, Timuassa, Doux, and Vespolina d'Henry are some of the varieties. Visit the company in Canelli to see their unique museum of distillation. The Bocchino brand is a commercial grappa made from Moscato; Antonella's grappas are much more expensive and are sold under the A.B. label.

Grappa is best drunk just slightly cool in small tulip-shaped glasses, in the best restaurants, of course. Older Italians are used to treating it with scant respect by putting a dash in their espresso coffee, the *caffè corretto*, or by mixing it with hot coffee in a wooden bowl with a lid and individual spouts, the *grolla* of the Aosta valley.

**SCHIAVON (Vicenza) Poli Distillerie** Via Marconi 46. Tel: 0444 665007. Fax: 0444 665637. (Jacopo Poli). All year. Jacopo Poli has created in Bassano del Grappa (Vicenza) a Grappa museum, the first in Italy. E.F.G.TF.WS.b E-mail: info@poligrappa.com www.poligrappa.com

*A grappa still in Piedmont. The art of distillation is a very ancient one, learned in part from the Arabs.*

# Reference Section

## PRINCIPAL GRAPES AND THEIR WINES

**Aglianico** (red). Southern Italian grape of great antiquity. Its name derives from Hellenico, "the Greek one." It produces robust reds for long aging in Basilicata (Aglianico del Vulture) and Campania (Taurasi).

**Albana** (white). Italy's first white DOCG is Albana di Romagna, made from this grape in central Italy. The wines are sweet or dry, still or sparkling.

**Barbera** (red). The staple grape of Piedmont, with Dolcetto. It makes intense reds for drinking within three years – such as Barbera d'Alba, d'Asti, and del Monferrato – and also fashionable boutique blockbusters.

**Brunello** (Sangiovese Grosso) (red). A type of Sangiovese used to make Italy's most prestigious wine, Brunello di Montalcino DOCG.

**Cabernet Franc** (red). Introduced to north-east Italy in the 19th century, this is widely used to make red wine with grassy characteristics.

**Cabernet Sauvignon** (red). One of the great grapes of the wine world. Hitherto only found on estates with Francophile leanings; now widely planted as growers explore its undoubted potential.

**Cannonau** (red). This makes one of Sardinia's successful reds, Cannonau di Sardegna.

**Chardonnay** (white). One of the wine world's most fashionable grapes. Chardonnay from Burgundy produces rich and long-lived white wines. In Italy, it is not generally aged in the same way (in small oak barrels) to achieve the same intensity of flavor and length of aging. Most Italian Chardonnay is fermented and aged in stainless steel, and therefore has a fresher taste.

**Cortese** (white). The grape used for Italy's most fashionable white, Gavi, and Cortese dei Colli Tortonesi, dell'Alto Monferrato, and di Gavi.

**Corvina Veronese** (red). One of the principal grapes of Valpolicella and Bardolino (together with Rondinella and Molinara).

**Dolcetto** (red). Piedmont's staple grape, along with Barbera. The name suggests sweetness, but it produces a smooth wine with a slightly bitter aftertaste, often used as a restaurant table wine.

**Erbaluce** (white). Little-known Piedmontese grape, producing still, sparkling, dry and sweet white wines.

**Freisa** (red). Still, sparkling, sweet or dry wines result from this grape with a characteristic strawberry aroma, from just south of Turin.

**Gewürztraminer/Traminer Aromatico** (white). Tramin/Termeno in Alto Adige claims to be the birthplace of this international grape. Used in north-east Italy.

**Grechetto** (white). The Umbrian grape that gives character to Orvieto; sometimes vinified as a varietal.

**Grignolino** (red). This grape from the Asti region makes a light red/rosé wine with a slightly bitter aftertaste,

**Lagrein** (red). Produces a rosé (*kretzer*) or red (*dunkel*) wine in Alto Adige; light and drinkable wines.

**Lambrusco** (red). In Emilia Romagna, the wine from this grape is intended to cut the fatty foods of the region. The wine is usually dry, unlike the exported versions.

**Malvasia** (white). An ancient vine of possibly Greek origins. Malvasia di Candia is one of the major grapes of Frascati, Galestro, Est! Est!! Est!!! and Marino. It is also found extensively in Friuli-Venezia Giulia.

**Marzemino** (red). This makes a red wine from Trentino celebrated in Mozart's *Don Giovanni*.

**Merlot** (red). The workhorse grape of north-east Italy is now being re-evaluated as producers in Tuscany, Friuli and Alto Adige make prestigious wines from better clones.

**Montepulciano** (red). Used on the Adriatic coast to make the red wines Montepulciano d'Abruzzo and Rosso Conero. Not to be confused with the town of Montepulciano in Tuscany which has its own wine, Vino Nobile di Montepulciano made from the Sangiovese grape.

**Moscato Bianco** (white). One of the great grapes of Italy, this is the source of the fresh grapey tastes of Asti in Piedmont and Tuscany's Moscadello di Montalcino.

**Müller-Thurgau** (white). An international grape variety giving a sophisticated but fruity white wine mostly in Friuli-Venezia Giulia and Trentino-Alto Adige.

**Nebbiolo** (red). The source of two of Italy's best-known and longest-lived wines, Barolo and Barbaresco. Also the base grape for several northwestern Italian reds.

**Negroamaro** (red). Puglia's most important grape.

**Picolit** (white). The legendary dessert wine of Friuli, Picolit, is made from the semi-dried grapes of the same name. It is high in alcohol and can be aged for several years.

**Pinot Bianco** (white). Similar to Chardonnay, mainly made in Friuli and Trentino-Alto Adige.

**Pinot Grigio** (red). The grape's red skins often give its white wines an attractive pink tinge. The wine has become popular as the thinking skier's white wine. It has good body with a characteristic aromatic twist.

**Pinot Nero** (red). The best reds of Burgundy are produced from this difficult grape, which has inspired producers in north-east Italy and Tuscany to attempt to do likewise.

**Prosecco** (white). Versatile grape of the Treviso area of the Veneto. Most popular for the medium-dry sparkling wine that is Treviso's house wine.

**Riesling** (white). The native Italico is less pungent than the Germanic Riesling Renano. Mainly used for varietals in north-east Italy.

**Sagrantino** (red). An indigenous grape in Umbria, used for red wines with aromas of blackberries and mushrooms. Can be *passito*.

**Sangiovese** (red). One of Italy's finest grapes, used in its various forms throughout Central Italy for wines such as Chianti, Vino Nobile di Montepulciano, Brunello and Carmignano (Tuscany), and Rosso Piceno (the Marches).

**Sauvignon** (white). The grassy green-stick bouquet and flavor of this international grape is less aggressive in Italy than in France.

**Schiava/Vernatsch** (red). The base grape of the red wines of Trentino Alto Adige, such as Santa Maddalena, Caldaro and Casteller.

**Sylvaner** (white). Better known in Alsace, this is also used in Alto Adige to make aromatic white wines.

**Tocai Friulano** (white). The most common white grape of the eastern Veneto and Friuli-Venezia Giulia.

**Trebbiano** (white). The grape responsible for most of Italy's white wines, especially Soave, Gambellara, and Frascati.

**Verdicchio** (white). The versatile white wine grape of the Marches area. It makes still or sparkling wine and can also be aged in small casks.

**Verduzzo** (white). Produces a white dessert wine from Friuli capable of being aged in *barriques*.

**Vernaccia di San Gimignano** (white). Responsible for San Gimignano's white wine.

## GLOSSARY OF WINE TERMS

**Abboccato** Slightly sweet; Orvieto Abboccato is the most typical.

**Acciaio** (or **Inox**) Stainless steel

**Affinamento** Aging (after fermentation, in barrel or in bottle).

**Amabile** Sweet.

**Autoclave** The tank in which sparkling wine made by the Charmat method (*Metodo Charmat*) gets its sparkle.

**Barrique** Small (225 liter) new oak barrel, now fashionable in Italy. Its use gives a smooth, initially vanilla, flavor.

**Bianco** White.

**Bicchiere** Glass.

**Botte** Large barrel, usually made from Slavonian oak.

**Bouquet** Smell of the wine, resulting from grape, vinification and aging.

**Brillante** Very clear.

**Brut** Very dry, applied to sparkling wines.

**Cantina** Cellar.

**Castagno** Chestnut wood.

**Corpo** Body and structure of a wine.

**Cru** Single vineyard.

**Da bere fresco** To be drunk cool.

**Degustazione** A tasting, the occasion for the **assaggio** (process of tasting).

**Dolce** Very sweet.

**Equilibrato** Balanced.

**Erbaceo** Grassy, especially applicable to Cabernet Franc.

**Etichetta** Label.

**Fermentazione** Fermentation.

**Frizzante** Slightly sparkling.

**Fruttato** Fruity.

**Giallo paglierino** Straw yellow.

**Giovane** Young.

**Gradevole** Attractive to drink.

**Invecchiamento** Process of aging.

**Liquoroso** Wine fortified with added alcohol, such as Marsala.

**Millesimato** Vintage wine.

**Morbido** Smooth and soft.

**Neutro** Without characteristics.

**Ossidazione** Oxidization.

**Ossigenazione** The process of letting wine breathe, especially desirable for older red wines.

**Passito** A rich wine high in alcohol, such as Recioto, made from semi-dried grapes.

**Pieno** Full, as in full of flavor.

**Pigiatura** Pressing, the first process of winemaking.

**Pronta beva** To be drunk soon after bottling.

**Resa** Yield (of grapes per plant or per hectare/acre).
**Retrogusto** Aftertaste.
**Robusto** A big wine, full of color, acidity, alcohol and tannin.
**Rosato** Rosé.
**Rosso** Red.
**Rotondo** Smooth.
**Rovere** Oak.
**Rubino** Ruby red.
**Sapido** Full of taste.
**Secco** Dry.
**Spumante** Sparkling wine. The sparkle can be produced by the *Metodo Champenois* or the *Metodo Charmat* (see above), or by artificially adding bubbles.
**Tannico** Tannin; in a red wine this indicates that it will age well.
**Tappo** The cork. The same word means "corked," that is, with a bitter taste from a bad cork.
**Tastevin** Small silver tasting bowl used instead of a glass in the cellar.
**Tipicità** "Typicality," meaning the wine is authentic and traditional.
**Torchio** Old-fashioned wine press.
**Uva** Grape.
**Uvaggio** Proportional blend of grapes, *cépage*.
**Vellutato** Smooth, velvety.
**Vendemmia** Vintage, harvest.
**Vigna, vigneto** Single vineyard.
**Vignaiolo** Grower of grapes.
**Vinificazione** Vinification.
**Vinoso** "Like wine," term used of a characterless bouquet.
**Vivace** Fresh and often slightly sparkling.

## RED WINES FOR LAYING DOWN

| | Barbaresco | Brunello di Montalcino | Barolo | Chianti Classico | Vino Nobile di Montepulciano | Amarone |
|---|---|---|---|---|---|---|
| 1970 | •••• | •••• | •••• | ••••• | •••• | •••• |
| 1971 | •••• | ••• | ••••• | ••••• | •••• | •••• |
| 1972 | • | • | • | •• | • | • |
| 1973 | •• | ••• | •• | •• | ••• | •• |
| 1974 | •••• | •• | •••• | ••• | ••• | •••• |
| 1975 | •• | ••••• | •• | •••• | | ••• |
| 1976 | •• | • | •• | •• | •• | •••• |
| 1977 | •• | •••• | •• | •••• | •••• | ••• |
| 1978 | ••••• | •••• | ••••• | ••••• | ••••• | ••• |
| 1979 | •••• | •••• | •••• | •••• | •••• | •••• |
| 1980 | •••• | •••• | •••• | •••• | •• | ••• |
| 1981 | ••• | ••• | ••• | ••• | ••• | ••• |
| 1982 | ••••• | ••••• | ••••• | •••• | •••• | • |
| 1983 | •••• | •••• | •••• | •••• | •••• | ••••• |
| 1984 | • | •• | •• | • | • | •• |
| 1985 | ••••• | ••••• | ••••• | ••••• | ••••• | •••• |
| 1986 | ••• | ••• | ••• | •••• | •••• | ••• |
| 1987 | •• | •• | •• | •• | •• | •• |
| 1988 | ••••• | ••••• | ••••• | ••••• | ••••• | ••••• |
| 1989 | ••••• | •• | ••••• | • | • | •• |
| 1990 | ••••• | ••••• | ••••• | ••••• | ••••• | ••••• |
| 1991 | ••• | ••• | ••• | ••• | ••• | •• |
| 1992 | •• | •• | •• | • | • | • |
| 1993 | ••• | •••• | ••• | •••• | ••••• | •••• |
| 1994 | •• | •• | •• | •• | •• | •• |
| 1995 | •••• | ••••• | •••• | •••• | •••• | •••• |
| 1996 | •••• | ••• | •••• | ••• | ••• | ••• |
| 1997 | ••••• | •••• | ••••• | ••• | •••• | •••• |
| 1998 | ••••• | •••• | ••••• | •••• | •••• | •••• |

**Key to vintage wine chart**
Vintages are assessed with star ratings. Five stars indicate an exceptionally good vintage. Remember that vintage wines need several years' aging in barrel and in bottle before they are released on to the market.

## SAMPLE LETTER/FAX/ E-MAIL TO AN ITALIAN WINERY

[Sender's name, address and telephone number; date]

*La presente per chiedere la prenotazione di una nostra visita alla Vostra stimata cantina.*

*Abbiamo sentito la fama dei Vostri vini tramite il libro A Traveller's Wine Guide to Italy, nel quale si nota la Vostra gentile disponibilità a dare ai viaggiatori intenditori una visita/degustazione alla cantina. Perciò, siccome siamo molto interessati a sapere di più sul vino italiano in genere e sul Vostro vino in particolare saremmo molto interessati ad approfittare dell'occasione.*

*Siamo un piccolo gruppo di [X] persone. Abbiamo intenzione di visitare la Vostra zona i giorni [dates] e chiediamo la Vostra gentile conferma della disponibilità di accoglierci.*

*Nell'attesa del piacere della Vostra cortese risposta e del piacere dell' eventuale incontro porgiamo i nostri più cordiali saluti,*

[Signature]

We would like to arrange a visit to your excellent Cantina.

We have heard of the fame of your wines through the publication *A Traveller's Wine Guide to Italy*, from which we understand that you are willing to accept visits from travellers who are wine lovers and who wish to taste wine in your cellars. We are very interested in learning more about Italian wine in general, and about your wine in particular.

We are a small group of [X] people. We intend to visit your area on the following dates [*** ] and would be very pleased if you could confirm that you would be able to accept a visit on one of those days.

We look forward to your reply and to the pleasure of meeting you when this can be arranged. With best wishes,

[Signature]

Italian dialling codes: Remember to keep the '0' in the local prefix, even when dialling from abroad.

## FURTHER READING
### (In English)

Burton Anderson, *The Wine Atlas of Italy*. From a technical point of view, the best book on Italian wines currently available.

Burton Anderson, *Vino*. A standard work on Italian wines, by the leading English-language writer on the subject.

Burton Anderson, *The Pocket Guide to Italian Wine*.

Nicolas Belfrage, *Life Beyond Lambrusco*. In-depth examination of the current state of winemaking in Italy.

David Gleave, *The Wines of Italy*. Well-illustrated guide to Italian wine by grape variety.

Marc and Kim Millon, *The Wine Roads of Italy*. Itineraries through most major wine-producing areas.

Bruno Roncarati, *Viva Vino*. A useful reference work.

Sheldon and Pauline, Wasserman *Italy's Noble Red Wines*. Comprehensive tasting notes on a wide range of the finer Italian reds.

### (In Italian)

*Guida all'Italia dei Vini* (Touring Club Italiano, 1985) Geographic guide to Italian DOCs and DOCGs.

Marco Trimani, *Guida ai Vini d'Italia* (Editori Riuniti, 1984). A basic dictionary of Italian wine, with notes on vinification.

Luigi Veronelli, *Le Cantine di Veronelli* (Giorgio Mondadori, 1989). Recommended wine producers with details of which wines to taste on a visit and how to book that visit.

---

**ITALIAN NATIONAL HOLIDAYS**

January 1: New Year
January 6: Epiphany
Easter Monday: (dates vary)
April 25: Liberation Day.
May 1: Labor Day.
August 15: Assumption of the Virgin.
November 1: All Saints Day.
December 8: Feast of the Immaculate Conception.
Christmas Day and Boxing Day.

**Local feast days**

Shops and businesses are often closed during festivities. The following is a selection only:
April 25: Venice.
June 24: Florence. Genoa. Turin
June 29: Rome.
July 15: Palermo.
September 19: Naples.
October 4: Bologna.
December 6: Bari.
December 7: Milan.

---

# Index

# Index